Simon Day began his career as a stand-up comic, winning the *Time Out* New Act of the Year Award in 1991. He worked extensively with Vic Reeves and Bob Mortimer before rising to prominence in the hit TV comedy *The Fast Show*, and as well as making many television and film appearances he has toured extensively performing as his comic characters. He is bald and does not turn down hot food.

COMEDY AND ERROR

SIMON DAY

They Really Were Marvellous Times

SIMON & SCHUSTER

London · New York · Sydney · Toronto · New Delhi

A CBS COMPANY

First published in Great Britain by Simon & Schuster UK Ltd, 2011
This paperback edition published by Simon & Schuster UK Ltd, 2012
A CBS Company

1 3 5 7 9 10 8 6 4 2

Simon & Schuster UK Ltd
1st Floor
222 Gray's Inn Road
London
WC1X 8HB

www.simonandschuster.co.uk

Simon & Schuster Australia,
Sydney
Simon & Schuster India, New Delhi

A CIP catalogue for this book is available
from the British Library.

ISBN: 978-1-84938-056-0

Typeset by Hewer Text UK Ltd, Edinburgh
Printed and bound in Great Britain by Cox & Wyman

For Ruth, Lloyd and Evie

Contents

'The problem of the actor has troubled me for the longest time. I felt unsure (and sometimes still do) whether it is not only from this angle that one can get at the dangerous concept of the "artist" – a concept that has so far been treated with unpardonable generosity. Falseness with a good conscience; the delight in simulation exploding as a power that pushes aside one's so-called "character", flooding it and at times extinguishing it; the inner craving for a role and a mask, for *appearance* . . . masters of the incorporated and inveterate art of eternally playing hide-and-seek, which in the case of animals is called mimicry – until eventually this capacity, accumulated from generation to generation, becomes domineering, unreasonable, and intractable, an instinct that learns to lord it over other instincts, and generates the actor, the "artist" (the zany, the teller of lies, the buffoon, fool, clown . . .)'

Friedrich Nietzsche

'Don't stand so close to the fire, lad – you'll burn.'

Charlie Chuck

Prologue

My elder brother once said to me: 'The trouble with you is you have no respect for anyone.' He was right. I was only seven years old, though, and hadn't yet met anyone that impressive, I suppose. As I grew up my catchphrase became, 'I know, I *know* . . .' I knew everything and yet I knew nothing. No one could tell me anything – not teachers, not family members, not any person in authority. The idiots I would listen to: the oddballs, the tramps, the funny fat kids who rode bikes too small for them and seemed to have no friends . . . Those guys got my full, undivided attention. I took my information from television and books and comics and whispered folklore. My parents might repeat things to me over and over and I'd seemingly ignore them, but it all went in and got stored away. I wouldn't give them the credit at the time, though. I'd just say, 'I *know*!' in an exasperated manner as if they were the children. Once, when I'd been instructed in some way by my dad, my brother stated that I'd looked 'like a wrestler receiving a public warning'.

I wanted to be different but not enough to really make a go of it. Maybe I've made a small difference. I've been called a maverick and a one-off but I'm not really. People in my field love to hear these words in the same way I hoped my dyslexia and Attention-Deficit Disorder might contribute to me being seen as some sort of idiot savant. These words, along with 'genius', have been devalued by thoughtless and deluded journalists. I'm not and never will be Ian Dury or Paul Gascoigne, Lee Perry or Brian Clough (obviously), but these people have inspired me; they've really uplifted me, made the hairs stand up on the back of my neck. I'm Simon Day and this is my story.

Chapter One

I was born in a nice little house in a nice little suburb of South East London called Blackheath, in 1962. Some two months after my birth Marilyn Monroe was found dead in her bed, the victim of dark forces in her brain and in her private life. When showbiz historians look back on our respective lives they will be forced to draw a number of parallels. One, we are both Geminis; two, we both took prescription drugs and slept around with powerful figures in organised crime and politics (local for me); and three, we both became much-loved comedy actors and talked in a silly voice for comic effect. But that was a world away. First I had to make my bones into funny bones – and that took quite a while.

It's hard being a child. One minute you're a baby and people are peering at you, saying, 'Ooh, he's so sweet; look at his little face!' Your mum picks you up and you suck on her tits for hours and when you've had your fill you stare into her eyes and do a great big shit – and then she wipes your arse. What a life . . .

Suddenly, around the age of three, it all changes. Everything you do is wrong. 'Put that down!' 'Pick that up!' 'Don't draw on that!' 'Don't snatch!' 'If you don't eat that foodstuff you can't have the slightly better foodstuff!' 'If you carry on you're going back to bed!'

It doesn't make sense.

No one warns you. You need someone from one of the Five Families to take you aside: 'From now on, kid, you gotta act like a man. You gotta use that potty: no more shitting your pants and crying 'cause you have to go to bed. You gotta stop hitting your sister or you're going away; you're gonna get whacked. Keep your mouth shut and don't rat on your friends.'

My earliest memory is of Mum crying and being comforted by my dad. A year after my birth my mum had a little baby girl, called Charlotte. She had Down's syndrome and died when she was two years old. They had no idea how to treat the condition then – it was 1963 after all. I remember Charlotte's face, her eyes particularly. Lying in her cot she looked perfectly Chinese; she had jaundice, too. I remember asking Mum questions about her, of the why variety, just as my boy does now. But his are questions I'm happy to answer. I've no idea what that did to my mum, her only daughter dying (the subject has never been discussed since), but it must have damaged her somehow. She was alone in a strange part of London with two kids and a man who, although kind, did not discuss emotions – yours or his. She dug in, I expect, and got on with it, which is what you did in those days. There was no recourse to any form of therapy, but you always had gin and tonic. And, trust me, I didn't give her a second's rest to ponder her feelings anyway. My name was Simon Day and I was alive and needed help with everything.

My mum was from Kenilworth in Warwickshire. Her parents had an outside toilet and grew all their own vegetables. My dad came from a large, prosperous family who had ties to St John's Wood and Henley-on-Thames. She told me once she married him because he seemed nice and had money. An earlier suitor had run over a rabbit in his MG and burst out laughing: he got the heave-ho. She was very attractive, my mum – still is – and Dad made quite a catch there. My dad loved to read – he had at last count more than 7,000 books, mainly about war and architecture, with his own little watermark on the first page of each; amazing, really. Everything is filed away. A good stamp collection too. After they got divorced I used to nick his books and sell them from time to time. One day he saw them in a junk-shop window and had to go and buy them back. I was a right little cunt or a damaged individual crying out for help – take your pick.

Every kid wants to be good at sport (apart from homosexuals). It's the ultimate high, scoring a winning goal in the World Cup Final, pinging in the last arrow to hit a 180, smashing your fist into a Mexican's liver in a hot room. All that adulation. The respect of your peers and beyond. I went to Brooklands Primary School in Blackheath. It was tiny by Inner London standards and there were only twenty-one boys in the top two years from whom to draw the football and cricket teams. But we had a secret weapon: Mr Davies. We called him Dickie after the ITV sports presenter. He was a superb example of seventies man-hero. He always wore a skin-tight old-school blue tracksuit; he had lovely sandy hair, a medallion and an MG in which he was frequently seen purring around Blackheath with leggy bits of stuff. In short, he *was* the seventies.

But beneath this seemingly shallow (and now much-derided) exterior there was a brilliant sports brain. We did all right at the football, though we didn't have good enough players to challenge the bigger schools. Everyone wanted to be good at football. Cricket was a slightly different matter. It was unfashionable, but cricket was Dickie's thing. The tiny pool of talent meant I somehow made the team. I batted at number 9 and fielded here and there. I was no Ian Botham but I could catch and I had an accurate throw. I was only a little fat fella then, yet to reach puberty. We had two very good players, Paul Cobb and Graham Wooldridge, both of whom played for the district. Paul Cobb was a sort of David Watts figure: he looked a bit like Paul Weller and the girls went mad for his broad shoulders, high cheekbones and dim nonchalance. (I'm assuming all this – at the time I had no idea why girls liked him; he was just someone I thought was cool because he was unlike me.)

I imagined myself as a scientific example of an unattractive boy: basin haircut, skinny legs; I had a lazy eye and wore National Health specs with an eye-patch. I often wore socks with sandals. Graham Wooldridge was a ginge but still had the wow factor both on and off the field. He once got off with a girl I fancied, called Janet Roy, while I was at my nan's. I was devastated, but what could I do? I had no pubic hair and at that stage I thought girls' vaginas were situated somewhere around their tummy buttons. I remember being told about Graham and Janet by someone on a patch of waste ground near where we lived. I was smoking a No. 6 at the time and the combination of the news and the nicotine rush forced me to lie down in some wet grass. I imagined them loving each other up, rolling about on a bed in a hot little room. It was too much to bear. I went home and read *Tintin and the Black Island* and pushed a half-eaten apple down the back of the radiator.

Dickie Davies was the first teacher to make me believe I could achieve something. Like Alf Ramsey with the England football team in 1966, he told us and the press (the *South East London and Kentish Mercury*) we could win the Cup and the League. *Is he mad?* I thought. Yet somehow we started winning matches. Our opening partnership of Cobb and Wooldridge was too good. They regularly put on seventy or one hundred between them – at that level it was enough – and they could both bowl too. We started moving up the League. I loved that season. I didn't have to do much: I caught a few people out, made the odd eleven or fourteen runs. Obviously with the Attention-Deficit Disorder I drifted out of games and started admiring trees and buildings beyond the boundaries, staring at people on the opposing team and wondering what they were like, where they lived, whether they'd read *Emil and the Detectives* . . . Suddenly I'd be brought swiftly from my reverie by a ball skimming past through my legs, or someone pointing to a red dot in the sky hurtling towards me. We'd all stare up at the heavens like a tribe of primitive pygmies witnessing the end of the world and a chant would rise: 'Don't drop it, Day! Don't drop it, Day!'

As the season reached its climax we were top of the League and in the semi-final of the Cup – unheard of for a school of our size. Dickie sent a letter to our parents requesting our attendance at school at seven-thirty in the morning for practice – seven-thirty! Everyone's parents agreed; we were on the verge of something extraordinary. On the first day of our dawn manoeuvres he put us in a circle and had us throw the ball to each other faster and faster. No one dropped the ball for ages – it was brilliant. I felt giddy with excitement. Then we ran around the playground for ages. I thought we'd done something wrong, but no – he was getting us fit. I didn't understand. I enjoyed cricket because fat people could still have a decent stab at the game; I had no idea that people who played cricket were in any way athletic. To me it was something like a John Major fantasy – all about the gentle *thwack* of ball on willow, and people dozing off in the sun. I didn't realise it was a proper sport. I kept my mouth shut, though.

After training I asked Dickie why he'd made us come before school and not after.

He said, 'At that time, around eight in the morning, your brain is at its peak and your reactions are quickest – you can learn more.'

Rather insolently I asked, 'Who told you that?'

'Colin Bell, actually. He's a good friend of mine.'

Then he walked away, his trim behind highlighted by his tight blue tracksuit bottoms and the sun glinting off his sandy-blond hair.

Colin Bell! Colin fucking Bell! The England and Man City midfielder. I was staggered. Dickie was friends with Colin Bell!

That night I told my dad. He was reading a book about Stalingrad and drinking a Martini Rosso.

'Really?' he said. It's not that he didn't care: he was distracted, deep in a book detailing one of the most ghastly and cruel battles in military history. When my old man concentrated he really concentrated – he may as well have been in one of those flotation tanks. He was constantly reading. Given the chance he would have read himself blind. He loved it, and I think he preferred it to interacting with other people. In that respect I'm my father's son. I have to admit that now, having overcome the dyslexia, I can read for hours, isolate myself, just the page and the quiet room. Sweet bliss.

We had to play John Stainer Primary in the final of the Cup and to decide the League. They were a massive school in Brockley, which is a racially mixed area bordering Lewisham and New Cross. To me they looked like the West Indies Test team with a few picture-postcard Cockney kids thrown in. This was my first experience of black kids up close. There were no black children at my primary school – not one. I'd seen them in Tintin books and on *Top of the Pops* but that was it. They were cartoon figures. In fact when I was very young I had a seven-inch single, 'Little Black Sambo', which was a song about a young black guy who got chased round a tree by a tiger. The tiger ran round the tree so fast he eventually melted into butter and Black Sambo's mum, being a resourceful jungle lady, cooked the liquefied tiger up into pancakes. My generation was the last to have a ridiculous, twisted prior knowledge of black people as 'golliwogs'. They smiled at us from our breakfast marmalade and at night we watched them dance about on *The Black and White Minstrel Show*. There they weren't even black: they were white people dressed up as black people. Very confusing.

Still, there were no happy golliwogs in this team. They bowled at seventy miles an hour and the only hoofing they did was of the ball over the boundary. This was a good team from a poor neighbourhood. Half the players didn't have proper cricket whites. Their sports teacher was a gnarly old badger who wore clown trousers that concealed cricket balls and bails. He craftily suggested we play two games, one for each competition. Dickie knew we didn't have the squad size to do that so he made them settle on one game, winner takes all. The venue: Blackheath Common. Blackheath is enormous. It's the main attraction of an area wrongly dismissed as a poor man's Hampstead – I think it spanks Hampstead or any other area of London. I've been beaten up on it, had my first drink on it, slept on it, run across it, had picnics, flown kites and had something close to sex on it. It's covered in cars now but you'll never destroy it – it's too big, too romantic, too alive. It was my home from the age of nought till I was twenty-nine, and one day I hope to return not in triumph but at least with my name on a bench. Or maybe I could have a curry named after me like Terry Waite in the Blackheath Tandoori. I mean, what's he ever done since he got off his radiator?

We won the toss and put them into bat. They made a good score, though I can't remember what it was – a hundred and something. Our lot made a good reply and when I got the call we were just fourteen runs behind. As I came into bat it started to rain, sweaty, misty summer rain. I was partnered with a podgy French-Arab boy called Matthew Le Merle. He wore glasses and I could see they were steaming up: he kept taking them off and rubbing them on his white shirt. I remember seeing his belly and thinking, *How fast can he run with that tyre?* I was terrified. The bowler hurled a full toss down at me and I hit it with the wrong part of the bat, the bit at the top near the handle. It flew slowly towards another boy. I was surely out, a disgrace. But he dropped it. He dropped it! We made two runs. I looked around me and swallowed, the blood crashing in my ears like waves on a beach. I was on Blackheath, my home turf. I could see the village clearly. I could see Stower's newsagent's, where I'd stolen sweets and cans of Coke, and the bus stop where the man approached me then changed his mind when he saw my haircut. Rossi's ice-cream van, the houses, the church, the sherbet lemon I found in a puddle and still ate, the disappointment of the helter-skelter at the fair, the good times, the bad times . . . It was all swilling around in my head. I tried to concentrate. I hit a single. The game crawled on. Le Merle made three runs. I looked at Dickie Davies. He was sort of fizzing and exploding underneath his haircut. Paul Cobb shouted, 'Come on, Si!' We stumbled on, singles here and there, then Matthew got a four. We needed one run.

The rain was filmy and slight; it made everything greasy. There was a rainbow behind me but I couldn't see it. Someone bowled at me. I hit the ball all wrong: it skidded off behind the wicket through the despairing slips. We ran towards each other, me and Matthew Le Merle. He was fat and I was an idiot, and it was our dog-day afternoon. As we ran our team were running towards us, white ghosts with red shining faces. People were shouting and laughing; everyone jumped on me. I was steaming. I'd somehow scored the winning run – we were the Cup and League champions. I was soaking wet and covered in boys but I didn't care: it was the greatest moment of my life. I was the hero of the hour and it seemed to go on for ever. The day fizzed and popped around me like a Latin American carnival. We walked back to the changing rooms like stick men as the gods drew back into the heavens.

I have absolutely no recollection of that evening at home but I must have been on cloud nine for weeks. I was boasting about scoring the winning runs at school later that week when Dickie snapped at me. 'Without Cobb, Wooldridge and Stefan Hohman's runs we'd have lost. You only scored eight!' I went all red. I'd been taught a valuable lesson, which of course I forgot immediately. *I scored the winning runs and I'm more than the sum of the cricket team's parts, OK? So fuck off, Dickie!* They gave me an engraved medal, gold with a little cameo of a cricket player on it.

Later, I proudly took it with me on my first day at secondary school and showed it around to everyone and anyone, filling them in on my own little Test Series victory. When I got home it wasn't in my bag; just the little box stared at me – a smooth little felt crater, devoid of jewellery. Someone had relieved me of my trophy.

Welcome to Kidbrooke. Welcome to the real world.

My extraordinary cricketing abilities meant I was put down for the team at my new concrete school. The trouble was I'd still not reached puberty: everyone else on the field seemed bigger than me, with huge Adam's apples and deep voices. Next to them I looked like one of those children who are led out by the captains in the Charity Shield, clutching a pennant and blushing.

On the first day of practice in the nets a boy bowled a ball at me so fast I thought I was imagining it. It hit my thumb. I screamed. It went all purple and swelled up like a weird vegetable. I retired, hurt, for ever. I never played cricket again, but I'd had a dangerous taste of adulation. I loved it! I'd felt fantastic. I'd seen the looks on those boys' faces and I wanted more. I wanted those looks on girls' faces too – that'd be more difficult but maybe I could be a contender . . .

I had to wait seventeen years to win something again. This time I did it on my own: the *Time Out* New Act of the Year, 1991. If I hadn't written this book I fear both these events would have been airbrushed from history.

I can't remember the first time I wet the bed. I was between three and six, probably: that's what it says on a website I found; that's the average age of the child when the soggy odyssey begins. Another website I looked at listed famous bedwetters! Can you believe it? It was an American site and the top name was Michael Landon, the actor from *Little House on the Prairie*. Jesus, I hope it was just him in the family. I mean, that's a hell of a lot of laundry.

I suppose in its own way the site was trying to say, 'Look, even wholesome, solid, kind men like this wet the bed, so don't worry about it.' Another big name was Bill Gates. That figures: the über-nerd cowering in his sodden sheets. Britney Spears too. (I think we're moving into a different area here, so let's move on . . .) I wet the bed three or four times a week right up until I was in my last year at primary school. It was soul-destroying for me and very boring for my parents. I used to wake up and think, *Oh no, not again – another Tintin book ruined* . . . (Actually the hardbacks were remarkably durable.) Poor Mum and Dad. I never thought about them having to strip the bed and wash the sheets over and over again. They must have worried, too, but it was the seventies and no one – least of all children – saw analysts or psychiatrists then. They couldn't ask an expert, so they used to ask me.

'Why have you wet the bed again?'

'I don't know,' I'd say. 'Do you think I enjoy it?'

I was sharing a room with my elder brother, Robert. We were in bunk beds, and I got moved down from the top bunk for obvious reasons.

My parents tried all the available cures. First off, no fluids after six o'clock. This didn't work – I was only six, so it wasn't like I was out drinking seven or eight pints of Ribena a night. They also tried offering me a treat or gift in the morning if I didn't empty my bladder in bed – a toy maybe, or a special lunch. I remember once they promised me a trip to the fair. I can clearly recall Mum tucking me in and talking about the helter-skelter and the dodgems. I went to bed with a smile on my face: no way was I going to piss this opportunity away.

I woke up soaked in urine again. I was gutted, and cried when she came into the room. They still took me to the fair of course.

The other precaution they embarked on was more proactive. It'd be midnight – the witching hour – and in my room silence would lie like careful mist; primitive robots and toy soldiers frozen mid-play, books stacked neatly, some orange peel rotting in the corner where I'd thrown it, a dead fly sitting crisp on the window sill. All at once the door would burst open and my parents would appear. The harsh sixty-watt bulb would blink into life, temporarily blinding me. I'd be dragged out of bed, half-asleep like some tiny political prisoner, and marched into the bathroom. More harsh electric light – a hundred watts! They'd then sort of hang me over the toilet and fumble my tiny cock out of my pyjamas and encourage me to pee into the bowl. By this time I'd be fully awake and the strange thing was that they'd always be talking about something completely unconnected to what we as a family were doing. Like the guttering, or renewing Dad's National Trust membership. Sometimes they'd actually be arguing about something while I was shaken down. It was odd, to say the least. I'd then be put back to bed – drained of liquid waste, happy, proud, and slightly traumatised.

Of course my brother would be woken up by the intrusion too, so he'd have the right hump. It didn't work, needless to say.

The last resort was a blanket they bought for me, which you plugged into the mains and placed over your offending child's torso. It had some sort of sensor and when the kid started to pee an alarm went off. So . . . On the first night, they tucked me in, lit the blue touch-paper and retired.

At around twelve-thirty they were woken by a furious beeping. They rushed into my room and found me fast asleep, the alarm going off as I peed on regardless.

I remained a committed bedwetter until the summer of '73. I was on a school journey on the Isle of Wight, that glamorous bit of rock off Southampton. I was in my last year at Brooklands. We were all crammed into a B&B/hotel in Shanklin – so crammed I had to share a bed with Graham Wooldridge (it was all good clean fun, though: we weren't at Eton). There was a single bed in our room, which Paul Cobb took. It was a shabby little garret, straight out of a Graham Greene novel, as was the rest of the hotel, but we children banished his Catholic guilt and seedy whispered conversation with shouts of joy and unconfined glee as we thrust pillows in each other's faces and hurled soggy spoonfuls of cornflakes at one another. I became the trip's Shoplifter-in-Chief: if you wanted something pinching you had only to ask and I'd snake it under my coat and hand it over outside the shop. The main gift on people's lists here was a funny little test tube of different-coloured sands denoting a visit to Blackgang

Chine, a bit of beach where such a miracle of nature occurred. Ten different colours of sand! All in stripes! You can keep the Hanging Gardens of Babylon . . . Actually at the time I loved my little knick-knack and kept it on my bedroom shelf for ages, often twisting it around in my little mitts, mixing up the sands into a kaleidoscope of grains. When my dad eventually saw the mess I'd created inside the glass he sighed and said, 'You've ruined it.'

I stole about four tubes and doled them out to happy hands on the pavement. I couldn't get any more – security was tight. They must have lost a lot of stock every summer, poor sods. Still, the sand was free, wasn't it? And test tubes cost fuck all.

I was very worried about my bladder letting me down and introducing Wooldridge to my own version of water sports. I didn't think he'd appreciate it – we were only eleven after all. But the captain of the football and cricket teams awoke at around seven-thirty one summer morning to discover a patch of piss under his left buttock. He shouted, 'Eeugh! What's that?'

I was mortified, having been awake for hours soaked in urine and terror waiting for him to stir.

What could I do? I'd crept out of bed and changed my pyjamas and put a towel under me, but there was too much fluid. I wished it had been blood. I wished I'd slashed my wrists – that would have been less embarrassing.

'Please don't tell anyone I've wet the bed, Gray. You won't tell anyone, will you! Sorry . . .' I was a stuttering, muttering fool.

I remember quite clearly that as he went to the bathroom he said, 'Don't worry, I won't say anything.'

We filed down to breakfast, girls on one table, boys on the other, the din, the teachers trying to establish order. Graham Greene had his pen out. I was fucked.

I remember all I was worried about were the girls finding out. The girls – why the girls?

I'd kept my eyes on Wooldridge like a sparrowhawk on a mouse since we'd entered the room. He sat opposite me with his back to the girls' table. At some stage I knew he would tell. Wouldn't you? He wasn't a care worker. I saw him lean back in his chair, his head entering the girls' atmosphere.

I can't remember which of the girls he spoke to, but she turned her chair round to face me as he whispered . . . something.

What? Was I imagining this?

Suddenly her jaw jacked open like a Pez sweet dispenser. She looked up briefly at me in horror and pity, then spun back to her cohorts.

I wished I was dead.

I never wet the bed again, though.

(I did, actually: seventeen years later in Dublin with an ex-model, but I *had* drunk fourteen pints of Guinness . . .)

My dad was a product of the public-school system. He was born in a house called the Mount in Surrey; prep school, boarding school, Cambridge. He enlisted and drove some oil drums about in Kent somewhere as the war was drawing to a close, then became a civil servant for a bit before working as an architect. He wore glasses like Eric Morecambe, had a study, drank Ruddles or Martini Rosso, and had fearsome powers of concentration. Like all human beings he was a mass of contradictions. To me as a child he sometimes seemed almost from another planet, while at others he was a normal loving dad. I wasn't an obedient child. I wanted it both ways: I wanted to rebel, to cock a snook, and to be admired and loved at the same time. My dad was strict, shy, kind, stubborn, academic and pompous. He was both distant and loving. He was very clever but in a way I couldn't get down with, a way I couldn't admire. I found his intellect to be very rigid.

He was Establishment to the core: Home Counties, Tory upbringing; very secure, he was, in his way. He did everything by the book, had magnificent handwriting and polished his shoes with an aggression and diligence I found overwhelming. He did everything properly: took his time, read the manual, purchased the right tools. Don't get me wrong, he could get quite steamed up indulging in DIY – 'damn' and 'blast' were the swearwords of choice – but he always prepared the ground. He left nothing to chance in everything he did – which is why he was a bit confused by me, a right chancer. I had a strange combination of insecurity and confidence that was hard to identify. He had a good sense of humour, though, and we used to watch comedy together. It was the seventies so we were spoilt for choice: *Porridge*, *The Likely Lads*, *Dad's Army* and of course *Morecambe and Wise*. It was one of the only things we really bonded over. A shared laugh is a balm to any relationship – that magic understanding; it brought a closeness we struggled to enjoy in other areas. He just didn't get me. I couldn't sit still, I couldn't write properly, I was hopeless at maths and fixing things, I used to drift off in conversation and stare out of the window. I should've run away and joined something, but what? The circus? The Royal Ballet? Like most kids I didn't know what I wanted but I knew what I didn't want: his world.

His grandfather had come from Essex, built up a property firm from scratch and passed it on to his son, my grandfather Frank. I never really knew Frank; he was heavily medicated whenever I sat on his knee. The firm was based in St John's Wood and was sold on at the time of his death to his partner, Michael Percy. I think my dad, his two brothers and one sister, Jane, got a nice wedge, but there was no trickle-down effect to me, thank God – I cannot imagine what a nightmare I would have become if I'd been a trustafarian.

My father's mother, Dorothy, could be summed up in one word: 'class'. She was good-looking, witty, charming and clever. She came from that select breed of women who'd appear in British films of the forties and fifties, formidable and resourceful, but always laughing. She was the sort of person who would have taken charge had there been some sort of calamity – a flood or a collapsed building – quietly instructing everyone, bandaging legs, marshalling children, occasionally raising her voice at the odd spineless man.

Every year she'd take me and my elder brother to see the new James Bond film at the Odeon Leicester Square. She often wore a mink stole and pearls and before entering the cinema we'd be taken to a posh London store and set loose on the pick-and-mix sweet wall. This was not the tired collection of fizzy snakes and stale hard gums you find now at your local multiplex, but was the best of British confectionery: individually wrapped chocolate caramels, proper humbugs, mints in a wide variety of strengths. I was like a pig in shit and would approach the till hopefully with four or five pounds in weight of sweets, smiling like an African dictator approaching Customs at Geneva airport. She'd then lead me back gently to reluctantly return most of my bounty.

Grandparents in general always seem more attractive than your parents. They always have more treats, for one, plus they only have to deal with you every other weekend, so you appear like a breath of fresh air and not the scowling, sulking horror you really are.

My dad had an older sister named Jane, a younger brother called Jeremy and an older brother who was never there. Jane was much like her mother, a bit taller but with the same slightly clipped way of speaking, frequently descending into laughter. Jeremy was an early hero of mine. He was suave and handsome; he played golf and had a large set of clubs in a leather golf bag that was always in the garage. I'd often wander in and examine these huge tools, engineered and built with as much care and precision as any Samurai sword. I was too small to pull a club right out of the bag and made do with examining the heads and handles, twirling the cold steel in my hot little hands. I enjoyed rummaging through the bag's pockets, the golf balls like giant gobstoppers you could not eat. I once bounced a few of them around the garage but was worried they'd smash into a thousand pieces.

We would visit my dad's parents around every three weeks, I think; all the family would be there. They lived in a huge house in Henley-on-Thames, and had thick carpets, lime-green shag-pile in the downstairs toilet (with matching carpet on the toilet seat – whizzo!), a large television, housed in walnut veneer, that we weren't allowed to watch, and an enormous garden with an ornamental pond complete with cherub fountain. The house was big, modern and light. I imagine the furniture came from John Lewis. Oh, and they had a gardener called Murket too – now that *does* sound posh.

On reaching the house I'd run through the living room, out the back door and into the garden shed to press the white switch that turned on the fountain. A small spurt of water would leap from the cherub's mouth and rain down softly on the fish beneath. I would watch for a bit, then turn it off and on rapidly, then trudge back into the house feeling cheated: it was never as good as I'd remembered it.

My dad's family were very close – clannish almost – and I think my mum struggled with this a bit. As a unit they were well-off and confident, certain in their political beliefs and unafraid of what the day might bring. They'd sit round the table like a *Punch* cartoon, laughing at jokes and events I was never really in on. I wanted to be part of it but never was, being much too young. There were loads of cousins and aunts and people twice removed who appeared now and then, a lot of whom seemed to be in the forces, but I only really knew the core group.

Once back from the garden I'd say my hellos and then wander around the house eating any boiled sweets I could find. At lunch table manners were important – not speaking out of turn, that sort of thing – but all in all I loved going there. It was a different world. They all still had that Empire confidence about them, which made me feel safe.

Chapter Two

I had two brothers. Robert was a year older than me and I tried to hang around with him as much as possible. My younger brother, Toby, went to boarding school when I went to borstal and I didn't really see him again until we were both living in Brighton in the mid-nineties.

Robert was always more grown-up than me. He was sensible and trustworthy and also talented and clever. He didn't have any obvious flaws as a person, which was difficult as we were growing up because I felt that my parents were comparing me to him constantly. We got on all right until he went to public school then a sort of gulf appeared. We had a fairly standard younger brother/older brother relationship: I was always breaking his things and doing things he got blamed for. I'd be kept out of his room and he wouldn't encourage his friends to associate with me. My main problem was clumsiness: excessive clumsiness. I was always spilling drinks and breaking toys; furniture would rebel and fall apart at my touch. I had a habit of worrying fabrics until they came undone. I pressed the wrong buttons, opened the wrong doors, drawers were always sticking then flying open, hurling their contents skywards. I was hopeless with any kind of machinery.

A lot of this stuff is quite normal, I suspect, but at the time each incident felt like a little crime. *What's wrong with me?* I'd think as people began searching for the hamster or sweeping up the broken glass.

At an early age I became the problem kid: by accident *and* design, I think. I started bucking authority, being a pest. I remember people used to say to me, 'You think you're clever,' and I *did*! But how can you think you're clever? What if you're insane? Where does that leave you? My dad was easiest to disagree with, as he had very strong views about what I should be, what I should like and how I should apply myself to my education: CONCENTRATE . . .

Every year Dad forced us kids to watch the Royal Tournament on TV. I hated it: idiotic, pointless, men in uniforms dismantling cannons and carrying them over makeshift walls. Then one year he took me to see it live. Cadets bussed in from Sandhurst, the stalls selling military paraphernalia, the smell of gunpowder and horse shit, my dad glowing with pride, standing for the National Anthem.

The Red Arrows were another family fixture. We'd stand in the burning sun, our tiny necks cricked as we stared into the clouds watching for those magnificent men in their flying machines. Now you see them, now you don't – wow, there they go! Superb. I must have seen the Red Arrows seven or eight times. My dad was always crowbarring in air displays and military bonanza into our family holidays.

Another annual day out was the Lord Mayor's Show. Squeezing through the crowds, asking to sit on someone's shoulders, cheering a fat man covered in jewellery. I remember asking an uncle what the Lord Mayor did for a living and being met with a stony glare. Is there anything more boring than pageantry? Dad was crazy for any of that shit – royal weddings, the Changing of the Guard . . . I remember nodding off to Winston Churchill's funeral, the somnolent, sober tones of the commentary washing over me like clouds of Mogadon gas.

I liked football and wrestling. For him it was rugby and cricket. I had no interest in yachting or any kind of spirited travelogue.

I suppose he was part of that Boy's Own generation, climbing mountains and suppressing 'fuzzy wuzzies', the stoic stiff upper lip. To him the British Empire meant Wedgwood china and Edmond Hillary; to me, Wall's ice cream and Brian Clough. One night we were brought downstairs to witness Sir Francis Chichester complete his round-the-world voyage. We had a tiny black-and-white TV at the time and I struggled to make out the image of the plucky pensioner wobbling on to shore – it was like watching an Etch A Sketch in a sandstorm. Don't get me wrong, it was great to be up at that time of night, but his achievements left me unmoved. It wasn't much of a spectacle, a man staggering off a boat. I was half asleep anyway and I just didn't get that type of endeavour. An awkward, ungrateful little sod I was then . . . Or was I?

On rainy days Pa would always discover an obscure war film on the telly and we'd watch it together. Some of them were good, actually (*Went the Day Well?* among others) but I couldn't get down with the army vibe. He was so proud of the British war effort, whether fact or fiction. Bursting with pride, he'd get the books out and try to interest me in the finer points of Waterloo and Dunkirk. *Jane's Fighting Ships*: an enormous series of volumes detailing every naval warcraft ever built! You needed a forklift truck to read it. I would have rather Braille-read a cheese grater but I didn't want to shatter his dreams. He bought me rulers and compasses, a set of woodworking tools, showed me blueprints of building foundations I didn't understand. The thing was, I never told him outright: 'This is shit, Dad! I have no interest in this.' I was as emotionally stymied as him, in a way.

Unfortunately my brother Robert didn't help matters. He was academic, didn't wet the bed and worked hard. By the time he followed Dad to university I was squatting, smoking pot and wanking in sleeping bags. My overwhelming image of Dad is one of kindness and love, but kindness and love that he found hard to articulate. I remember once when I was in court he was asked by the judge if he had anything to say. He stood up.

'Yes,' he said firmly. Then he faltered; the words wouldn't come. He 'um'ed and 'er'ed for what seemed like for ever. My friend in the dock with me was laughing, but to me it was awful – I really felt for him that day. I wanted to hug him and tell him it was going to be OK: we'd only been arrested for breach of the peace. Of course it wasn't OK. His marriage went down and so did I – not then but soon after.

My mum's dad was gassed in the war and had a market-garden shop-thing. They lived in a terrace and you could pump rain-water from a barrel for their outside toilet. They had toilets in the house too but I liked the outside bog – the spider webs, the yellowing newspapers, the overwhelming smell of must and creosote. It had a pale light that appealed to me and I'd sit there now and again imagining the olden days. Margaret Grindrod was my mother's name. She was clever but the family couldn't afford to send her to university so she went to work as a nurse in London, giddy London. After a few false starts she married my dad and moved to leafy Blackheath where she gave birth to me. As a child I loved my mum but this was dependent on her working tremendously hard for me as an unpaid servant. It seemed completely normal at the time that I didn't lift a finger. I wasn't spoilt as such, but she cooked and cleaned and organised for me and my brothers and just did not stop. I remember she'd say things like, 'This is the first time I've sat down all day,' and it would be eight o'clock at night. It just didn't register with me; I just thought, *Yes, but that's your job.*

Food-wise she was immense. She cooked three meals a day, every day, with all the puddings too: apple crumble, steam pudding, syllabub, gooseberry fool, queen of puddings, apple pie, baked apples . . . She did this every fucking day! And all the classic main courses: steak and kidney pie, toad-in-the-hole, spaghetti bolognaise, Lancashire hotpot, macaroni cheese; six kinds of potatoes, and all the veg.

Are you listening, women of today, with your hummus and your tiny sea-bass fillets? Get your aprons on and get stuck in! The kitchen is meant to be full of steam, not cocaine-driven conversation and bunches of dried chillies you'll never use.

I'm proud of my mum. She brought us all up, educated herself, qualified as a teacher (remedial English), started smoking Silk Cut, joined the SDP, then met and fell in love with a man she still dotes on today. As the Americans would say, she really grew as a person. I'm not being patronising here: after sixteen years of grafting for the family she started thinking about herself. I can understand that. I started thinking about myself the minute I was born and haven't stopped since. Not a day goes by when I'm not mired in self-obsession; having children has helped but it's all about me in the end.

She was strict with us, though. She smacked our legs now and then, shut us in our rooms, the usual fare. I think we three kids drove her mad but I was the worst. As a kid I did the normal stuff – fighting, teasing, not sharing – but I also had a sort of death wish as far as my relationship with grown-ups was concerned. I'd push and push my parents' buttons until they cracked. But they never hit me properly, even though I deserved it often enough.

We'd visit my mum's parents quite a lot. We often spent whole weekends there, which suited me down to the ground – the main reason being my nan. Eileen Grindrod spoilt us rotten. We had eggy fingers for breakfast – French toast, the Yanks call it. This was Mother's Pride dipped in egg and fried in butter. It was delicious and all the better eaten in bed with a *Whizzer and Chips* or a *Victor*. My brother Robert and I shared a room upstairs at the back of the house. I loved the slightly musty smell of the numerous bedcovers that weighed you off to sleep every night. Even in summer we'd have two sheets, two blankets, a knitted blanket of some sort and a small silky eiderdown. I always felt very secure under that lot but as I got older having a hand shandy proved difficult.

Lunch was often a full roast, with beef or pork absolutely annihilated in the oven. The meat was always brown and the veg (often from the garden) was cooked for ages. I was a potato man and the roast spuds were always good, as were the new potatoes (again from the garden). She kicked on again with the pudding: homemade jam roly-poly with egg custard (I never ate that, though: too sloppy).

We'd have homemade scones for tea, with homemade jam. And she made us egg and chips every Friday when we arrived, the chips scattered on to newspaper or kitchen roll, then put into bowls, good eggs thrown on top, the wire holder thrust back into the murky boiling lard. She made bread and dripping for my mum, too, which I found a bit scary: I wasn't a war baby.

For obvious reasons I was very, very happy whenever I was under that roof. My gran liked me and frequently called me a 'card', which in reality I later came to be.

My nan would wake at seven and start knitting immediately. She'd get dressed – a twinset or jumper and thick skirt – and start cleaning the house, emptying fire grates, washing steps, sweeping yards. Like my mum, she didn't stop. My mum would try to get her to sit down but that was an alien concept to her; if forced, she'd just start knitting again. Her joints were always bandaged, it seemed to me, ankles and elbows, knees and wrists, and she twittered rather than had a straight conversation. She was too busy to sit down and have a chat, even when we were there.

She had a catchphrase – 'I didn't like to say anything' – which often ended a particular strand of conversation. She'd be reporting some terrible events involving Mrs Arkwright from number 89, a friend of hers who had just discovered her son was a murderer and her husband a paedophile, and she'd pause in her knitting and say, 'I didn't like to say anything.'

Granddad was the strong but silent type. He said hardly anything but if I resemble anyone in the family it's him, with his large frame, bald head and slightly slitty eyes. He had a ruddy complexion and almost blistered hands from working outdoors all his life. I remember his hands, hard and calloused, when he was hurling me about under the pretence of bouncing me on his knee.

Once, after a family outing in Blackheath, my nan shut my finger in the door of the Cortina. I started screaming but she – still inside the car and a little hard of hearing – thought I was joshing; she was laughing, pointing at me saying, 'Ooh, you are a one!' Suddenly a spurt of blood hit the car window and I clearly remember the colour draining from her face instantly. She'd gone into shock and slowly, slowly released the door to free my little finger, which was hanging on by a small piece of skin. I was rushed into the house screaming like a napalm victim.

My mum turned off the telly, causing my little brother, Toby, to burst into tears (he was watching *Tom and Jerry*). The thing I recall was this: Mum said to her father, 'Go and look after Mum, she's upset.' Nan had come into the room silently, white as a sheet and not speaking, her body bent forwards as if she was pushing herself into a great wind. With my little finger wrapped in a tea towel, I watched Granddad as he looked at my grandmother.

'She's all right,' he told Mum and went and sat in a chair, ignoring his wife.

That really hit home, that; the hardness of it. He didn't seem to have the ability to comfort her – nor the desire.

That generation didn't make a fuss. He'd been gassed in the trenches and I doubt he ever moaned about that. What would he have made of *Big Brother* or Premiership footballers, *Jeremy Kyle* or Peter Mandelson?

I would constantly steal any sweet foodstuffs in the house and eat them all, then stuff the remains and wrappers down the back of sofas, radiators, wherever.

I mean everything, from a family pack of Club biscuits (which were intended for the whole family) to all the chocolate digestives, flapjacks, rock cakes – gone! All the packs of raw jelly. I've been known to box down sugar in any form: caster, icing, brown, refined, unrefined . . . If Mum made any cakes I'd get in the tin like a fox in a hen coop and leave the contents torn to pieces. Also any cake decorations: hundreds and thousands, those little silver balls, bits of candied peel, sultanas, raisins.

Nothing would escape my lunatic gorging.

My dad had a sweet tooth and his more adult and glamorous sweetmeats would be savaged too. Pontefract cakes, Liquorice Allsorts, glacé fruits – all dispatched. Of course my prime hunting season was the Christmas period, when I'd be constantly chewing: After Eights, Matchmakers, Quality Street and – the *pièce de résistance* – the liqueurs.

I was showing early signs of an addictive nature; but my parents didn't know and nor did I – they just thought I was thoughtless and greedy. I was, but I once ate four packs of lime jelly in one sitting and that's not normal, is it?

And the interesting thing about the liqueurs was that I didn't like them! I hated the taste of the booze and yet I'd still eat them all, just for the chocolate. I'd wince and gag the little bells and angels of chocolate down my gullet and then burn the box. I was never sick, though, never ever. I didn't do that bulimic vibe and I now have the love handles to prove it.

Vision On was a popular children's programme featuring kindly, shabby Tony Hart. They did arts-and-crafts stuff and it featured Morph, a Plasticine creature who got up to fancy tricks. My favourite bit was at the end, when the camera panned over all these pictures on the wall that were painted by children (they were handicapped, I think). They told you in sign language in no uncertain terms that they couldn't return any of the pictures. I thought this cruel and unfair: the pictures were brilliant – watercolours painted by four-year-olds! The standard was much higher than now. On CBeebies now they encourage kids to send in pictures of CBeebies characters, which is shoddy and smacks of greed: it's only so they can sell merchandise.

Tony Hart was doing a live PA one day and my mum took me to meet him. He sat sweating behind a table looking persecuted, a long line of children (including me) snaking away from him. It was very exciting – I'd never met a TV star before. We inched forward; he was drawing pictures for people and smiling. I stared at him like a girl looking at a blouse in a shop window. Finally I was face-to-face with the great man himself.

'What would you like me to draw?' he said.

'Snoopy, please.' I was mad on the *Peanuts* cartoon strip.

'I can't draw Snoopy but I can draw you another dog.'

I faltered. 'No, thank you; Snoopy, please.'

'I can't draw Snoopy but I can draw you a different dog.'

My patience was wearing thin. I looked up at my mum; was he taking the piss?

'Can you draw me Snoopy, please?' *(Just draw it, you sweaty fucker . . .)*

He stared at me for a bit too long. 'I can't draw you Snoopy but I can draw you another dog.' He was quite firm.

My mum hushed me up. I was astonished by his behaviour – how hard could Snoopy be?

He drew me a shit dog, a sort of Thelwell friendly-hairy-dog thing.

I have no idea why Tony Hart refused my request – was it some contractual thing with the BBC, or did he just hate Snoopy? Maybe he was jealous of Charles Schulz's wealth. I was absolutely gutted. My mum couldn't understand why I was so angry; she told me to shut up after a while. That was the first time the BBC let me down. It wouldn't be the last.

Apart from Obelix my first real hero was my friends Ben and Dan's dad, Ray Joseph. I'd known his two sons since I was five. They lived in a basement flat in a huge Georgian house round the corner from us. Their mum's name was Thelda; she was a handsome woman with a dry sense of humour and she was pals with my mother. She had a funny way of looking at you, and I found out much later she had a glass eye. This was drawn to my attention by a bloke called John Gordon, who asked Dan if he could take out her glass eye and fuck her eye socket. Nice of him to ask. He also asked if he could fuck my mum. I found this really funny but my elder brother was deeply upset. Was there something wrong with me? Do comics have a broken moral compass?

I felt a connection with Ray as soon I met him. He woke me up as if from a long sleep. He was the first grown-up to treat me like an adult and he didn't seem puzzled by me. He laughed at a lot of the things I said and this made me feel special – something I hadn't felt before. He was Jewish, very clever, slightly hangdog and ruffled-looking with wiry hair. He kept odd hours and never seemed to have any clothes on in the house, just a selection of dressing gowns and robes.

He was a professional gambler by trade and got a black cab up to town every day at eleven sharp (how cool is that?). When he was at home he sat around most of the time, playing mah jong or backgammon and listening to the Who or Ten Years After. This was where I first saw the album *Quadrophenia*, and I was very taken with the giant photos inside. When I listened to that album and looked at those images – the fry-up, the kid in the tunnel (a tunnel I'd walked through), the sea, the emptiness of it all – a majestic melancholy soaked through me like sea spray, all that rage and frustration. It's the ultimate adolescent album; I can't describe how affected I was by it. Much later, when I was homeless, I became obsessed with the film and used to travel down to Brighton to watch it. Lingering around on the beach, thinking about dossing down for the night under the pier, I'd stare up at the cast-iron arches of that Victorian monolith, as distant and forbidding as any cathedral, while under my feet the shingle slipped and slid in the waves like the penny falls in the arcades above, on and on mercilessly with no winners. But I found the whole thing too wet and spooky: those mods must have had waterproof sleeping bags – two-tone shell with mohair inside, probably. Later still I lived in Brighton, a compelling town but not restful, not peaceful. It's no place to lay your weary head.

Ray Joseph had been a genius maths pupil. He'd gone to a top boarding school until he was expelled after being caught using the phone in the headmaster's office to put a bet on (again, how cool is that?). His excellent maths brain meant he was immediately offered a place at Manchester Grammar. I think he flunked out of there too. My dad had told me this over lunch one day, relaying this information as evidence of how Ray had wasted his life. He summed up by saying, 'The man lives completely outside the system.' Of course that last line completely confirmed Ray's reputation for me: he was the king of everything! *He lived completely outside the system . . .*

Ray taught me to play backgammon and by some crazy fluke I beat him the third time I played him. His sons loved this and ribbed him mercilessly. The victory also sealed my friendship with Ray and he took me under his wing after that, teaching me different card games and even trying to teach me mah jong. He introduced me to his whacky friends, odds and sods who were vaguely hippified and often sat in a sort of lotus position. Ray did yoga and meditated – although he was probably meditating on the gee-gees. He put me in a yoga pose once and told me that monks could sit in sub-zero temperatures in that position for hours and feel no chill; they'd have a fire in their bellies.

'Can you feel the warmth?' he said.

'Yes,' I lied, wanting a wee.

I have no doubt he was smoking pot in the house but I never saw or smelt anything. He told me a story once: he'd been watching the con guys on Oxford Street doing 'find the lady' on a packing case; he'd watched them for ages, until it started to rain, then Ray counted the number of rain spots on the queen and took them for 150 quid. Another time he'd sped round in a cab putting money on different horses in different bookies, driving the odds up on a horse he fancied.

The *Sporting Life* later called him a 'gang of crooks'. Him alone, a gang of crooks! Of course, I was eleven years old so he was like a god to me. My poor old dad couldn't compete with a man who played me Jimi Hendrix while discussing *Zen and the Art of Motorcycle Maintenance*.

My dad gave me Hornblower books. My dad went to work on the train and walked home with his briefcase, swinging his umbrella.

Ray ate egg and chips at two in the afternoon and had a pair of silver balls he'd swirl round in his palms to help him think.

My dad had Allen keys.

Ray had Rizlas.

My dad had a Black & Decker Workmate.

Ray had a chess set designed by the same guy who did the cover of *Yessongs*.

One day Ray took me and my elder brother, Robert, out for a treat with Ben and Dan. I wondered where we were going . . . Only to the Hard Rock Cafe! It was the most excited I had ever been in my life. This was when hamburgers were still a mythical dream: we'd heard about them, seen them in films, but unless you were lucky enough to have been taken to a Wimpy (and, of course, being middle class our parents shunned the Wimpy) they were a divine mystery. We had to queue up – so exciting! There was a red rope between two gold posts. We went in, and the walls were covered in guitars and pictures of bands that I'd heard in Ray's house, like the Stones and Pink Floyd.

I'd been at Ben and Dan's the fateful day Ray entered the room with *Wish You Were Here*, Pink Floyd's follow-up to *Dark Side of the Moon*. Again the artwork amazed me and we sat, the four of us, and listened to the whole album.

At the end Ray got up, gathering his dressing gown around him.

'It's not as good as *Dark Side of the Moon*,' he said.

No, I thought, and I proceeded to tell anyone and everyone I met the same thing.

'It's not as good as *Dark Side of the Moon*,' I'd say when I saw it in someone's house. How they respected me then.

I told people who'd never heard of Pink Floyd, too, like the Greek barber and the postman. All would nod reverently.

I had a down-home double burger and Devil's food cake; also a big Coke full of bobbing ice. The ice was so sophisticated. I held the glass up to the light and chinked it. Jeez, we were really living. I remember it as if it was yesterday. I'm not sure of the wisdom of letting eleven-year-old boys add their own relish, as we judged the condiments on colour rather than flavour, but the whole experience was mind-blowing and we jabbered about it the whole way home.

We badgered my dad to return the favour and naturally we asked if we could go back to the Hard Rock, as we now called it. He kept saying he was too busy and such. I must have really bugged him about it because I was sliding up and down on the back of his chair whining about it one day when he suddenly lost his temper, which was very rare. Ben and Dan were duly phoned and Dad, still fuming, dragged us on to a train up to Charing Cross, then marched us towards Leicester Square.

I was still droning on about the Hard Rock, saying, 'I don't think it's this way,' and, 'There'll probably be a queue.'

He took us into the first burger joint on that little strip leading to Leicester Square – a Golden Egg or something. How embarrassed we were. It was a far cry from the framed prints of the Moody Blues and Chuck Berry's Rickenbacker pinned like a butterfly above the toilet door. The walls were barren and there was no relish. Then – horror of horrors – he made us eat our burgers with knives and forks! How square can you get, Daddio? Ben and Dan were laughing into their hands.

I was mortified. He'd really shown me what he thought of Ray's world, and once again had inadvertently cemented Ray's genius in my tiny mind. I don't know why he'd been so against the whole thing; it may have been that Mum had nagged him too – that would have really put his back up. I know that when I have something to do and then my wife asks me to do it, it suddenly becomes the most disgusting, most difficult task in the world.

It's hard being a parent. You step out of line once and you're branded a clown for ever. Still, the knife-and-fork thing: that was unforgivable.

It's strange how addicts locate each other, like vampires or werewolves – there must be hidden signs along with the more obvious ones. I'd never gambled then but would later embark on a disastrous gaming spree. Ray still gambles now. He's been through millions. He lives in a council flat with three tellies, betting on different sports in the middle of the night.

When I knew him he made most of his money in prestigious backgammon tournaments across Europe. I imagined him playing poker with Omar Sharif and Sean Connery. He made it look easy. He was shortcut man and so am I.

Now everyone is a gambler; everyone plays poker online and they all tell me they do all right, but someone must be losing.

It's weird. If Ray had been my dad I would have probably turned out very different. I would have seen through the black cabs and the packs of cards, the broken promises and the skint birthdays. As it was, from the age of eleven till I was fourteen he was one of the single most impressive people I knew. Raymondo, I salute you.

Blackheath was a brilliant place to grow up, a leafy, lazy suburb that seemed enormous to me. We went wherever we pleased, sunup to sundown. There was very little violence, certainly no poverty; there weren't even many cars. We smoked, spat, shoplifted and spent. It was like the country without cow shit and cattle – which was what the suburbs were meant to be, I suppose: the best of both worlds.

I was lucky that in my life as a kid it all went to plan: there were no short, sharp shocks, no one betrayed me. It was exactly the same as the children's books I read. Everyone was clean and nice, there were monsters around but I never smelt their breath. We sat in gardens under trees and drank our lemonade, and went to Devon or East Anglia for our hols. At Christmas our stockings were always full of interesting and imaginative little gifts, and on Bonfire Nights we sat gorging on hot Ribena and baked potatoes while my dad took charge of the fireworks. We lived on a small-span estate and he'd place the fireworks in tubs of sand, using very long tapers to light them. Everyone was kept well back – in those days, the only real dangers posed to middle-class kids were fireworks and being run over. If a lit firework didn't go off, I'd be the kid who approached it jauntily while the rest of the kids hung back in awe. My dad would shout, 'Get back, Simon!' but every time the blue touch-paper didn't ignite I'd creep forward, like a junior bomb-disposal expert without any training.

Like I said, I loved growing up in Blackheath and it all seemed completely safe, but from what I hear there was a lot of paedophile activity around there in the 1970s. Many different people have told me of encounters and close shaves with dirty old men and the like throughout their childhoods. In those days there were many more available open spaces and patches of waste ground on which offenders could strut their stuff. I somehow missed out on that kind of attention. I was approached, I'm sure, but I think I got on the men's nerves, annoyed them during the early part of the chat-up procedure, so nothing more ever happened to me. They'd offer me a sweet and I'd mash down the whole packet in seconds. I remember a man approaching me on Blackheath once and striking up a conversation about Wimbledon. He told me they used more than three thousand balls in the tournament. I was impressed.

'Do you know what they do with them after?' he enquired. Then: 'They sell them abroad,' he said triumphantly.

I walked away at that point, a bit freaked out – I'd thought he said 'ball *boys*', not 'balls'. *Three thousand ball boys sold abroad? The man is some kind of cretin ...*

There was a guy called Jim who worked at Deptford railway station. He had the uniform with gold braid on the hat and everything and was in some sort of position of authority – I've no idea what. Anyway, in the summer he ran a project involving the restoration of the Tenterden light railway in Kent. There was no doubting his enthusiasm for railway transport in all its forms, but he also had great enthusiasm for young boys stripped to the waist and wielding pickaxes and shovels.

My elder brother, Robert, was just such a boy. Jim was a clever man. He came to our house in the evening in his full British Rail livery. My dad was impressed. He showed our parents blueprints of the task ahead, the re-laying of the sleepers and suchlike. He used to wait outside for Rob, sweating in his peaked cap, and they'd go for little walks up the road and back. Of course I wanted to go with them but Jim didn't like me: I had yet to reach puberty, which may have naused it for me. I'd try to join in their little conflabs but Robert would tell me to go away.

One night my brother was upstairs and I went out to have a chat with Jim. He grunted a few times at me before telling me to piss off. I was appalled. I told my mum and I think his days were then numbered.

Rob stayed at Jim's house one weekend and was given Guinness and slept on the floor. He went on a few Tenterden weekends too – how I envied him! Nothing happened, though: Jim never put any moves on my brother. On the weekends in Kent he had about a dozen boys to choose from, and I suppose it was a careful selection process and Robert may have fallen at the final hurdle. He missed his chance with me – I'd have given him a run for his money, that's for sure.

Chapter Three

After the bedwetting incident on the Isle of Wight I was very glad to be leaving Brooklands. I had a clean slate: no one knew me as that person, so I could reinvent myself as anything I pleased. A year earlier my elder brother had got a half-scholarship and gone from Brooklands to Dulwich College, which was a very good private school. From the word go I was amazed by the amount of homework he got – an hour and a half a night. Apparently he became so arrogant during his first year at Dulwich that my mum vowed I would go to a comprehensive. I think my academic results helped realise her dream, being as how I couldn't write or spell and was a world-class daydreamer. (My partial dyslexia and Attention-Deficit Disorder remained undiagnosed, of course.) So the local comp was a foregone conclusion.

My new school was Thomas Tallis in Kidbrooke, which is a shithole bordering Blackheath. Basically, north of Blackheath are interesting poor areas – Deptford, New Cross and Lewisham – and south of Blackheath are uninteresting poor areas – Kidbrooke, Eltham, Welling. The deep south, really. Once you get over Shooters Hill it all gets a bit ignorant and racist. Stephen Lawrence was killed in Eltham and the BNP get a lot of votes from round that way. I realise these comments will hit my book sales in places like Blackfen and Erith, Swanley and Thamesmead, but c'est la vie: you can't write a whole book without some crass generalisations.

To get to Thomas Tallis I had to walk through the Ferrier Estate, a huge concrete jungle that was (is) the gateway from Blackheath to Kidbrooke and beyond. It mainly housed people from the surrounding areas but also a large amount of overspill tenants from Bermondsey, which was another very rough working-class area past New Cross down by the river. I knew a bloke who went to school in Bermondsey and he claimed the only way out of there was football or robbing banks. According to Wikipedia, the Ferrier is one of the largest and most-deprived estates in London and is due for an overhaul; it could have done with one thirty-five years ago! It was a stereotypical failed-experiment nightmare-bunghole of a place, with smashed windows and graffiti everywhere. It was grey all over, grey walls, grey floors, grey faces. It had walkways high up linking the towers – all that jazz that was considered futuristic when they built it but just became a boon to muggers. I went past the other day and someone has painted all the balconies different colours, like putting a hat on an elephant, but it doesn't effect the overall dismal and gloomy look.

I was quite shocked when I first walked through the Ferrier. I trod carefully, swinging my new briefcase, my shiny basin haircut (washed in Silvikrin) hopefully warding off evil spirits. And when I first saw my new school I was taken aback by the sheer scale of it. It was just an extension of the Ferrier Estate, grey concrete and dirty glass. It looked like a huge military base. There were so many kids in the playground – more than a thousand! I'd never seen so many kids in one place. It was like China, or *The X Factor* car park except no one had a dream.

On my second day I saw a fight between two third-years. They both had big boots on, and one wrestled the other down and started kicking him in the head. He was jerking around on the tarmac like a rabbit on a string, obviously unconscious. I was frozen in fascination and fear. Then the boy walked off and stood with some other kids as if nothing had happened. After a while a policeman arrived with a teacher and hauled him off. The boy on the ground was in hospital for a month, with a broken jaw and severe head injuries. The victor had been wearing steel-toecap boots. What's amazing, looking back, is that everyone had these Dr Marten boots on, these weapons of mass destruction; pupils were never banned from wearing them. I had a pair, of course (no steel toecaps), having graduated from monkey boots, but I wasn't allowed to wear them to school; I wore mine to climb trees and stamp on the occasional wasp, not maim people.

Thomas Tallis had started out with lofty ambitions. When I was there it had been open only four years. This was the first comp to have carpets throughout, and the girls were taught metalwork while the boys did home economics. Mum was very excited about the whole thing, as she was essentially left-wing and quite forward-thinking. I didn't give a fuck if the floors were covered in taffeta as long as my head wasn't smashed against them.

It was a brave experiment but ultimately a failed one. For some reason the deputy head and the head left soon after I arrived and it all went downhill very fast, like some utopian dream in a J.G. Ballard novel. The carpets became mired in chewing gum and graffiti was sprayed on to the walls and stayed there. The plants in the staffroom withered and died, and the brand-new lockers were bent out of shape from repeatedly having small children hurled against them. The doors were ripped off or hung limp, making terrible groaning noises when you pushed them. The fibreglass roof insulation was suddenly discovered to be dangerous and was all ripped out; what was left, we'd rub in each other's faces.

It was like a concrete ship on a doomed voyage full of cunts. Of course there were nice people there but they never came up and kicked you in the bollocks. There was an undercurrent of fear and loathing that I found hard to shake off. No matter how many friends I made, I felt out of place.

What would become of our podgy sensitive hero?

Spitting was all the rage in those days. Long before it was hijacked by punk rock it was a staple of school life. It carried such menace and evil, to have someone gob a huge greeny right into your eye; a horrible act. There were different disciplines, of course. These would depend on the consistency and actual amount of saliva in the mouth.

The greeny was the cudgel or broadsword of spitting: a huge mulch of green snot would be dragged up and held in the mouth before being gobbed or flobbed on to a victim (all the better if the gobbee had a chest infection). This was mainly deposited on to someone's back, where it would be found later, leaving the culprit safe. When spit was scarce or very white in colour boys would flick it from the end of the tongue, jerking their heads to help launch the fluid in one motion. This was a totally silent manoeuvre, snake-like, the cut-throat razor of spitting. I used to marvel at it. Not much spit would land but the whiteness would stand out. This was to me a classy move – in a way, non-confrontational, and easier to clean than a greeny. A similar thing was the squirting of thin spit through the teeth, making a little noise. There was also a form of action where the spitter would eject the gob just with his lips, making a sound like a comedy ejaculation.

Other crazes were sticking pins in people (the arse, mainly), using rubber bands as catapults, and folding a piece of paper many times, until rock hard, then firing it at someone.

Later the metal tags were removed from the green-lace folder bindings and used as pellets; a teacher had her cheek cut open in this way and the pupil was expelled. Kung fu made its way kicking and chopping into the classrooms. Nunchucks were confiscated and throwing stars banned.

Some detonators were stolen from a British Rail storeroom and exploded. All good clean fun. Walking from lesson to lesson was invigorating to say the least.

The average hooligan and main danger to me resembled Rod Stewart circa 1974: lank, greasy hair, long-limbed with pigeon's-forehead buttocks, a scrawny chest and puny, bony arms, a vicious temper and, of course, wearing great big boots, which would be swung at the intended target after the preliminary verbals.

Butterfly-collar shirts, sleeveless pullovers and high-waistband trousers with huge side pockets. Kids would walk round with their hands thrust deep into their pockets, bent forward, scuffing their boots on the carpets. There were girls there too, obviously, but I was still a tiny mouse person, yet to reach puberty and squeaking around largely unnoticed.

One day my little brother had a few friends round – he was about eight at the time and I was twelve. There was a knock at the door. It was another kid – Laurence Bundage was his name – and he ran past me into the house. I looked up at his dad, David, who was hovering, unsure of what to do.

'I'm afraid there're already quite a few people here; you'd better not come in,' I said. He looked uncertain. 'Sorry,' I said. 'It's really quite crowded in there.'

He left looking wounded, but I thought no more of it. Later that day I was watching TV when the door flew open.

'What possessed you?' my mum roared. 'What possessed you?'

Apparently I had really upset the guy. He was fifty years old, and I just couldn't understand what the big deal was – could a twelve-year-old boy hurt a grown-up with words? It was completely beyond my comprehension. I'd just stated a fact: there were already a few people in the house and he would have made it more crowded still.

My mum was furious. I had to go round and apologise. It wasn't far. I felt very strange on the way – surely if you're a grown-up you don't do what a kid tells you; you laugh and push him aside. Very odd behaviour. It was a span house with a red door. It was open so I walked into the house. The living room was empty and David Bundage was upstairs sitting slumped on the bed. He looked ill – my dad would never sit like that, like a broken ape. Next to the bed was a huge pile of dirty magazines, *Club International* on the top. The place was messy.

I went forward and spoke in my best BBC 'young-child actor' tone.

'I'm very sorry, Mr Bundage.'

He looked up briefly and nodded then looked at the floor. I stood there for a while. I wasn't offered any orange squash. He wasn't behaving like any adult I'd met before. For an adult to sit before me like this just staring at the floor, was amazing. There were plates on the sofa with bean juice on them; the radio was on quietly. I hovered a bit taking in the strange vibe then ran off home.

I told my mum about the scene and she seemed annoyed, as if I was trying to erase my crime by slandering Mr Bundage. When I told her about the *Mayfair*s by the bed she went quiet and cleaned something vigorously.

When I was growing up there were three cinemas within walking distance from my house: the ABC at Blackheath Standard plus the Six and Seven and the Odeon in Lewisham. I saw many films at the Odeon, though I was never a fan of Saturday-morning pictures. Too noisy, and people would throw hot dogs at the screen and launch Kia-Ora fruit drinks at you. It was full of what I considered to be common people; much later I'd be forced to study their language and speak it at times to avoid being set upon.

The cinema is a place of great reverence for me, almost womb-like. I'm very happy in a darkened cinema, the shadow-land – the silence fills me with wonder even now. Pearl & Dean, the low mechanised sound of the curtain moving across the screen . . . I always go to the pictures on my own, lunchtimes on weekdays only. I can't be having people destroying buckets of popcorn and eating imitation-Mexican snacks during the film – all that time and money spent on the soundtrack, on the atmosphere, only to have it ruined by a group of people chomping and whispering, slurping and crunching. I've been very close to violence in those velvet pews, taken many deep breaths to avoid a custodial sentence. I've spared many lives. Take note: I wouldn't want to drown you in your bucket of 7-Up. *Ssshhhh.*

The Six and Seven was the venue that my brother Rob and I decided to visit in order to see a cracking double-bill of *Stardust* and *That'll Be the Day*. They featured the most glamorous of all gypsy entertainers, David Essex. He was the Adam Ant of the 1970s, made girls go gooey and turned many of my early crushes' knees to jelly; I wanted to have a closer look. There was just one problem with our plan: both films were rated AA, which meant you had to be over fourteen to get in.

At the time, I was twelve and Rob was thirteen. All it would take to get in, so various friends told us, was a parent standing behind us in the foyer ready to say, 'This child is fourteen years old.' In those days grown-ups didn't lie – why would they? Enter my dad, one of the most honest and least conniving men in London. We badgered him for days and eventually he agreed to take us.

We told him in no uncertain terms: 'If they ask how old we are you have to tell them we're fourteen. OK?' He nodded grimly, sighing. That journey to the cinema was as fraught with tension as any bank robbery.

We knew he was the weak link – how would he hold up under fire? I explained his role again calmly; he told me to be quiet. He parked the car. I was very nervous: my brother looked thirteen and I looked about ten. We entered the small foyer and my dad approached the counter. In a hesitant manner, he asked for three tickets.

'Are the boys over fourteen?' the nice lady said.

He faltered. 'Erm . . .' he said, as if she'd asked to see his genitalia. *Here we go*, I thought. He looked back at us as if not knowing who we were, then said, 'Erm . . .' again.

The nice lady, sensing weakness, turned into someone who might have worked at the dole office. She said harshly: 'How old are the boys?'

He peered at us and laughed nervously. 'Erm, twelve and thirteen,' he said. I felt for him then, seeing him exposed like that. He wasn't like me: he wasn't deceitful; he was good. We walked down the steps. He'd blown it, blown our chance of seeing naked ladies and Ringo Starr acting. We gave him a lot of stick on the way home.

He was an honest man. Thinking back now, I'm proud of him. That kind of decency and all-round good-egg behaviour is sadly lacking in today's society. He was like that American president George Washington: he could not tell a lie.

At school I got good reports for the first two years and less good the next two years. All the teachers said the same thing: 'Simon must smarten up the presentation of his work.' It doesn't matter now we have computers, but in those days you were judged solely on your handwriting. My dyslexia meant I had terrible handwriting and couldn't spell. I still can't, and writing this is painful at times. By the time you read it some editor-type will have smoothed it all out, but basically every third word is wrong. It's boring and trying.

At the start of the third year I found myself left behind in other ways. I'd returned to school still unburdened with pubic hair or bum-fluff moustache. As Miss Armstrong took the register I looked around and noticed that certain boys had changed: they were taller, they had enlarged Adam's apples and the veins stood out on their hands; when they answered the register, they spoke in booming voices like Bernard Bresslaw. They had become men.

I seemed to be the only boy in the showers with no tangle of light-brown hair around my cock and balls. This was a worrying state of affairs. I'd slipped off track somehow. In reality most people didn't give a hoot and it was all in my head, but that's all you have to go on, isn't it? What's in your head.

I had two close friends, both off the Ferrier Estate. One was called Mutley after the dog in *Wacky Races* – he laughed in the same way, shaking his shoulders. Also like a dog, he seldom spoke but was loyal and had a good heart. You sensed this somehow, though like a lot of kids of that age he seemed enormously physically frustrated. If ever you had a bit of play-fighting with someone you'd pick up on an anger, as if they wanted to really let go and do a Godzilla and smash you all over creation – nothing personal, just an adolescence thing. Maybe sexual, who knows . . . ?

My other mate was Jimmy Whitton. He would have been really cool but for the fact he was very uptight and a borderline psychopath. I don't use this term lightly: he was way nuttier than anyone I later met in the prison system. He had an attaché case instead of a bag and his uniform was immaculate – pressed trousers, sharp blazer, big tie knot, leather-soled shoes. Naturally, being middle class I had the regulation school uniform: awful blazer, funny trousers, and of course Start-rite pasty shoes. The parents from the estates made sure their kids were dressed in the height of fashion – Jimmy's blazer alone cost seventy-five quid! It was the same with school journeys and day trips. My dad would give me exactly what it said on the letter, say five pounds ('More than adequate,' he'd tell me), whereas some of the other boys would have thirty quid on them. They'd say, 'How come your dad ain't given you any money? You're posh!' I never had an answer for this. It used to annoy me.

Jimmy Whitton's written work was very neat and he had a nice Parker pen. I remember he did a homework project once in the summer holidays about the Egyptians and he drew all the hieroglyphics and statues using a gold felt pen; it looked amazing and he got five gold stars. He would have been popular with the girls but apparently he played too rough, so another kid told me. This was still at the stage when if a boy fancied a girl he'd humiliate her verbally then throw her bag out of the window or steal her hairbrush. These things would result in a tussle, often ending with the girl being pinned down on the floor. I'd had no idea there were possible sexual overtones to all this.

Jimmy Whitton's dad was a butcher and he often hit him full in the face if he'd done something wrong. When Jimmy told me this I was shocked. I had no concept of it: how could a man hit a boy? It was beyond my comprehension.

When Jimmy had a fight all the colour would drain from his face and he'd calmly take his jacket off and fold it neatly before steaming in. All that confined rage would pour out and he'd have to be physically dragged off his opponent – he never gave up. Mind you, he didn't have many fights: word got round that he could look after himself. He was never one of the chaps; he was too weird. I think he wanted to better himself, wanted to get off the estate. He was always calling people 'thick' and deriding them for eating too much fried food.

When I went back to Thomas Tallis for the fourth year I was slipping into bad ways. I still hadn't reached puberty and I was losing interest in school work. I felt alienated from most other kids at school and had already begun to perform Monty Python sketches and do Basil Fawlty impressions to try to gain some sort of acceptance. Boys would come into my lessons demanding a 'Basil'. I'd leap up, regardless of what the teacher was saying, and do my stuff.

On 1 December 1976 I was watching TV. I was fourteen. I'd been told or had read somewhere that the Sex Pistols were going to be interviewed by Bill Grundy on an early-evening news programme. They were on last and sat about in the studio like a group of kids who were in big trouble in front of a headmaster. What followed was probably for my generation the most important piece of TV ever. I was absolutely astounded by it and each swearword got me more and more excited. I was right behind them: no one had ever spoken to a grown-up man like that, not on television. It was brilliant. I felt as if I'd won some sort of Cup final. It united everybody who saw it, and gave the teenage nation a huge fillip. I think a lot of people became punks after seeing that footage; that's what sealed it for them – to be that disrespectful and look good doing it. The Pistols were smoking fags throughout the interview, too. My favourite line was Steve Jones', right at the end: 'What a fucking rotter.' I've always loved that word and it really made me laugh out loud. I think John Lydon taught our generation a lot, by showing us that fear was a trick played on us by so-called grown-ups. Although he had a dark world view it was ultimately inspiring: 'Be what you want, do what you want; it's your time, have a laugh and don't listen to anyone old.' It wasn't going to be good for my school career, though.

I hated school. I was happy enough away from there, though: I rode bikes and went swimming at Greenwich baths, hurling my clothes on to the floor while that strange echo of conversation and splashing bounced down from the ceiling. I chewed beech-nut and laughed with my safe middle-class friends. The fair and the circus came and went. But I could see my school across the fields. I wished the Thunderbirds would come and blow it up but they were busy doing other shit. The last 200 yards of my journey home it would come into view across the sports fields like something from a bad dream, striking a chill in my heart.

In Blackheath I'd developed a reputation as a laugh, an idiot – someone who'd go a bit further than 'knock down ginger'. Even then I was known as a person who'd do silly things. A combination of boredom and an unquenchable desire to be accepted meant I'd volunteer as a guinea pig in situations involving anything illegal or dangerous.

Not only was I the first to return to lighted fireworks (with mixed results), but I also held fireworks and pointed them at things as required. Aerial bombshells were the best but the plastic spike often dug into the chest. We used to slice fireworks open and make piles of gunpowder, which I'd then light. Hooray – eyebrows gone! Never mind . . .

When the ponds on Blackheath froze over I was always the first on the ice, testing its suitability for skating. I went under countless times. The pond was only three feet deep, so I wasn't Evel Knievel, but it sure froze what gonads I had.

It was on one such occasion that I was pulled out of the pond with everyone laughing and Dan said, 'We're laughing *at* you, not *with* you.' This line really bothered me and I forgot how cold I was for a second. *We're laughing* at *you, not* with *you.* I hadn't really understood the difference before he said that.

That afternoon I rushed home and got changed, shivering in my bedroom. I must have had the light on and the curtains open because later a note was pushed through our letter box. My elder brother snatched it up and read it, holding me off with one hand. He was really laughing. I knew it was about me and I went cold.

'Hey Superman, come outside and show us your baked bean,' it began.

I'd been seen changing by someone (presumably girls) we knew. The 'baked bean' line was in reference to my grotesquely shrunken cock and balls; admittedly they weren't very big prior to me falling into the frozen pond but I was so embarrassed. I wondered who'd sent it and whether they'd tell the world. Being laughed at in nakedness by boys is bad enough, but *girls* . . . I was really upset. I went upstairs and closed the curtains and ran the whole thing over in my head endlessly. It seems funny now but at the time it was devastating.

One day we had the bright idea of rigging up a pulley-swing thing, like the soldiers use to get about in the jungle – you know, from one tree to another. We had the tree, a big horse-chestnut, in Ben and Dan's garden, and we also had the hand-hold thing somehow; all we needed was the rope. I was dispatched to the hardware store in Blackheath village and duly returned with some rope/twine stuff (this wasn't really my area) and we assembled the slide part. Someone tied the rope to the top of the tree and then we pulled it down and harnessed it to a smaller sapling, near the house. Of course I went first. I climbed nervously to the top of the tree. It was fucking high up – I could see the church where my funeral would be held. I gripped the little handle bit and jumped. Everything worked perfectly except that the twine wasn't strong enough: basically I jumped down from a high tree holding a bit of wood. But the branches broke my fall and I wasn't seriously hurt. In fact I was secretly proud in moments such as this; I don't know why. I had a role, I suppose. That was who I was – the nutter.

Ben and Dan had a massive garden. The excellent horse-chestnut tree was a brilliant climber; there was enough room for all of us up there and we had a lovely view of the surrounding environs. The three of us hung out a lot and went through all the important changes and experiences together. In the seventies fags were still seen as exotic and sophisticated and everyone smoked. We'd try out different brands, suckered in by the gimmicks: Lark (with the crush-proof box) and Winston (with the charcoal filter); and the menthols, of course – both Everest and Consulate went down well with a *Men Only* and a tin of Coke. Don't get me wrong, we smoked the working-class brands too: Kensitas, No. 6, Embassy and Sovereign – which I think were the smallest, cheapest brand you could buy and a lot of dinner money up and down the country was squandered on those rancid little buggers.

We had a camp at the bottom of Dan and Ben's garden – basically a hole with a rug in it and a corrugated-plastic roof. We used to sit in there with tubs of John Player Special reading dirty magazines. Occasionally one of us would toss ourselves off – jaw jutting out, knuckles white, eyes fixed on a big-knockered lady dappled in sunlight wearing nothing but an apricot scarf. It could take ages, depending on whether you were bothered by your mates sitting two feet away. Afterwards you could relax with a Lambert and Butler or maybe a Peter Stuyvesant. We were living the dream. Our hole in the ground was our own Playboy Mansion, without the Bunnies servicing us (which was OK, as the girls we knew didn't look anything like the girls on the page – they fell a bit short in the tit area and they didn't take all their clothes off and bend over).

One day we decided to try roll-ups. There were those little rolling machines then – Cadets, they were called – and it looked like fun. As usual I was sent in to do the buying. I didn't look any older but I always got the nod for this sort of thing and I felt I needed to go the extra mile to be liked. I bought all the rolling equipment but had no idea which tobacco to get. I chose one, paid, and left the shop feeling pretty grown-up.

We repaired to the tree in the garden, where the branches were wide enough for us to all sit in comfort and we each had our own little favourite knobbly seats. As we started assembling the roll-ups we realised I'd bought pipe tobacco. Borkum Riff, to be precise: a particularly foul-smelling whiskey flake with a picture of a schooner on the packet. The strands were too big to roll properly and we sat there cursing my stupidity and the greasy brown worms of tobacco. When we finally lit the things the rush was incredible. I thought I saw a ghost ship looming out of the branches, sea shanties rang in our ears and we clung on to our leafy crow's-nest as it lurched from side to side. Later we climbed down gingerly, double-checking hand holds, our skin pale and clammy. Up the tree that day I'd smoked my first joint and laid the foundations for a lifetime of altered states. Oddly enough the only thing I smoke now is the occasional roll-up (Golden Virginia, liquorice papers) but I don't smoke in trees any more.

There seemed to be so much time, then. Everything moved slowly. You'd go somewhere with your mum as an appendage; she'd have conversations and you'd just sit listening, seen and not seen. People now are in constant contact – calls, texts, 'See you in five mins', 'I'm outside', 'Oh, I can see you' – but in those days you'd go and call on a friend, ring the bell and wait for ages. *Are they in?* You'd look through the window, go round the back, and eventually a kid would appear, half asleep.

He'd beckon you in and you'd sit down and do nothing for ages, just talk turkey, the house quiet. No mobiles, no telly on, no computer screens. Better conversations were had by all, with less distractions. My young life was uneventful, comfortable. I did my best to spice it up: I put my hands in cages, messed around with flammable materials, ran out in front of cars, the usual stuff.

I was once asked to babysit by a couple; they must have been friends of my mum or friends of someone else's mum. I think I was about fourteen or so. I have absolutely no idea who stuck my name up for such an important job – it was a girl's job really – but I was earning a tenner so I agreed. They lived on Shooters Hill Road in a basement flat. I remember the slightly dank feeling of the rooms. The couple were quite arty and the place was sort of messy but interesting, with lots of prints and books slung about and burnt-down candles, the wax creeping on to the table like lava. I have no recollection of seeing a child at any stage but there must have been one there. It didn't wake up, though, which was the important thing for me and the parents. I would have dropped it on its head or tried to wash it with bleach or something.

I remember they told me to help myself to the fridge and left the flat smiling and nodding. The woman was attractive, as I remember, with olive skin and brown eyes; she also had small white teeth and a gold pendant thing. She and the bloke were quite funky. Anyway as soon as they left I put *Hunky Dory* on the turntable, poured myself a large whisky and began searching their home in earnest, picking up books and opening drawers. I had some toast and pâté and switched to sherry (I still don't like whisky really). I started to feel at home with the soft lighting illuminating the bookshelves. I could have done with a place like this to live myself: I'd spend the days writing and having dinner parties in the evening.

At some stage I wandered into their bedroom and started rummaging through their drawers. I discovered some French money, huge brown and yellow franc notes – they seemed enormous to me. I studied them by the lamplight. A wonderful currency the franc was in the seventies; why has money got so small? In those days a whole family could have a picnic on a ten-franc note. I took some of the money and left the rest as I found it. I tried to remember the exchange rate from previous school journeys so I could determine exactly how much I was pinching, but nothing came to me. I felt a bit guilty and returned to the living room where the gas fire was blazing. The booze had made me sleepy. I silenced Bowie's caterwauling, turned down the fire and lay down on the sofa with a book. I was woken suddenly, as two anxious faces looked down on me. I had a splitting headache.

'Jesus – are you all right?' said the white teeth. The couple picked me up and brought me a cup of water. There was a smell in the room I didn't recognise. The guy opened a window and the night air came in quickly.

'You left the gas fire on,' she said, and there was real concern in her face.

Apparently I had turned the flame off but left gas leaking from the tap. The room stank. I was bewildered but not dead. Hours had passed as I lay like an accidental suicide, the only sound the hissing of the gas and my laboured breathing. They were so relieved I was alive – and that their child was, too, obviously. I remembered the francs in my pocket and felt terrible: they were so concerned and I'd robbed them. I couldn't put the money back now. They gave me a lift home – all's well that ends well and all that. Had I nearly died? How awful when they stripped my little white carcass and found the francs: 'He died in our home but he took some of our money to see him all right in the afterlife, plus the tenner we gave him for falling asleep on the job . . .'

It could have been worse: I could have done the same trick in the kid's room.

On the Saturday I walked into Barclays Bank in Blackheath village and proffered my francs. I received thirteen pounds sterling and some coppers, which I spent largely on sweets, and sadly learnt nothing from the affair.

By my fifth year at Tallis things had gone from bad to worse. Punk rock had broken out properly and my gang from Blackheath had become vaguely new wave in our dress. We used to steal punk singles from the record shop in Blackheath and rush home to play them. It was so exciting being young then; there was an electricity in the air and you felt you were part of some secret society. If only I didn't have to go to school.

Somewhere at this point three things happened. First, my father's father died and Papa inherited a bit of money. Then, after Dad got wedged up, we moved to Granville Park, a nice road that curls down to Lewisham from Blackheath. Things were looking up. Our new home was a big four-storey Victorian house and Rob and I were very excited as we had a floor at the top of the house all to ourselves. We intended to pack it with our friends and smoke fags. Unfortunately Mum had other ideas: whenever we turned up with a group of pals she'd say, 'You can only have two friends in the house . . .' Being forced to choose was tough and of course we refused to be that cruel – we'd just all mooch off somewhere else.

On the surface things looked good for the Day family, but it was also during this time that Mum (unbeknown to us) began enjoying secret trysts with the headmaster at the school where she worked. So who knows what tensions were flying about? I had my own problems, though, and they've always seemed more important to me than anything else.

Robert turned sixteen while we were at Granville Park and asked if he could have a party. After some deliberation my parents agreed. We were very excited – I was going to wash my hair and everything. We had a whole floor to ourselves! It was going to be a real hoedown, with young girls vying for our attention as we danced across the floor, people being sick in comfort, ashtrays throughout, loud music . . . I couldn't wait.

On the afternoon of the party I heard Rob arguing with Dad about something. Then my brother stormed upstairs cursing.

'He says I can only have forty people – there'll be about a hundred! And he wants a list of names.'

'Don't worry,' I said. 'Give him the list. What's he going to do? He won't know how many are there on the night.'

Rob smiled. 'You're right,' he said.

Three hours later my brother and I stood dumbfounded as Dad dragged a table and chair across the room and positioned it right by the front door. On the table he carefully put Robert's list of guests (in beautiful handwriting) and laid a ruler and various marker pens on top of it. And that night as the great and the good of Blackheath teenaged society gathered outside in their finest garments, they were met by the head of a man wearing glasses peering at them through the crack of the door.

He asked them their names, frequently returning to the crack to get them to repeat themselves before he ushered them in. My brother was distraught: he'd been fast becoming a face on the Blackheath scene and this was a shameful, shameful experience for him. Older boys were being treated like children – and woe betide anyone not on the list: they were met with a stony glare and a firm rebuttal. Anyone trying to give a false name or returning after being sent away was treated as if they'd got one of us pregnant. The door would be flung open and they'd be sent off into the night clutching their tins of beer. Actually, though, forty people were enough. I didn't get off with anyone. I kept putting the Jam on the stereo, scratching the vinyl in my drunkenness; that's all I remember.

I was going through my mum's handbag one day, looking for money to throw into fruit machines or the greasy palms of chip-shop owners, when I came across a handwritten letter. I didn't recognise the handwriting. I had a gander and it seemed a bit steamy; I felt a mixture of shock and confusion when I realised it was a love letter to my mum. The meat of the prose ran as follows: 'I want to touch your eyes, your nose, your mouth, your knees . . .' Well, not knees, perhaps, but that was the gist.

I told Robert, who said nonchalantly, 'She must be having an affair.' I then told Ben and Dan and they in turn told their mum, Thelda, which was a bad move. She confronted me and had a quiet word. She told me that it was a prop from a school play. I was annoyed that the grown-up's union were trying to pull the wool over my eyes; this really bothered me. I know now that I was a lot more sensitive than I tried to appear, and I think that letter accelerated my addictive behaviour. I was very confused and I started playing truant in earnest.

I think I became properly depressed at this point. I had a set routine: I'd get up with the family, have breakfast and leave the house in my uniform, having unlocked one of the back windows; then I'd hang about on the heath for a bit, wait till the house was empty then let myself back in through the unlocked window. Once I found my chosen window locked and thought it would be a good idea to break in. I chose the smallest window, thinking of the cost of repair, but unfortunately it was too small for me to get through and I got stuck. I huffed and puffed and wriggled like a crazy worm until eventually I got in and fell on the floor. I'd cut myself on some glass left in the frame and bled for hours. Life seemed very difficult at this stage. I felt completely disconnected from everything, and there seemed to be a huge chasm between who I was and who I was supposed to be. Each time I got back into my home I'd relish the silence – on my own, thank god, no responsibilities, no one looking at me. I always stuck to my routine. I'd put a big potato in the oven, read while it was cooking (an hour and twenty minutes on gas-mark five), then eat it with baked beans and slightly too much butter. After that I'd go to bed and sleep until late afternoon, get up and put my uniform on, leave the house and then return as if I'd been at school. I did this three times a week, sometimes four. I was sleeping too much:

I'd sleep from ten till morning, too. I'd sit around the house in a towel, brushing my hair like one of the Liver Birds – but never went out.

As I said, my elder brother was quite cool by this time. He had an expensive Italian 50cc trial bike – a Husqvarna, I believe – loads of records and a girlfriend. He and his friends viewed me with disdain. I was like a chrysalis waiting to hatch as something. I wanted some pubic hair desperately.

There were boys in my year with beards and children. They were doing scaffolding in the summer holidays, driving cars into rivers, killing donkeys and smashing birds' eggs, fingering girls on waste ground in all weathers. They seemed so alive. I got beaten up quite badly at school once for being a punk. I was a massive fan of Dr Feelgood – we all were – and word had got out. I had a Lurkers badge on one day and this second-year, Chris Heffer, who lived in a children's home, knocked me to the ground and his mate started kicking me in the head. I'd never been kicked in the head before; it was like *Tom and Jerry* but not funny. And being kicked stupid for a band as shit as the Lurkers was hard to take.

I'd really had enough of school. Then one night we were having supper and my dad suddenly piped up.

'As you may know, your mother and I are splitting up.'

That was it: no rows, no recriminations, no nothing. My brother and I went down the pub. I remember feeling completely fine with it, totally cool.

I left school with one CSE. I'd blown my education. It was OK, though; it was the punky thing to do. (I didn't brush my teeth either.) My parents were too consumed with their own problems to sort me out, but they must have been very worried.

Chapter Four

After my parents got divorced my mum moved to a flat in a little fifties cul-de-sac called Crown Court in Lee Green with her new man, John Vincent. He was a Yorkshire man, loved cricket and had a bit of a temper. Coincidentally, the school where he and Mum worked was John Stainer in Brockley, whose team we'd beaten at cricket. She and John Vincent had fallen in love. Good luck to them. I say that now, but obviously at the time I hated the man and the situation.

'He's not your dad, Simon – he'll give you a good clout,' Mum would say, and that cheered me up no end.

At this stage I would wander from parent to parent soaking up both real and imagined dislike from my folks' new partners.

I used to stay at Crown Court sometimes. I'd leave a window open so I could climb back in when they'd gone out and sit about in the warm, and I remember one time I returned and all the windows were locked. Headmasters are not idiots: he had my number. That day I went down to the Eltham Road roundabout and looked in on the World of Leather; all those sofas, all that leather – what did it all mean? I walked for miles, right out into the countryside. I sat down exhausted, like a pilgrim, then I walked back to civilisation. At Crown Court I tried all the windows again, but eventually Mum returned and I went in and had some tea. It never felt like home there, though. It was all over: I'd been chucked by my mum.

So I used to do this all the time – walk and walk around, walk and walk around. I have long legs and am good at walking. I've never had any interest in cars and didn't pass my test until I was forty. As a young man I walked everywhere: my lack of funds and homeless periods gave me the chance to walk about almost non-stop. You see much more when strolling. I've walked in all the styles – hurrying, strolling, pacing, mooching and moseying. The motor car is a barrier to real life; most people are insulated from what happens on the street from the age of seventeen. You see images at different speeds, snapshots of events, but they are gone as soon as you set eyes on them. You're not forced to meet and interact with other human beings nearly as much. People like this: it's one of the benefits of being wealthy. You move to an area where there are less people to bother you, you go from car to house to car to house . . .

The only way to really experience the area you live in is to walk around it, to go in every shop, stand on corners and look both ways, go up and down and look at all the houses and buildings. If I had my way I'd go and look in people's houses too, have them sit down while I poke about asking the odd question. I used to walk and meet other gentlemen of the road, older than me most of them, but they'd nod and go on their way like me. People used to toot me in cars and I'd wave, not knowing who they were sometimes. I was lucky: virtually all my walking days were spent in and around Blackheath and Greenwich, both beautiful areas with fantastic architecture; it wasn't so much fun in Deptford and New Cross, plus there was more chance of meeting volatile characters there who might impinge on your person.

I remember the first time I went to Lee Green to see Mum's new place. I was horrified to see posters of animals on the walls – a chimp on the toilet with the slogan 'Have a nice day' and a chewing camel whose caption read 'What you looking at?' I realised my mum was no longer middle class: she'd returned to her roots. My dad wouldn't have let her put up those abominations.

I stayed at Crown Court when I had nowhere else to go. It was obvious they could do without me in their lives. I wasn't much fun and I was always on the lookout for spare cash. More to the point, I wasn't above taking stuff without asking. Sometimes I'd get back in through the open window, climbing in like a burglar. You had to be careful doing this, trying to make sure you only ate food that wouldn't be missed, returned objects to their correct places, flushed the loo. It's strange being in your own home when you're not supposed to be there – although this was never really my home of course. You drop to the floor and listen in the silence, listening for sounds inside and out. The first time I did this the house was very tidy. There was nothing of my dad there: everything felt unfamiliar, very tidy and clean; I could have been standing in a flat in Munich or Oslo. There were ornaments I didn't recognise and a tree mug in the kitchen made of pine. The monkey on the wall was staring at me; he was holding a cup of tea in his hand and there was a roll of bog paper on the floor by his hairy arse (did they want us to think he was going to wipe his bum?). His eyes followed me around the room and his teeth were slightly bared. 'Have a nice day.' I had seven grapes and went out.

My mum helped me find a bedsit in Lee Green, right at the top of Burnt Ash Hill. It was £12 a week. The house was enormous; it was run by an Eastern European woman who was tiny with a slightly sinister and regal bearing. She spoke very slowly, savouring her sentences – she reminded me of Gloria Swanson in *Sunset Boulevard.* There was a feeling she'd once had people scurrying round her and hanging on her every word – one of the first things she said to me was, 'Once my family had great riches and now we have nothing.'

My room was cold and there was no lock on the door. The shower was outside the house; when I moved in it was December and you had to freeze your nuts off every time you wanted a wash. One night I was getting dressed and my landlady swept into my room like Marlene Dietrich. She looked me up and down.

'When you wash you must dry yourself lightly with the towel.' Her eyes lingered on my young flesh. I was freaked out – I got rid of her and sat on the bed.

Where exactly did she come from? Was she a Nazi? I was worried she'd slip me a Mickey Finn and I'd wake up in a terrible cellar, bound and gagged with her looming over me, naked except for jackboots and holding a whip. She had that arrogance of the master race: I'd catch her regarding me with a mixture of avarice and contempt as I pottered about. The house was so big and she was so small it made her seem like a cartoon figure. The rooms were lit oddly and she cast huge shadows as she strutted about. She'd enter my room as if on stage and stand for a minute, her back straight, hands clasped together tightly, before summoning me to a freezing room to point out a forlorn mangle or a socket for an iron. She was definitely after something. The odd thing was I seemed to be the only tenant – I'd been so consumed by self-pity I hadn't noticed that. Was there such a thing as bedsit noir? Were there really Nazi war criminals holed up in Lee Green? I wasn't even sure there were any female Nazi war criminals . . .

At Christmas my mum came round with a box containing satsumas and biscuits and general seasonal stuff. I asked if I could stay at Crown Court; she said no. We were both pretty upset. It was sad but I had my hands full with the landlady drifting in and out of my room like some randy ghost.

My landlady invited me for a drink at Christmas below stairs. I didn't go. In those days I'd think nothing of walking to the Rose and Crown in Greenwich three nights a week, an eight-mile journey there and back. At least I slept well. My social life was still quite normal: I went to parties, smoked a bit of pot. I spent Christmas at a mate's. His name was Ian Sutherland; he lived with his mum and his stepdad, Michael, who was twenty-two stones and wore a Stetson at Christmas dinner. It was rumoured that Michael and his dad used to bend down lampposts then rip them out of the earth and take them down the scrap yard. He was an ambulance driver and had put his wild past behind him. Ian's mum, Sheila, got a bit tipsy and put on Elkie Brooks then started asking questions about my mum – why wasn't I having Christmas dinner with her? She was a bit upset for me, which made me sad. I wanted to defend my mum; I still had a childlike need for her that I couldn't admit.

That New Year's Eve our lot went to a party out in Croydon – big house, lights in the garden, a huge synthetic tree badly dressed, some rugger-buggers being disrespectful. In those days at twelve midnight everyone used to try to get a kiss off someone they fancied. That year two wobbly older girls lined me up with five other youths, like an identity parade, and walked down the line French-kissing us in turn. One of them kissed me then went, 'Wow!' and came back to give me a second snog. I was the only soldier to get a repeat kiss. She was pretty, too. I was so happy – and very turned on. I followed her into a bedroom where she passed out on everyone's coats. Later she was sick on someone's jacket and got told off while she was green and drifting in and out of consciousness.

'Leave her alone,' I said. I brought her a glass of water and she sat up a bit.

'Who are you?' she said. Then the car I'd come in had to go, so I left her, but I kept that word in my head for ages: '*Wow!*' I had the wow factor.

On New Year's Day I returned to the bedsit somewhat frayed and the landlady met me on the stairs, her eyes blazing.

'How dare you spurn my request? Do you think you are a great man? Do you think you are better than me?' She shimmered with anger. Petrified, I followed her downstairs into the basement flat where she had her quarters – another room of huge dimensions, another crazy film set. There were stuffed animals everywhere and plastic bowls of fruit and flowers, huge bevelled-glass ornaments. A giant owl sat on a plastic tree; his eyes glowed. There was a box of chocolates on a nest of tables – I think they were made of something synthetic too. It was like Jeff Koons had gone berserk while depressed.

A man sat in a soft chair. On a table in front of him was a cheap pie and some carrots; next to that, two slices of Mother's Pride on a saucer, the margarine glistening. On another saucer sat a Mr Kipling apple pie. I think the man looked at me – he was cross-eyed. It was too much. She paced up and down the room seeming very agitated. I couldn't tell if the man was looking at me or not and I wanted to burst out laughing. The bars of the electric heater creaked as they contracted; I noticed that everything was covered in dust. She poured me out a small dark spirit into a crystal glass. She had one too. It tasted like Calpol.

'Where were you at Christmas? she barked.

Was the man glaring at me or looking at the ceiling and the window?

Suddenly she screamed: 'If you want to go, then go!'

The man hadn't moved. As I said, he may have been staring at me, showing his displeasure. I was hoping for a Kipling cake but decided not to mention it.

I moved out soon after that.

At this point in my life I was obsessed with music, and living where we did meant we were lucky enough to follow Squeeze, one of the greatest post-punk bands. They were an awesome live band and I must have seen them twenty times. We'd pogo around a bit but they weren't a punk band and spitting was *verboten.* They also had some South East London faces from Deptford at their gigs and you wouldn't want to gob on *them*, trust me. Squeeze were very much the archetypal local band. We didn't have much to be proud of in South East London but we were fiercely proud of them.

Chris Difford's bittersweet lyrics were a big influence on my comedy: from him I learnt how to tell a story in an urban language. Those hilarious yet savage little poems backed by the music really bashed their way into my bent little brain (Tommy Cockles was very influenced by his work with Squeeze). And of course I was also influenced by Ian Dury – but who wasn't? I don't see how you could have alternative comedy without Ian Dury: for me he was the first alternative comic. Such a wonderful poet.

After much discussion and fearful dreaming we decided to form our own band. I was the singer, Ben Joseph was on bass, a guy called Seamus Beaghen was on guitar and Nigel Preston was on drums. We were called Simon and the Virgins. Some of us were virgins and maybe we hoped this name would goad some local girls into deflowering us, I've no idea: we were sixteen and we weren't very good.

We practised like a real band in a dark room, the walls covered in foam rubber and egg boxes; we argued like a real band, we did drugs (pot and speed) like a real band. We *were* a real band!

From the debris of my parents' relationship I rose, like a phoenix from the ashes, to claim my place on the grubby post-punk podium. Luckily in my sixteenth year I'd also finally reached puberty and started gaining height rapidly, so suddenly everything in the garden looked rosy. OK, I was well on the way to being homeless – but I was *in a rock-and-roll band.* All those nights staring at Lee Brilleaux and Wilco Johnson, Glenn Tilbrook and Gilson Lavis, Paul Weller and Joe Strummer – I could be any one or a mixture of all of them. I wrote some songs. One was called 'Tube Train' and the chorus went: 'Oh that tube train/Why do I always take the blame?'

That particular lyric was quite prescient as my reputation as a petty thief had by now grown to such an extent that if anything went missing in the Blackheath area people would say, 'Has Simon Day been round your house?' We were once playing a gig and a cry went up in between songs – 'I want my mum's jewellery back' – which soon became a chant: '*We want the jewellery back!*' The terrible thing was I was completely innocent. I'd never met this kid whose mum's bits and bobs had been swiped. It was weird to be on stage defending my honour: 'Look, it wasn't me, so fuck off. This one's called "Stepping Stone" . . .'

I *loved* being in a band; it was brilliant. After one gig Glenn Tillbrook appeared on stage and said, 'I loved your set. Do you want a beer?' Then an Asian girl came and sat really close to me and kept holding my hand. She was quite ugly but so what? How had this happened? How had I become Elvis?

I remember we were once doing a sound-check and some black guy shouted, 'Oi, mate, you've got stage presence!' When I heard things like this I melted into a ball of self-love and egomania. I thought I was already there – wherever that was – and all my dreams were going to come true.

But of course I couldn't deal with the nuts and bolts of being in a band: rehearsing, working on songs; I wasn't a very good singer, either. We looked all right, though – sort of mod-dy in our dress and we had acne, too, which you don't see nowadays in young bands.

We used to drink in the Bricklayers Arms in East Greenwich at that point. There was a small bar off the main pub run by a guy called Harry; it had the best jukebox ever in the world – I've looked and looked but no jukebox ever comes close to it for just-brilliant songs. I mean that. I'd always put on 'Itchycoo Park', 'In the City' and 'Tap Turns on the Water' by CCS. It was our little scene and it even made its way into *Time Out* as a top punk hangout. Bikers used to come down and sell us blues and downers; we used to take three Tuinal, have a couple of pints and fall about the place. I was doing acid as well, and my addictive nature started to sabotage my dreams of *NME* covers and *Top of the Pops* appearances. I was struggling to hold it all together. I kept blowing-out band practice and in the end they lobbed me out.

I was shattered by this and added it to my list of woes – *I could have been a contender* and that sort of thing. I was seventeen, and I thought I was washed up. I'd had my chance of the cake and not eaten it, I'd missed the boat . . . What now?

I'd be a nobody for ever.

The strange thing was, the other band members all went on to make serious inroads into the music business. Seamus has played with Paul Weller and Madness and is an all-round top musician; Ben played with a number of people too, including the legendary Jimmy Cliff. Sadly the real star of the band, Nigel Preston, died very young. He was a brilliant, instinctive drummer and we knew he'd outgrow our band. He was such a beautiful-looking kid, so full of energy and life, but he never saw thirty – fucking pointless and sad. I like to remember him behind me smashing the fuck out of his kit, grinning, white teeth, and his hair falling in his eyes, or standing laughing holding his drumsticks tightly in his right hand, ready for anything. Ready or not, rest in peace.

At that time I was staying a lot at my friend Rupert Moy's house in Greenwich. Despite his name, Rupert was a right laugh. He had a basin haircut back then, and a lumpy nose, but at school had somehow convinced everyone he was the third-toughest in our year. He came from a big family in Greenwich: his dad looked like a Victorian explorer, with an athletic physique and a huge beard, and was known as 'Mr Greenwich', as he owned a couple of antique shops and an excellent French restaurant, the Spreadeagle. He's dead now and they've put a blue plaque up on the front of the building.

He'd split up from his wife, Vicky, and they'd shared the house out between them. He lived in the middle floor with his girlfriend, surrounded by copper pans and fantastic antiques; she lived on the top and the bottom with all the kids – three boys and two girls. There were five bedrooms upstairs, a small living room and kitchen downstairs and few creature comforts – they had a telly, of course, but it was quite Spartan.

Vicky was a lovely woman. She became a sort of surrogate mother to me and somehow kept five children, me and numerous other waifs and strays fed and watered. She worked in drop-in centres and homeless hostels, and often brought home various tramps who'd fall asleep on the sofa smelling of piss, shit and Golden Virginia. She was gentle and kind and I'll always be grateful to her.

Jeremy was the oldest of the Moy brothers. He was good-looking in a pre-Raphaelite way, with curly blond hair, and very bright. Like a lot of bright people who engage in verbal wordplay he could be a bit of a bully. He was a chain-smoker, quite cultured, knew how to cook and had a mate who handed out booze from an off-licence where he worked. He always had a cupboard full of spirits and a silver box containing 200 Senior Service in his bedroom. Mad as a hatter. We all were: it was a very competitive environment and probably the last thing I needed after my parents' divorce, but it was so interesting, so unstable and vivid – anything could happen – and after the sterile distance of my parents' relationship it seemed fun. I would occasionally feel very insecure there, though; I'd suddenly think, *You're not part of this family – you're an outsider and always will be.*

Rupert was the middle brother. He was my friend from school and was a brilliant laugh – he could have been a comedian, I think. We were very close and I suppose I looked at him like a brother as I didn't see mine any more. He'd got a job for Greenwich Council as soon as he left school, and later gave me a job working for him after he'd set up on his own as a landscape gardener. He shared the family traits of quick-wittedness and love of nicotine, he supported West Ham and did very well with the girls – all the Moy brothers did. I was so full of self-hatred at that time I seldom had any success. I just spent my time counselling the brothers' rejects. Toby was the youngest boy of the Moy family: blond hair, extremely agile – like a cross between a cat and a monkey. He was his father's son: by fourteen he'd started a collection of lighters which by the time he was twenty was worth ten grand. He was always in and out of skips and house clearances; like his dad he befriended people in museums and markets and got first refusal on stuff. He did amateur taxidermy and you'd often find sparrows and mice in the deep freeze among the burgers and fish-fingers. Toby never ever wore shoes – he even took his driving test in bare feet – and he once sewed a leather patch on to the sole of his foot. He was a nice kid, though, open and positive.

Mandy was the oldest girl. She was brunette, attractive, had quirky boyfriends and would sit in her room listening to Dory Previn and Leonard Cohen. I suppose she was quite a normal teenage girl but I had no real experience of girls. She had an excellent dark sense of humour, was another chain-smoker and loved a drink. She'd inherited a strong social conscience from her mum and worked with handicapped children. Both Mandy and Vicky had a slightly ghoulish side and used to go up to the Old Bailey for murder trials. I remember they both fancied Alex Higgins like crazy, too: he was their ideal man.

Polly was the youngest. She was blonde and pretty. I didn't really see so much of her at that point; she was a lot younger than me.

I learnt a lot from that family and they were there for me when others were not.

To say it was a madhouse would be an understatement but everyone was so full of life. There was a constant stream of oddballs coming through the house – runaway kids and battered women as well as all the tramps. Vicky and Mandy tried to look after everyone, but there was nothing worthy about it – some of the vagrants got the piss taken out of them mercilessly. One such bloke was Pete, an Irishman whose catchphrase was, 'I don't give two monkeys' fucks!' He claimed you could get drunk on any fluid – even milk – provided you drank enough of it.

We'd all been taking the piss one day and when the others left the room Pete turned on me.

'You're like me: you're light-fingered. You'll do bird . . .' I was really freaked out by this and afterwards kept turning it over in my mind. I often felt an impending sense of doom at this point in my life, felt disjointed and disconnected.

By now I was a trainee tramp myself. I read the papers in the library with other tramps, walked the streets like other tramps, sat in cafés making my tea last like other tramps. I smelt better than some of them but I was just as confused and insecure. I stayed where I could. I divided my time between Rupert and Jeremy's bedroom floors, and when I'd outstayed my welcome there I'd slope off elsewhere and sleep rough or cadge a bed if I could. At times it was great and I felt part of something – we had such a laugh; we used to stay up all night and wander through Greenwich, running up and down the tunnel leading to the Isle of Dogs.

I made my first appearance in court around this time – though really the whole thing was a joke from start to finish. A friend of mine, Jason Bratby, was the son of the painters John Bratby and Jean Cooke, and was an accomplished artist himself. He also had a grey Morris Cowley – a big old fifties British saloon with a stick shift and a bench front seat. Being slightly older than us, and with that car, Jason was sort of our leader. On this occasion me and Rupert Moy were sat in the back, returning from Jason's family seat in Eastbourne – which was in fact a hovel perched on top of a cliff and has since been reclaimed by the sea.

His family were proper bohemians. Their home in Blackheath looked like the Addams Family mansion, and all they ate was beans: the fridge was full of half-used tins of beans covered in mould; they used to scrape off the mould, put the tin in the oven, wait a bit, then eat them. I'm sorry – I'm better than that, aren't I? The Eastbourne cottage was worse than a squat and I'd been very disappointed. Being semi-homeless I was already missing home comforts such as fluffy towels and decent bedding; the least I expected was an Aga and a clean single bed, a nice few biscuits and a Dick Francis – was that too much to ask? But the place stank! Why drag us all the way down there? I'd imagined I'd be leaning against a radiator, wistfully gazing out to sea while eating a homemade scone, not staring at an overflowing toilet.

Really, artists: from Picasso to Damien Hirst, they're all a bit remiss with the soap. It was so damp I think we slept in the car. Jason kept apologising and giggling but I wasn't pleased.

On the drive back we stopped alongside a milk float and stole some potatoes, a bag of flour and a load of eggs, which we proceeded to distribute among the good people of Sussex. I hit this bloke who was gardening with the flour amidships and he went over. Eggs were flying out of the car every few seconds. We were careful with the spuds, because we didn't want to maim anyone, but they boomed nicely off garden sheds and garage doors.

Suddenly the Old Bill were upon us – flashing lights, screeches of brakes, the whole kit and caboodle. It was hardly *Badlands* but we were a little nervous. Jason was whining and blaming it all on me, as I had thrown most of the groceries. He was twenty-one and we were both seventeen so he was worried he'd get all the flak.

Just in case of emergencies I was wearing a purple bondage suit: handmade belts and buckles and tartan trim – the lot. At that time I still had my basin haircut, so I looked like a junior Morris dancer who'd spent the day treading grapes.

One by one we were asked for our names.

'Name?'

'Jason Bratby.'

'Full name?'

'Jason Sovereign Bratby.' He chuckled.

'Name?'

'Rupert Moy.'

'Full name?'

'Rupert Peregrine Moy . . .'

'Are you taking the piss?'

I was OK, my full name being Simon William Day, but they thought we were having a laugh with them. They seemed very angry, the police, as if we'd done something very serious. I couldn't see what the fuss was about; a clear case of high jinks, youthful spirit and all that. But they kept threatening us with

Eastbourne CID. What were they going to do – fit us up with a sub-Post Office or murder?

I stood about in my ridiculous outfit trying to look callow. Unfortunately it came up to my knees. I was also wearing fourteen-hole Dr. Martens boots, painted red so no one thought I was a fashion victim.

We got booked to appear at some magistrates' court in the backwoods and drove on our way. Jason kept moaning about his licence. What was his problem? He lived in a huge studio flat above a garage and had recently started seeing this world-class punk-bird sex menace; her name was Tracy Marks and she looked a bit like Sharon Stone in plastic trousers and black lipstick. Jesus, she was dangerous. She'd call you by your first name in that way, and look right in your eyes. She was out of my league, and even Jason couldn't hang on to her: by the time we appeared in court she'd transferred her affections to Rupert (taller, better-looking, more of a laugh). The problem with that was that I was staying on his bedroom floor and they used to fuck each other while I lay four feet away on the other bed, pretending I couldn't hear anything. She wasn't averse to talking during sex and kept up a torrid dialogue that only heightened my excitement.

They used to whisper to each other as if I was asleep. Were they mad? How do you sleep through that? I'm sure a more confident person would have tried to engineer a threesome but that sort of thing was a world away to me.

Jeremy Moy had a steady girlfriend I was a bit in love with. She was called Lucy Flowerdew (what a great name) and she always wore fishnet tights and suspenders with sixties dresses. It was easier to be fixated on someone else's girlfriend: no responsibility. I really liked Lucy but I think she felt a bit sorry for me. Rupert had loads of girls. I had my moments but they were few and far between. I couldn't really take a girl back to someone else's bedroom . . .

Chapter Five

The first McDonald's restaurant in England opened in Woolwich in 1974. Woolwich is a prime McDonald's site: a shithole, basically, with high crime-rate, mass unemployment and terrible housing. Just the place to start infecting children and their parents with ghastly plastic worm-food. Of course I write this now, having read *Fast Food Nation* and having seen Morgan Spurlock's documentary *Super Size Me*. In the seventies it seemed like a wonderful spaceship had landed containing future food: delicious golden fries, tasty burgers, those sexy dangerous thick shakes; the packaging bold, all vivid reds and yellows.

Then there was the place itself, science fiction with a large Coke. It was so bright and clean, the tills like humble robots, the chairs seemingly part of the floor. There were no sweaty vinegar bottles on the tables. As a child raised on a takeaway diet of greasy spoons and forlorn chip shops it made my heart sing.

Soon after leaving school I saw an ad in the local paper for staff at Woolwich McDonald's. The money was good – £2.20 an hour – and you got free food: yippee! I hotfooted it down to the bus stop and picked up a number 53, which scooted me all the way from Blackheath's lofty Georgian mansions to the squalid mess that was Woolwich High Street. I then sat on a shiny slippery seat carefully filling out the application form. I wanted this job – I needed this job. I had fruit machines to feed.

I handed the form in and returned home. Three days later I got a letter with a golden arch branded on to the top of the page: I was in. They had room for me, and if I played my cards right I was off to Hamburger University. It's a bit sad to think that back then I thought this was a real job, that the top brass had seen something in my application form that my teachers had missed. This was long before the expression 'McJob' would be used to define a pointless waste of time and effort.

I arrived on the Monday nervous but excited. In those far-off days all the top brass were real-life Americans, gritty pioneers eking out their time on the far-flung space station instructing the English droids in the fine art of fast food. How they must have wished they could've gone home to their friends and family: what had they done to deserve this godforsaken posting? Woolwich High Street, for fuck's sake. Saturday mornings always saw bloodstains on the pavement, soldiers from the nearby barracks *v.* casuals *v.* immigrants. I was half a mod at the time, wearing Sta-Prest, Ben Shermans and desert boots. I didn't have a scooter or a parka. I always thought scooters looked like a pain in the neck. All those mirrors – who was going to clean them?

I was sent upstairs and sat down facing a semi-attractive American lady. I'd never spoken to an American before, never mind an American chick. She laid my future out before me: focus, be punctual and above all work for the team. Noble sentiments indeed, but this was the seventies and the unions were still in full effect. The idea was that you got a job, joined a union and did as little work as possible for as much money as you could get. This is what had been hammered into me by virtually every working-class person I'd spoken to. People talked about mythical perks like six months' paid sick leave and treble time on bank holidays. I had mates who worked for Greenwich council who'd told me of the Accident Book, a huge dusty tome that would be opened as soon as you cut your finger or tripped over a onion and in which your name and vastly exaggerated injury would be written down quickly before you were cloaked in a blanket, hustled out of the building like a paedophile and sent home to await your pay-out.

At McDonald's you had a badge with space for five stars on it. Each star you got meant you'd mastered a certain station in the kitchen: fries; shakes; production (making sure everything ran smoothly) . . . I can't remember the others.

I was put on shakes to begin with. That gorgeous thick confection you slurp with your Happy Meal is made up of just two things: a syrup, which comes in five-litre tins of chocolate or strawberry flavour; and the 'milkshake mix', a thick viscous, slightly obscene slurry that comes in huge unwieldy sacks. The smell was odd. In fact there were a lot of odd smells in the kitchen – it didn't smell like my mum's kitchen, I can assure you. It was all a bit *Soylent Green*. The other thing I noticed was that the further you went away from the counter the more smelly and sad it seemed: the massive freezers with boxes and boxes of fries, dry ice steaming and swirling, great gas bottles of Coke-fizz sticky to the touch, the bins, which stank, and all the time the mechanised corporate language of the American managers, hushing you and shushing you about your business.

'Hey, Simon, we don't do that here at McDonald's . . .'

This referred to me picking a bun off the floor and putting it back on a burger. Fair enough, I suppose, but the floor was spotless and I'd once eaten a pineapple chunk that had fallen in a puddle with no ill effects.

Of course I was hopeless. On my first day I spilt five litres of chocolate milkshake syrup all over the floor by the fat fryer. I went bright red and tried to wipe it up with a grey floor-cloth. It looked like brown gloss paint. Two kindly dinner-lady types moved me aside and mopped it up with skill and dexterity.

'Oh, don't worry, love – it's your first day.'

'He's nervous, bless him.'

Ten minutes later I knocked over five litres of strawberry syrup in exactly the same spot. My two old-lady friends stared at me in disbelief, as if I'd spent their bingo money on crack. I was very embarrassed. A large American told me to go and move some boxes.

I never got my milkshake star – I never got any stars. I never saw the inside of Hamburger University either. I think the thing that ultimately got me the chop was my refusal to work overtime for no money. I was getting ready to go home one night when a septic tank had the audacity to ask me to wash the stairs down.

'Is that overtime?' I enquired.

'No. Here at McDonald's we all pull together as team . . .'

I told him straight: 'If I'm not being paid I'm going home.' And I did, feeling like a cross between Paul Weller and Arthur Scargill.

For some reason I'm very, very proud of that moment. I felt ten feet tall.

So I was let go after my two-week probationary period. I remember being taken upstairs to see the same lady. The strange thing was she wasn't angry; she seemed concerned to hear whether I'd been treated decently by McDonald's. It was all very odd. In nearly all my jobs the person who fired me was angry: angry with me. I left the building feeling good about myself.

I think history will serve to show I gave the world far more than McDonald's ever did.

At this stage of my life I was casual-employment crazy. I'd get up, go to the Job Centre, select a card from the rack, get the job, get sacked and go back for more. I always chose jobs with no skills and especially no responsibility: warehouseman, packer, labourer, shelf-stacker, whatever. Until I started doing stand-up I'd never had a proper job – I mean one using my brain. I deliberately sought out employment that wouldn't tax me mentally. That way I couldn't fail, could I? It's easier not to attempt to fulfil your dreams, be you a budding singer, painter or poet. It's easier to drift and wander off track.

I just wanted to get by, but all the time I was storing up resentment and bitterness. I did have dreams. I wanted to be famous, as an actor or a singer. (Yes, folks, I was normal.)

The lady would ring the employers and more often than not I'd be told to start on the next day or the following Monday. There was a reason I got those jobs: no other fucker wanted to do them. I was doing the work that English people would later decide was beneath them and would hand over to the Poles, when the English working class exchanged the lathe and the fork-lift truck for the TV remote and the sofa.

However, I wasn't working class, as you know – I was middle class. I was slumming it. It was all a bad dream, and one day soon someone would take me away from all this and let me curl up by the fire with a good book. I didn't know who. Certainly not me; I certainly didn't seem to have the wherewithal to extract myself from the mire.

D.G. Electrics was just off Lewisham Way on a site that's now occupied by Tesco. It was winter and I was living in Hyde Vale and I walked to work in the inky-black mornings, the chip papers blowing around my feet like tumbleweeds. If you want to know where you are in the grand scheme of things then a low-paying manual job on Monday morning is a good indication.

Everyone looks so sad and defeated, their faces blank and green on the buses, doors slamming, women clutching their dressing gowns to their necks as they take the milk in, beefy men holding tiny Tupperware containers with awful sandwiches just visible through the grey plastic (maybe a Penguin or a Club too on Fridays). And the cold – all the time the cold – chipping at your fingers and your toes; and all the clever people sleeping in their beds.

I started at D.G. on a Monday. I was mostly moving plastic boxes of screws and washers around. There were four other people in the warehouse and I was at the bottom of the ladder. There was a guy there who was the spitting image of Walker, the spiv in *Dad's Army*, plus two old men and a Pakistani rockabilly with a quiff and steel-toecapped boots; he thought he was the ship's biscuit and joshed and japed around with me, taking the piss in a general manner – by the Wednesday he'd become quite confident and was putting me in headlocks and tripping me up when I was carrying tea and suchlike.

When he approached me on the Thursday, his arms held out like a wrestler, I kicked him in the bollocks then went and got myself a cup of chicken soup from the vending machine. He was in some distress and rolled around a bit; I was a bit shaken up but life was hard enough without his homoerotic horseplay. When he finally got up we tussled around a bit and my earring got ripped out before we got broken up by the spiv. He never bothered me again. Mind you, I got fired the following Tuesday by a Jamaican foreman for wanking in the toilet.

However, before that, on the preceding Friday, I was shocked and amazed to open my pay packet and find not the £26 I'd expected but £84: I'd been granted a tax rebate from out of nowhere. I immediately told everyone on the shop floor and even the Hindu rockabilly rebel was pleased for me. Within an hour the spiv had sold me a girl's sheepskin coat that didn't fit me for £45. At the time I had no concept of 'a fool and his money are soon parted'. I was so young – how stupid could you be? I mean, he looked like Walker, he spoke like Walker – how much warning did I need?

Down the pub that night I stood with pockets full of cash, puffing on a quality cigarette. The jacket fitted me like a condom. Someone who thought he was clever pointed out it was a girl's coat because it buttoned up the wrong way, and later on someone else said the same thing. But I didn't care: I had forty quid on me and was drinking tequila sunrises without ice.

I put most of it in the fruit machine. The jacket was so tight I could barely raise my arm up to the slot but I wasn't taking it off – it was a genuine sheepskin and it was mine.

* * *

After D.G. I got another job, at a printer's in New Cross called the Brindle Press. It was round the back of Goldsmiths in a cul-de-sac, and was a quaint little firm – a bit Ealing Comedy (actually more Ealing Soap), run by a small family. The boss was a little chap in a three-piece suit with a fob watch. His son worked there and his sister, too, in the office.

I worked in the warehouse. It was tiny, like a little mouse's house, and lining the walls were racks and racks of different kinds of paper that would slice you up if you handled it wrong. I was very wary of it and always got someone to help me move it if possible; it was floppy and heavy and sharp at the edges, a lethal combination.

I used to come into work early, do a bit then try not to fall asleep in the afternoon. The foreman used to come in and say, 'Are we keeping you up?' which he thought was hilarious. He also admitted I was the first person he'd seen sweep up with only one hand.

One weekend I blagged the keys so I could open up on Monday morning. On the Sunday night I nervously let myself into the building, having drawn a blank trying to cadge a bed off people in the pub. I lay by the gas fire like a huge paranoid dog. I didn't sleep a wink – I knew the secretary had keys too and didn't want to be caught slumbering. It's horrible being homeless. You walk around like a ghost all night, looking at the lights in flats and houses, wondering if you could creep into a garden and doss down in the shed. The foxes stare and the cars rush by and there's no relief from the paralysing thought: *There's nowhere for me to sleep* ... You just walk and walk. I've slept in cars, graveyards, warehouses; I once slept in a garage in Lewisham and the family came home and tried to park the car on me. That was so embarrassing! When they realised it wasn't a neighbour come to borrow some sultanas they were horrified. They must have expected a tramp, a smelly old codger with shoes made of rags and a frightened dignity in his eyes, not a young man in Levi's and a Ben Sherman. I could have been their son. I slipped off into the night muttering apologies.

The odd thing was, not that many people in my immediate social circle knew I was homeless. It was just when the last bell sounded that my problems began – as Charles Bukowski said, 'Give a man four walls long enough and he could own the world.' I couldn't bring myself to go to a doss house: that would have been admitting defeat. I saw myself as someone permanently hitchhiking. I went to my dad's or my mum's occasionally but I'd been caught pinching money from them so they were always a last resort. They both had new partners who didn't like me (or so I thought), too, and most of my mates had had enough.

During the day at work I tried to present a chipper and jaunty disposition but it was a thin veneer. I always made sure I was presentable when I was socialising in the pub or at parties. In fact I kept myself spotless the whole time I was homeless or staying in intermittent accommodation. I was always washing: the first words out of my mouth on arrival at someone's house would be, 'Can I have a bath?' People would go to the toilet and find me washing my feet in the sink; when I stayed the night with someone I'd slip off after a while and have a shower. Some people would get quite shirty about this – 'You can't have a shower now, you'll wake the whole house up!' *But you live on your own* ... I'd think.

I had few clothes but they were kept clean – I was always hand-washing shirts. The point was that being dirty represented poverty and failure. I didn't want to be thought of as a tramp; I refused to be smelly. A man must have standards.

In the storeroom at Brindle there was a small dumbwaiter lift that carried paper up to 'the girls', a tiny room full of lovely old ladies who folded and stapled things. One day I put my hand into the lift shaft and started playing chicken with the lift, pressing the button to send it up and stopping it just before it trapped my hand against a reinforced metal rod. There was something satisfying about the feel of the big primary-coloured buttons. I was leaving shorter and shorter gaps between arm and steel, and suddenly my arm was trapped.

One half went white and the other half went red. I started squealing up the shaft at the ladies like a drowning miner: 'Help! *Help!* I've got my arm stuck!'

They thought I was messing about and fell about laughing. I begged to differ: 'My arm's stuck – help!' Eventually they realised I was in pain and suddenly the whole shop floor was crammed into the tiny room.

'Shall I shut off the power?' said a man with a beard who was good at darts.

'Ring the fire brigade,' said the bloke who never let anyone read his paper.

The boss asked me quietly, 'Which way was the lift going, son: up or down?'

'Up I think,' I said.

'It's your fucking arm, son. Was it up or down?'

'Up.'

He pressed the button and the lift slid down. I carefully freed my arm.

Everyone went quiet. I felt very stupid.

'Why the *fuck* would you do that?' the boss said.

I didn't know either – an early mechanised form of self-harming, perhaps?

They didn't fire me but I wasn't invited to join the print union SOGAT either. I got bored soon afterwards and left.

I got a job in Deptford High Street in a shabby carpet store. There was me and a young Asian guy hoiking and dragging great rolls of carpets around. The man in charge asked me if I supported Millwall.

'No,' I said.

'Good,' he replied. 'Only, we had one working here used to nick the Stanley knives and hand them out down Cold Blow

Lane to his mates. They're animals, those people: they'll slice you up for nothing.' He shook his head in disbelief.

'It's no fun any more. I remember when it was just a punch-up, cuts and bruises, now they sling ammonia at yer.'

That lunchtime I put the last of my money in a fruit machine in a café. I'd often do this. Unfortunately the machines were often by the counter, so I'd lose my money before I'd actually ordered any food. I'd leave dejected, staring at huge plates of sausages and chips, starving hungry.

The following day I saw a tenner on a desk and whiffed it. It was already late afternoon. No one said anything, and I went home.

I arrived the next day a bit nervous and was greeted by the manager.

'All right, Si? Can you sling that underlay through there, mate?'

After a while I realised the Asian boy wasn't there; I asked where he was.

'He nicked a tenner out of the office, Simon. Little cunt tried to deny it, too – they're all the same, fucking Pakis.'

I felt awful for a bit then went and had a massive fry-up with the blood money.

The lady at the Job Centre knew me by now and had a soft spot for me – I was the only waif on the books, I suppose, and she must have felt sorry for me. I guess she was used to people going for jobs and never coming back, whereas I was the exact opposite: her own little boomerang boy; wherever she flung me I'd come arcing back into her hands.

'Didn't it work out, Simon . . . ?' she'd say. She never asked for a proper excuse, which suited me.

I'd return to the 'jobs vacant' boards hoping there'd be a job in a record shop. This was an early Hornby-esque fantasy that never panned out, the only job I could think of that I'd actually like to do.

The next thing she offered me was working nights in a factory. The only people I knew who worked nights were people in novels who were betrayed sexually by their wives while they toiled away. But I wasn't married so I'd be OK on a night job, coming home on the milk float swinging my legs and downing a bottle of gold top then sleeping all day. Actually I hated milk but it still sounded brilliant.

The factory was nondescript, off Evelyn Street in New Cross. I arrived at nine o'clock and the place was dark and dingy, virtually deserted. It felt odd to be starting work at the same time as *Minder* would be starting on ITV, but I put such silly thoughts aside and strode in.

I was to be working until six the following morning with two half-hour breaks – Jesus, in that time your wife could be taken to Paris and rogered senseless. A man with glasses set me to work then vanished. The job entailed putting little plastic containers like Berocca tubes on tiny metal poles that whizzed past you on a conveyer belt. *This will be a piece of piss*, I thought.

The tubes slotted on quite easily but I soon realised that the belt moved too fast to ever get in front and have a rest. You had to concentrate the whole time or you fell behind. I didn't know what would happen if I stopped and I was too scared to find out. It was exhausting. The noise of the machine was awful, everything in the room was filthy and there was nothing to take your mind off the task in hand. A lot of the places I'd worked in had page-three calendars, with some girl clutching a spanner to announce April, or posters of Farrah Fawcett-Majors tipping her tiny breasts forward. Here there were just greasy magnolia walls and empty Styrofoam cups. The sink looked like it had been used to wash dead bears before burial, and the floor was sticky with something strange. But the job, the job – all that rapid hand-eye coordination – it was a nightmare. With the strip lights above my head buzzing, bearing down on me, I felt like Batman at the end of the show when the razor saw is coming towards him, pinned down on the table.

I looked at the clock: I'd been there only forty minutes.

I wondered why I was on my own. What happened behind the greasy plastic curtain that led to the main building? What were they manufacturing there? Just then a fat black lady came in and asked how I was getting on. I was overjoyed to see another human being and struck up a conversation with her. I explained my problems and she showed me how to get a march on the machine by collecting lots of plastic tubes by your left hand and then suddenly doubling up, using both hands. Eureka! I hadn't thought of that. I, the one-armed sweeper, was away. After smoking a few fags at me she shuffled off.

I began to make my move like a crack cyclist in the mountain stage of the Tour de France. I shot to the front of the pack; I had the machine on the rack. I was well in front . . . I had time to get a cup of warm water and eat a bag of peanuts.

I started to feel like I'd cowed my machine and would just pop tubes on now and then like a skilled printer or lathe operator. It was weird to be alone with such a large piece of machinery. *Where was it built?* I thought. *Who had been its last master? Will we forge an unlikely partnership and become rich and successful?*

At around eleven-thirty I got cocky and went for a dump. When I came back I was well behind: I had to really graft to get back in front again. It was the middle of the night – what was I doing? It was like trying to push custard uphill, and I suddenly felt depressed.

I went outside at some point, into the sweet night air, got the night bus home and went to bed.

I returned the following week as if nothing had happened and tried to claim for five hours' work. A man shouted at me, calling me a 'waste of space' and a 'clown'. Apparently I'd halted production for several hours. I somehow got a cheque for seventeen quid, though.

⋆ ⋆ ⋆

Trafalgar Road is a busy thoroughfare that links east and west Greenwich. At one end is the Royal Naval College and the Queen's House and at the other Tunnel Avenue – the gateway to the Blackwall Tunnel. Here Royal Greenwich becomes a rough collection of buildings and factories made grubby by the vast slew of traffic streaming into East London.

Mr Carter (seventy-two) had chosen me from nine applicants to be his right-hand man at Frisby Menswear, which at the time gave me a little Ready Brek glow of pride. He had two shops, one opposite the builder's merchants and one further down near the tunnel entrance. His premises were old-school high-street gentlemen's outfitters reduced now to selling jeans, underwear and Fred Perrys plus any other accoutrements required by the good citizens of Greenwich and beyond. In the afternoons I'd loosen his tongue with tea and biscuits and he'd regale me with tales of the old days when labourers would come into the shop, their pockets stuffed with cash, and buy underpants, vests, shirts, socks and even handkerchiefs, then repair to Greenwich swimming pool for a slipper bath; after ablutions it was straight to the pub for beer and fags. Now, he'd say, 'we're lucky if they buy a sweatshirt'.

He had the old cabinets in the shop, with drawers for cufflinks, collar studs, ties and cravats now all sadly stocked with casual wear. He was a nice old man, a bit dodgy on his pins and slightly overweight. He smoked like a trooper – like many of his generation he'd been forced to climb down from the proper fags (Senior Service, Embassy) and now smoked Silk Cut. He'd often puff while dealing with customers, put his cigarette down somewhere and forget it; then he'd light up another one, which he'd place carefully in another ashtray. Consequently he'd often have three fags on the go at any one time, burning away like little signal fires around the shop. It was only a small place and I'd have to weigh up which fags to stub out and which to leave: if he returned to an extinguished ciggie he'd look briefly in my direction, a bit annoyed, but he'd never show this to the customer.

Like Vito Corleone he'd be mortified if we ever let a customer know what we were thinking. Much like a con man, a good salesman treats his customer like a 'mark', there for one purpose: to be relieved of his money. There must be a stillness and silence about a salesman working in a gentlemen's outfitters. It's not like a street market – you can't barge into the conversation whinging about your piles or the foibles of the England football team. There's a softness and lightness of touch displayed by a good salesman. Patter is a good word, denoting that light, almost sensuous stairway of remarks leading to the top of the stairs where the deal is done. Obviously some people need to be led right to the top floor before you get a result, but selling is human behaviour at its most fascinating and even now I love to watch people flogging people things.

Later on, when I worked at the Blue Mantle fireplace shop in the Old Kent Road, I was privy to one of London's great masters of the art: Mick 'Ginger' Godden, a proper salesmen who'd learnt his trade on the stalls at Battersea funfair. The thing with selling is that some people like to be coaxed, some like to be bullied and some don't want to talk at all – it's up to you to gauge and deliver the performance they want. Mr Carter was pretty good. He belonged to the world of the pervy salesmen of *The Fast Show*, all little compliments and hidden hints of great expertise. He could sell a shirt all right but he wasn't in Mick Godden's class. Mick was an animal. He sold me a wooden toucan bookend for three quid once and was buzzing for days afterwards – he never thought he'd sell it, you see, and he loved me for taking it off his hands.

Mr Carter lived in Catford and got a cab to work every day from home, which must have cost him at least twelve quid each way – a sum that seemed extraordinary to me at the time. It lent him glamour and kudos that had been sadly lacking in my employers up till then.

He had another old boy, called Tom, who helped him out on Saturdays. He was even older than Mr Carter and very gentle and kind: his catchphrase was, 'Yes, I will do that small thing for you,' which says it all really. He was *old*, though. One day he left early, saying he was going to walk through Greenwich Park, and returned later unable to breathe, gasping like a fish. We sat him down and got him a nice cup of tea. It took him about three-quarters of an hour to recover. Mr Carter was furious.

'I told you you wouldn't make that hill,' he said.

They were very fond of each other and, like many old couples, would each try to convince you that the other was the more feeble one.

It was a lovely warm environment in which to work after the harsh industrial workhouses I'd thrust myself into, and I really looked forward to the shop each day. I was living at the Moys' at the time and could walk through Greenwich Park to work each morning. Unfortunately it wasn't all tea and cakes at Frisby Menswear, though. On Saturdays I had to help out at the other shop, near the tunnel. This branch was run by Bob. Bob wore brown clothes, had a bulbous nose and was very angry at the world. He was like those people you saw in the sixties kitchen-sink films, having a pop at Tom Courtney or Albert Finney, a dyed-in-the-wool, clock-watching menace to free thinking and love of life. He hated me – I could see it in his beady eyes the second I first walked through the door and he was forced to put down his sandwich.

I think he thought Mr Carter should have consulted him about my appointment; perhaps he thought the firm didn't need another assistant – who knows?

He was right about me, though: I robbed the place blind. Mr Carter put me in charge of stock and a steady supply of jeans and Fred Perrys were siphoned off for me and my pals. Boxer shorts had just come into fashion and I purloined these too. I never thought about what effect my pilfering was having on the business. I saw every employer as being part of some huge central mass from which I could help myself. A lot of my friends pinched stuff from work – it was kind of all right, wasn't it? Also it was just great to have clean underwear every day. I started to feel good about myself. I had a proper job and I could put fresh denim next to my skin. I used to listen to 'Jeans On' by David Dundas and think, *Yes, that's me*.

Prior to this I'd walked round in the same clothes for weeks, having to borrow shirts and socks from people. I'd stay at people's houses, get up in the morning and change my socks, taking from whichever drawer in the house was convenient. Consequently I'd sometimes be found by my host hopping around trying to drag an eight-year-old's socks on to my size-twelve feet. I never took pants, though – that was beyond the pale even for me.

Saturdays were a drag. Bob would stare out of the shop window remarking on the general lowering of standards in life (much as I do now, which is frightening): how the buses never ran on time, how the window cleaner used to polish the whole window with hot water then buff it up with a shammy leather, leaving it sparkling, whereas now, he'd say, his voice dripping with disgust, 'he just swings that scraper over it, leaving marks'. This was the same window cleaner who'd had the round for twenty years. Imagine that. He did the whole street, a mile long, and he used to buff up every window, sometimes with newspaper in the old days. I bet he was pleased when the scraper was invented.

I found out the real reason Bob moaned about him: he had a big fuck-off house in Bexley Heath. *Good luck to him*, I thought. He'd earned his house and his arthritis.

Of course my enthusiasm at Frisby didn't last. The familiar traits began to creep in – days off, lack of application. I felt trapped in the shop. It was so quiet some days, like a tomb. I'd make excuses to run out and do errands that didn't exist. It was so boring standing in a shop all day; sometimes during the week you wouldn't have a customer for hours and you just had to shuffle boxes around. I'd often go upstairs to the first floor, a dusty shuttered room full of broken mannequins and empty boxes, where I'd sit in a daze and zone out, the dust mites wavering in shards of sunlight.

In all my jobs before stand-up I located a room or patch of ground that was very still, a place where no one came any more. There'd always be mementos of the business – broken machinery or old advertising paraphernalia – and always an anonymous stillness I could wallow in, almost meditate, until the familiar cry I'd heard all my life: 'Simon, where are you? What are you doing . . .?'

By this time I was trapped in a little-window world of bells and lemons, watermelons, cherries and pears. I was always getting subs from my wages and all my money went into fruit machines at night and lunchtimes. I knew every pub on that mile-long strip – the William IV, the Vic, the Bricklayers Arms, all of them.

I would arrive, the anti-customer, and hurry up to the bar for a small lemonade or Coke then head straight over to the fruit machine. Depending on how much money I had I'd hop backwards and forwards to the bar changing fivers and tenners. I never bought a beer when I was playing them on my own (in fact I didn't really get a proper taste for booze until I was twenty or so). It was a strange existence. I led a sort of double life in pubs. There was my solo gambling life, when I'd be incognito, just feeding coins into a slot, never looking up. This could be anywhere in London – in fact sometimes I'd be spinning the reels in Bromley or Wapping at midday and would meet someone I knew from Greenwich on their lunch break. 'What are you doing here?' they'd ask and I'd mumble some story about something, make my excuses and leave. Other times people I knew would hail me and I'd just walk out of the pub, my cheeks burning.

And then there was my normal social life, when I'd meet friends, play pool, buy rounds and chat up girls. Although if there was a machine in the pub it could all go wrong: I might just wander off in the middle of a conversation or game of pool and begin playing. I missed out on lots of sexual opportunities in this fashion. People would say, 'She liked you – where'd you go?' and I'd just shrug. My close friends eventually got very frustrated with me ('You're not going to play the machine tonight are you . . . ?') and often took me to pubs where there were no machines to distract me. I usually enjoyed these evenings, as I'd get drunk and make people laugh. I think the general feeling was that if I was kept off the fruits I was brilliant company, capable of both verbal and physical comedy. This was even more the case when the people around me were under the influence of hashish: then I'd really come into my own and just take over, conducting conversations with members of the public, winding them up without them realising. My friends would laugh their heads off and I'd feel fantastic. Here I had a role – a job, if you like.

Of course in pubs with machines I'd lose my money early on, most times anyway, and be dependent on handouts. This and my on-and-off homelessness helped to develop my showman personality: I felt I had to offer an all-round entertainment package to compensate for having no money of my own. I'd try to make my benefactors laugh and offer to get rounds in with their money; when I stayed at people's houses I'd roll joints and rush out to the garage to buy munchies. I was a Joey and a gofer and it didn't do wonders for my self-esteem, but I got on with it.

But my solo fruit-machine playing was the strangest. If you took the machine out of the picture you'd just be left with a boy facing the wall, over and over again, in different rooms all around the area. Why would someone want to do that? I didn't know. I've played machines in every pub within about a mile radius of everywhere I've lived. I think I must have played machines in every pub in Brighton – every pub! That's a lot of boozers and no booze. (Though I later rectified the whole no-drinking thing, of course.)

Most days I'd catch the overground to Leicester Square and hang round the arcades. Occasionally I'd meet other lost souls like me and we'd bond over a particular machine, helping each other, punching and flicking the buttons, our eyes never leaving the spinning reels. If I wasn't playing machines I'd be watching other people play them, creeping nearer and nearer like a pyromaniac gazing at a fire. Sometimes people would get angry, especially if they were losing, and cut me with a look so I'd shrink back like a dog to watch from afar. Other times they'd shake their heads and talk to me after losing a gamble or not understanding a feature. Here I'd be in my element. I'd offer advice, whispering in their ears like a politician, the original spin doctor, helping with nudges and features if they'd let me. You never asked for money or were offered any, though. In the arcades the little skunk monkeys might ask for a coin but I never did.

I was an addict, pure and simple. Approaching a fruit machine, my arm swinging up to poke a coin in the slot: that was all I lived for.

It sounds ridiculous, doesn't it: addicted to cherries and lemons and bells and bars. But, let me tell you, it was no fucking joke. I begged, borrowed and stole so I could lose over and over again. I stole from my family and my friends. I stole from shops, houses, libraries, the swimming baths. I took anything I could and cashed it into ten-pence pieces to offer up to the metal gods. I knew every machine that was on the market, all the supposed ways to win – but I never did win, because I could never walk away. I wasn't there to win; I was there to lose. That's the essence of the addictive mind: I WANT TO LOSE.

I became properly homeless. I had holes in my shoes and went without food. I was a walking ghost, forever staring at the blinking lights through pub windows while the good people inside laughed and drank their beer.

I was stealing all the time: pushbikes, cheque books, clothing, books, records, cassettes – anything I could sell and lots I couldn't. I once stole a catering tub of margarine from a café, a rope and a spade from a perplexed man up a tree. I stole a bottle of vodka and a steak from Safeway's every day for about three weeks; I got two quid each time from a builder I knew for the vodka (I ate the steak) – two pound notes straight in the fruit machine. I tried to sell a wooden clotheshorse to a pawn shop, a lamp from a library. I stole something every day.

I became bolder and more careless. I was in and out of car windows like a chimp looking for bananas. I began to get hooked on the buzz of stealing – brilliant, now I had two addictions! – the tightness in the chest, the feeling of fear as I laid my hands on the goods, then running and running till my lungs burnt. And all for what? An empty bag, a folder containing papers, a plastic clock . . . What the fuck had I become? As the addiction took hold I started staring at women's bags and men's briefcases. I nicked two Fred Perrys from a shop in Oxford Street and was caught red-handed and held in Ryman's by a skinny man with an over-developed social conscience and bad breath. 'I hate people like you,' he muttered. *Fair enough*, I thought, *I hate myself.*

Chapter Six

I carried on for a while at Frisby Menswear, mooning about and pinching bits and bobs. That job and the short-lived social status it gave me was my last hurrah before borstal, really. After I left Frisby the jobs petered out and Vicky Moy threw me out. I'd stolen some money from her son's – my best mate's – Christmas card (classy). She said she couldn't trust me in the house; I'd have to go.

One night I crept back in and hid behind the sofa, trying to get some sleep. In the morning everyone came down and was eating breakfast in the living room when suddenly someone saw my leg and the sofa was yanked back. They all laughed at me, which at the time seemed worse than them being angry. I remember Vicky came in and looked astonished. I was in a bad way mentally at this point: I really didn't know what I was doing. I just wandered about pretending I was normal but people were looking at me sideways more and more.

I must have made my peace with the Moys, though, because I was fast asleep there one bright and early morning when the Old Bill piled in and arrested me for seventeen counts of theft.

It was quite dramatic, plainclothes men swarming round my mattress on the floor. They were looking for cheques – I'd nicked a cheque book from a Range Rover and naively tried to cash a cheque at the bank named on the book: *derr!* My signature was different to the owner's, obviously, and the teller said those terrible words: 'Can you wait here a minute, please.' I fled.

Toby Moy led them into my room. I remember he had a bit of toast in his mouth. I didn't blame him – it wasn't like they were going to hide me in a priest's hole then smuggle me out of the country. They must have been sick of me.

I remember I had to get dressed in front of a copper. It's a weird feeling, that, pulling your pants over your cock and balls in front of plod. Something inside of you dies; your shoulders go down a bit and you can't meet their eyes.

From that moment I didn't see another fruit machine for a year – nor a naked lady, for that matter. I was on my way to jail: do not pass Go; do not collect £200; do not win first prize in a beauty contest. All that and more.

Once arrested and in the system you often find yourself travelling across the country in police vans and prison wagons. You look out and see people going about their daily business: you can see them so clearly, sometimes hear them, but they're people in a film, in another country. They're living in normal time but you're not; you're in black and white and they're in colour. You're no longer part of real life, suspended in custody. Nothing moves for you, except your bowels, and they wouldn't see you even if they wanted to. You're in prison.

When I got sent down it was a bit of a shock, though not totally unexpected: I'd already been up before the same magistrate twice in two weeks.

First I'd stolen a handbag from a wall outside the National Gallery – somehow I'd thought that it didn't qualify as an actual mugging because I hadn't wrenched it from the lady's hand. I was chased into Soho and rugby-tackled by two off-duty coppers. One of them punched me in the face, dislodging a tooth, but I was so full of adrenaline I didn't feel it till later. I'd been given a two-year conditional discharge for this crime and the atmosphere in the court was quite genial: they seemed to think it was a one-off. However, eight days later I was standing before the same beak having been caught red-handed stealing from a shop off the Strand.

He spluttered in disgust.

'You were up before me last week. Well, I feel it totally beyond my powers to sentence you and therefore remand you in custody to be sentenced at Crown Court.'

That was it. I was led below court by an official and placed in a cell.

I was in shock but it was tempered by a strange feeling of relief. My real life was over and I was about to start an unreal one – at least I'd be fed and given a roof over my head. In the real world I was homeless and my life had become almost unbearable. This was where I deserved to be.

My holding cell contained a tramp and two Dickensian criminals, one tall and cadaverous and one small and rotund. All three ignored me. Little and Large were pacing the cell near the door, lost in angry recrimination and a huge sense of injustice. They frequently banged on the door and demanded to see the screw, shouting, 'Come here, you fucking dog.' From what I could gather someone had grassed them up and if he sang properly they'd be going away.

'He won't say fuck all.'

'He fucking might, John. He fucking might.'

It was all so real and odd. This was it: the start of my adventure. I was in a prison film but I didn't know the ending. The thick glass tiles that served as our window lent us all a ghostly pallor, and the tramp studied the rest of us with a strange magisterial calm. At some point some food arrived on metal trays: gala pie and cold veg. I stared at the grey pork and greenish boiled egg and felt depressed. Not a good start on the food front: gala pie is the worst pie of all – and I love pies. My punishment had started. The angry men ignored their food and pretty soon the tramp had siphoned their victuals on to his plate. I watched him, fascinated, as he produced from his pocket two small wraps like cocaine parcels, one with an 'S' on it and the other a 'P'. Salt and pepper! He seasoned his food carefully and replaced the packets in his ragged garments. I remember that scene very clearly but the next three months are a jumble of places and memories.

At the time of my arrest there was a prison officers' dispute going on throughout England, which resulted in many screws not showing up for work and many jails being forced into lock-down. Also admissions were restricted: there simply wasn't the staff to deal with prisoners arriving, so convicts were kept in police stations.

In the three months of my remand I visited five jails: Wormwood Scrubs, Lewis, Leicester, Brixton and Maidstone. I met a multitude of people, some good, some bad and one completely insane. I did a lot of twenty-three-hour bang-ups, which is where you're confined to your cell all day and night because of lack of staff. It suited me down to the ground so long as I had a book and my cellmate wasn't an eight-foot predatory homosexual (and I didn't meet any of those).

It was a strange three months. For some reason I did three days in Wanstead police station, where I met a tiny Irishman who'd stolen a tray of rings from a jeweller's and run off as fast as his little legs would carry him (not very far). He was in a terrible state as he was missing his daughter's fifth birthday. I didn't think about my family; I was on my own. I tried to freeze my feelings out, crush them, or they'd make me weak.

The days became a blur of whitewashed walls, slamming doors, tasteless food and smelly feet. On my first day in the Scrubs I awoke and went out for a wash, still half-asleep. Suddenly I was in this huge prison with the landings and metal stairs, shouts and cries, hollow metallic banging. I chose a sink next to a huge pair of hairy shoulders. I splashed some water on my face and looked to my left to see a huge bald man eyeing me. He was horrible, staring at me as if I'd strangled his mum (maybe *he*'d strangled his mum). I ran back to my cell.

In Lewis I was billeted with a young black guy who remained deep in thought the whole time I was there. He used to pace up and down the cell, ruminating, and eventually I asked him if he was OK.

'It's my girls, man. I worry about my girls.'

'What girls?' I said innocently.

He swung his head round. 'I've got four girls, man, in Spain; they're on their own. I worry about them . . .' He then proceeded to tell me about his four girlfriends, who apparently all lived in Spain in a beach environment. They all worshipped him and he used to spend his days rogering them. Not much else seemed to happen in this part of Spain – he never discussed the food or the architecture either.

'When I laid with her, man, it was wicked.'

'Which one?' I said.

'Karen,' he replied, a little put out, then spun back to his lonely vigil, pacing up and down lost in thought.

In one jail I was put in a cell with a tall lad with a harelip who had some sort of speech impediment and was a bit simple. I started a chinwag with him and soon discovered he was an arsonist. Arson's a very serious crime, second only to murder, and as time went by I started to rib him a bit and sort of take the piss. I told him that his crime was disgusting and said he must be some sort of idiot. I was soon dislodged from the moral high ground when I found his hands round my throat. I nearly shat myself; he was hissing at me to shut up and he appeared to be very strong. I apologised profusely and he let me go. I used all my powers of persuasion to get back in his good books and by suppertime we were buddies again.

I was obviously very angry and confused at the time and this had come out in our exchange. I'd wrongly thought the guy to be a bit of a mug and had tried to verbally bully him. I'd never done that at school, so what had changed? What had made me do it? I didn't do it again. From then on I kept my opinions to myself. It was a valuable lesson.

When I was in Maidstone I had my first really dangerous cellmate. He was fairly short and had thick black hair; his face was red and he came from Manchester. He was also very talkative, which I thought was a good sign but after a while he started telling me things about his life that were a bit disturbing. He told me that his mum had been taken off to a mental hospital when he was nine years old, and that his dad used to hit him in the face for no reason. After his mum was interned his dad started bringing women home. One night he'd crept downstairs and his father was sitting on the sofa with a girl of about fifteen – she was crying and her top was torn. While he was telling me this he really stared at me as if I thought it might be funny. At one point he started shaking and seemed to be on the verge of attacking me. His normally red face went purple and white and his eyes narrowed to slits. *Here we go*, I thought, but luckily he thought better of it and flung himself on his bunk.

After lunch one day he came into the cell and said, 'Are you taking the piss?'

I was confused.

'What's your towel doing there?'

I kept very calm as he started ranting and raving. He was shaking again.

'Do you think I'm some sort of cunt?' he fired at me.

'No,' I replied.

After a while he calmed down and apologised.

'You're all right, really,' he said. This gave me a warm feeling.

He disappeared the next day and I didn't see him for a week. When he walked back into the cell one day I asked him where he'd been.

'Down the block. I smashed a black bloke across the head with my dinner tray.'

'Why?'

'He was nicking my chips.'

Fair enough, I thought.

They say when you die your whole life flashes before you. Well, in jail the good parts of my life played constantly over and over in my head like a Pathé newsreel of a perfect childhood: orange squash and Club biscuits, holidays in Cornwall, egg custard and homemade chips at my nan's house in Kenilworth, my parents drinking gin and tonics and eating peanuts from Sainsbury's in the good old days before they broke up and I became forlorn. Was I depressed? Knowing what I know now about my mental health, yes, I probably was. But no one was bi-polar in those days; you didn't have therapy. It was all stiff upper lips and pull yourself together.

All my friends' parents broke up – five out of my seven closest friends experienced this. I'd sat at home and listened to tape cassettes. Punk had fizzled out and people had traded in the Sex Pistols for Spandau Ballet, ideas for silly hats. We were entering the worst decade of the twentieth century, both politically and culturally, and I wanted none of it. I was already selfish and obsessive – the calling cards of the addict-in-waiting – and I could have become addicted to drugs or alcohol or anything. But I was still a child at heart, I never grew up, so it was no surprise that I became addicted to fruit machines. I'd always been fascinated by them, lingering in the arcades on holidays watching the penny falls and the one-arm bandits. Fuck what the butler saw, I wanted to gamble and as an addict I didn't have a lot of choice in the matter.

People are learning more and more about addiction all the time, but in the seventies and early eighties you were just dubbed an idiot. I didn't live in California – I went right through the prison system undiagnosed. I only stole to play fruit machines. I didn't want to be a proper criminal; I had no ambition to have a

Jag and buy a chain of launderettes. When I was standing in front of a fruit machine I was happy. I was shut off from real life and didn't have to deal with my feelings.

That's what an addict is searching for: dislocation from how he feels. Whether it's cocaine, masturbating, smoking weed or just eating a really huge bag of crisps, you can get obsessed with anything. (By the way, I've done all these things at once and the hardest part was finishing the crisps.) For me, all the things I've been addicted to led to one thing: shame, shame and more shame. I carried it around on my shoulders, like a living thing weighing me down. When someone screams at you, 'Why do you do these things?' all you can say is, 'I don't know, I don't know,' and you think, *Who am I? What sort of person am I, to steal my brother's birthday money or try to sell my dad's umbrella to the toy shop? Am I mad?* In a way, yes – but this isn't a dressing-up-as-Napoleon madness. It's very hard to pin down. Addictive behaviour comes and goes – there have been periods in my life when I've held down jobs, drunk moderately (three pints a night), felt good, wore nice clothes and avoided addictive pastimes. It can flare up at any time, and your preference can switch. No sooner have you put down the booze than you start online betting; you get off the sleeping pills only to develop a fondness for buying up model soldiers. You can get lost in anything – everything can be taken to an extreme. I've had problems with gambling, booze, drugs and overeating – sometimes overlapping. But the fruit machines really brought me lowest. I was mad for them.

I was glad to be banged up. I'd become a walking shame dog, a pariah, a menace to society, a doughnut without any jam in the middle. At least now I'd get fed and have a bed.

Breakfast: the most important meal of the day. Mmm . . . Powdered egg and bacon like pickled pigs' ears on toast, porridge, of course, if you wanted it, and fucking boiling red-hot tea – honestly, it was like lava and was the most dangerous weapon in borstal, used only for special occasions.

After I was convicted and sentenced I was put in the allocation unit at Latchmere – now *there* was a bad atmosphere. No one knew where they'd be sent and the borstals differed greatly. It wasn't like university: you didn't get a choice. There were about eight borstals in all and three of them were closed. Portland was the worst, this being where they sent all the lunatics, the arsonists, the no-hopers. Stories abounded about rapes, suicides and general mayhem. Other inmates assured me I wouldn't be sent there, first time inside and all that, but they often mixed it up. One day they just put everyone's name up on a board, like exam results. I got Hollesley Bay in Suffolk. There was an Asian lad who was also a first offender and he too had been told he'd be going to an open borstal. I was there when he saw Portland next to his name on the noticeboard. He looked like his mum had died; he went to pieces, wringing his hands and hopping up and down. People were laughing at him.

A ginger boy leant over and said to me, 'A Paki in Portland? He's fucked.'

I'd befriended a chap in the snooker room; he was tall and wiry with pointed features and sported a fashionable wedge cut. He looked not unlike David Bowie. I didn't talk to many people on remand because of the bang-ups, but that was fine with me. I was left alone to my rapidly enlarging penis and shrunken balls and they had a decent library.

I read *My Family and Other Animals* by Gerald Durrell while I was there, about a wealthy family living in a large house in Corfu surrounded by the wonders of nature. I'd never been transported by a book like that before: the heat, the fireflies, the kids swimming in the Aegean . . . I could smell the eucalyptus. When I shut the book at night it was like running out of heroin, though – I felt bereft, utterly desolate. Suddenly I was back in my cell. I tried to sleep and dream of Corfu but the shouting and the wailing drowned out the cicadas. I thought perhaps I should read something else.

I forget the chap's name but we bonded over music. It was a relief to talk to someone about a subject I was familiar with. Inmates were constantly ridiculing each other's perceived ignorance about criminal activity or sexual behaviour. I couldn't box or play football; I was a petty crook, a plum, a sap, but so were a lot of people. I'd seen people try to set themselves up as major players 'on the out' – but sooner or later someone from their neck of the woods would arrive in the prison and tell everyone what they really were. For the first time in my life I kept my mouth shut.

I'd sat opposite him at breakfast and struck up a conversation about the merits of Echo & the Bunnymen. That evening we hotfooted it downstairs to the TV room and sat in the front row to watch David Bowie, the man himself, who was Number One with 'Ashes to Ashes'. This guy was a Bowie nut and my extensive knowledge of England's greatest-ever singer-songwriter's previous albums stood me in good stead. I couldn't help noticing that my new friend was being greeted by all the top boys in the unit as they sat down; it seemed he was some sort of face. I felt a bit like one of those Italian girls who realises her date is a made guy. One boy even came over and gave us both fags, with filter tips! I was floating on air.

That night at lock-up I was entering my cell when I saw my new friend walking down the landing towards me. I waved and slammed my door shut. I felt safer doing that: I never liked looking at a screw's face last thing before bed. They'd often try to say something funny or kind. Of course even if you did shut your own door they'd look through the spy-hole, in case you had a bear in there or were trying to set yourself alight. As I began to undress I heard muffled raised voices, then a scream like nothing I'd ever heard before. My hair stood on end. My new pal, the thin white duke, had thrown boiling tea over the boy in the cell adjacent to mine. I stood at the door in shock. It was such a horrible sound – he kept screaming and screaming. The last thing I heard was the screws saying, 'Just bathe it. Just bathe it . . .'

The following week during *Top of the Pops* I sat at the back. David Bowie was no longer Number One.

In prison the smallest thing can start something off – whether it's someone nicking chips or custard getting spilt. At Hollesley Bay this bloke Marsh was enjoying his pudding one day when he was pushed from behind; he span round. Cherrington hadn't been there very long – no more than a week – and didn't realise who he was dealing with.

'What you doing, you soppy cunt?' said Marsh.

'I'm just trying to sit down, innit.' Cherrington had a high lisping voice and seemed to be balding prematurely. Unfortunately, with his big eyes and round face, he did resemble a friendly toy from yesteryear. I imagined him slumped against a toy box somewhere.

Marsh stood up, pushing Cherrington against a table full of spotty oiks frozen in terror and fascination.

'I'm having my dinner here, you black cunt.'

'Don't speak to me that way, guy.'

'Guy! Guy! You saucy cunt. Fuck off and sit down.'

A little shiver of excitement ran through me and I felt a strange sense of pride. Marsh was our leader. Twenty-one going on forty, he was already a hardened criminal: this was the fourth time he'd been incarcerated and it wouldn't be the last. He was completely fearless and was rumoured to have stabbed someone in the leg over a can of 7-Up in Latchmere on Christmas Day. Realising I had a year to do in jail, I'd attached myself to him and was a sort of protégé – although he was appalled by my lack of aggression. He led me to his cell once and opened a box containing packets and packets of digestive biscuits, some peanuts and Old Holborn. He said: 'You could have all this but you got no go in you.' Often he'd punch me repeatedly on the arm and chest, each punch harder than the last, until I was forced to sit down or just stare at the floor. I think he expected me to head-butt him or kick him in the bollocks. He would have loved that; he'd have lain there groaning, saying, 'That's my boy,' like the bulldog in *Tom and Jerry*.

I'd decided when I first arrived that I'd have to make some sort of stand, a show of strength, or certain people would make my sentence a misery. One day in the plasterers' shop, where I was learning a trade that would stop me being a criminal for ever, a little stocky bloke from Essex told me to take a barrow of muck outside. I refused and he just said, 'D'you wanna know?' then ran at me. I didn't have a lot of time to think: I just swung my prison-issue boot up and somehow kicked him in the chest. Someone shouted out, 'Day can fight!' I felt as light as a feather, as if I was floating in space. The last time I'd fought anyone the Bay City Rollers were Number One. He manhandled me to the ground then sort of wormed his way his along my body – it was an odd move but effective. I saw his little head coming towards me; he was focused and grimacing. I was fascinated. It was like a circus trick. Before I had a chance to think he was punching me in the face repeatedly. He'd obviously done this before. I was out of my depth, dazed and confused. 'Screw,' someone shouted, 'in the storeroom.' It seemed we'd have to continue fighting in an enclosed space. I'd already had enough, and as I walked into the corridor someone hit me unseen in the temple and I went down. That's when Choc, a six-foot-two mixed-race inmate with hair seven shades of ginger decided to join in by kicking me in the head. I blacked out. I woke up outside, lying on the concrete, my head cradled by a screw. Suffolk was laid out before me like a Constable painting – gently undulating hills, copses, cows, sheep gambolling. I, however, resembled something by Francis Bacon only not as valuable. My face was a mess.

'How many people attacked you?' the screw said. Laidlaw, the kid who'd started it, had been caught kicking me; the other two had melted away. Laidlaw was stood panting with cut knuckles. I felt sick.

'Just him,' I said. They didn't believe me but I stuck to my story. By not grassing on Choc and the other guy, Blueit, I became visible: I was someone. I was not a grass but the very opposite. This was a good thing and had currency – 'There goes the Elephant Man: he looks a mess but he's not a grass: hooray!' When I got back to the unit I was summoned to Marsh's room. I told him what happened.

'Don't fucking cry,' he said. 'Don't fucking cry.' I went back to my room and wept.

A month later, after an internal inquiry, Marsh pulled Choc and asked him why he'd kicked me when I was already half-senseless.

'He kept mixing the plaster wrong,' Choc said. 'It was always lumpy.'

The hardest thing was going back to work the next day. I was in a state of shock; people sniggered and stared at me. I just tried to get on with it. Blueit just laughed at me – he was the worst of the three. He was constantly on the verge of anger and probably had a difficult upbringing. Shall we forgive him? No, let's not: he came at me from the side and it wasn't his fight. Over the next few weeks I just dug it out. I'd gained some sort of respect from Choc. He was a genuine one-off: he was a giant of a kid, from Lowestoft of all places, so he spoke like Pam Ayres and was built like George Foreman. Then there was his hair, which was hallucinogenic – it seemed to change colour as you were talking to him, from red to brown to ginger . . . He carried on bullying me in a minor way, flicking plaster on me, spitting at me, the odd slap; it was nothing personal, just something he could do to help pass the time. One day he said, 'I hope you go straight, Day: you're not cut out for all this.'

But he'd been wearing big fucking boots that day and if the screws hadn't arrived he could have really hurt me. If he'd given me brain damage he would have got seven or eight years and he'd have done them happily in his way, having borne me no malice. I wonder whether that would have been the main thrust of his defence: 'He kept mixing my plaster lumpy, Your Honour . . .'

* * *

The year was 1981 and Britain was in the grip of something new. In the annals of civic unrest, race riots, poverty, unemployment and the Sus law had ignited a brush fire that was sweeping the country. Black – mainly Jamaican – youths were fighting with the police whenever and wherever they could and this situation inflamed Hollesley's already fractured and twisted atmosphere. Black youths made up about 40 per cent of the population in our unit and had incredible solidarity. They shared everything with each other – foodstuffs, soap, tobacco (or 'burn') – and even had control of the laundry, where they'd have the best-fitting clothes starched and pressed (by white boys). It must have been an almost exact reversal of how life was in apartheid South Africa. Very few white inmates stood up to them and those who did were lionised by both the inmates and the screws. I was all right: I was in Marsh's inner circle and their top boys were extremely wary of him.

My feelings about the black kids were confused to say the least. Growing up in an affluent suburb of South East London I'd no black friends and at school in the seventies there'd been only two black kids in my year. In jail I was torn between feeling very sorry for them and being very scared of them – and of course when I was with the 'chaps' I had to pretend I loathed them as well. It was all very complicated.

Back in the dinner hall, Cherrington was now standing with two other black inmates, who'd leapt to his side and were quite wisely trying to calm Marsh down. But Cherrington was intent on not losing face.

'You want dead, innit.'

Awful grammar, I thought. I did – I really thought that.

'I'll see you upstairs after lunch,' said Marsh, and with that he sat down and finished his pudding.

After lunch we clustered round Marsh in his cell like eunuchs round the queen. He was changing into his pumps, as if he was going to play tennis – he was slightly excited and even started limbering up, throwing some punches. We were his seconds and he was the champ. We were silent: what was there to say? He knew what he was doing. There were three of us in the room: me, Waller from Norwich (a bit thick but nice enough) and Woolridge. Woolridge was tall and a bit plump, with curly hair – a bit effeminate-looking, though you wouldn't tell him that. Of all the other white kids he was the most available in a tear-up and quite happy with the black *v.* white tensions rising within the borstal. Come the day of reckoning he'd be there, ready for the black uprising.

As I stood transfixed by Marsh's shadow-boxing I wished I had the courage and inclination to be a useful member of our little firm but I was in a state of voyeuristic shock. I didn't hate enough; I was frozen. I felt my destiny was to endure, keep my head down, read and wank my way to freedom.

Marsh bowled out of his cell flanked by us, his backing singers: *shoo-wop de do-wop*. Cherrington was stood outside his cell, which was next to mine. He turned and faced Marsh, looking furtive and bewildered. Marsh was on centre court and about to serve.

Where were the screws? They must have known what was afoot. In a room somewhere, taking bets, muttering racism and laughing courage, hoping Marsh would do what they couldn't (let's put it in plain English): beat the fuck out of a wog.

Upstairs in the corridor that was our home, flanked by the cells where we dreamt of steak and chips and Daisy Duke, Marsh opened the verbal exchanges.

'Have you got a problem?'

'No. You have: you want dead, innit!' *Is this to be his catch-phrase?* I wondered.

Cherrington produced a small blunt dinner knife. He held it in his right hand, tight to his hip, and moved his other arm forward, swaying, ready to deflect any blows.

Marsh had shown me this exact stance the week before during some self-defence and attitude tests in the kitchen. I'd been horrified and bemused in equal measure: would I really have to fight someone with a knife before I was released? I was a long way from home, Greenwich Park, the ponds on Blackheath Common, people poking fires in their back gardens and drinking tea, watching *Morecambe and Wise* in my pyjamas . . .

Marsh launched himself at Cherrington, knocking him over, then began to smack him in the head and neck at great speed. Cherrington's knife was useless – any one of us could have told him that. You couldn't kill a squirrel with it; it was blunt and lightweight, designed by the authorities not to be dangerous. Cherrington couldn't get any purchase on or momentum from the spotless linoleum. He was being destroyed. Marsh had him pinned to the floor. He head-butted him twice and Cherrington's head bounced with a dead, squashed noise. Marsh jumped back and kicked him twice in the mouth, blood everywhere. Cherrington seemed to be in shock: he actually went white. It was odd, I really don't know what I felt – this was just my life now. It wasn't me on the floor, and that was all that mattered. Where were the screws?

Marsh stood back, panting. It was over before it had begun. Cherrington was picked up and dusted down. One of his teeth had been driven through his lip and he was talking nonsense, jabbering, trying to make sense of what had happened.

With an uncanny sense of timing two screws appeared, Mr Pitt and Mr Branch, two of Norwich's finest prison officers. They all seemed to be ex-army or ex-Old Bill or ex-something or other. Marsh and Cherrington were taken down the block and locked up in solitary confinement, where they stayed for three days without privileges.

Other people drifted off to play draughts and listen to tiny radios and talk about the finer points of Marsh's display.

I went to my cell and felt a growing sense of unease.

That night I lay on my bed and listened to John Peel on the radio. Music in prison to me was like water in a desert. It was my only connection to the outside world and my former life. I'd been in the band, briefly, and had absolutely no other interests apart from fruit machines and books and girls and clothes. Every night Peely would be there, quietly confident and reassuring. The Jam, the Specials, Ivor Cutler, obscure reggae . . . These artists spoke to me and were there for me every day of my sentence (so much easier than real relationships). When 'Ghost Town' entered the charts at Number One, the whole unit gathered to watch the video on TV one Saturday morning. The atmosphere was electric! Fuck Johnny Cash at San Quentin – we were up and mooching to the one record that crystallised how we were all feeling, a haunting, poisonous love letter to the country that had abandoned us. This was Jerry Dammers' masterpiece and it oozed malice and frustration. Sadly it only added to the racial divides already smouldering in Hollesley. Marsh started taunting the black inmates: 'It may be your music but it's a white man singing . . .' Some chairs went over and there was a standoff. It was a good job we weren't allowed to watch *Top of the Pops* that Thursday night as anything could have happened. Soon after that Talking Heads released 'Once in a Lifetime' as a single and the TV room was spellbound once more – all this and Tenpole Tudor too.

There were some records that reflected my own feelings of despair and self-pity: 'Lately' by Stevie Wonder (I always tried to walk away when that was on); 'Celebration' by Kool and the Gang (I felt they were taking the piss somewhat); 'Embarrassment' by Madness (for obvious reasons the end line – '*You're an embarrassment* . . .' seemed to hang in the air taunting me, though I'm sure it was nothing personal). Another record in the Top Ten at the time was 'De Do Do Do, De Da Da Da' by the Police. I'm sure Sting thought he was being clever, but I thought he was being a cunt. Nonetheless that was prison in a nutshell – *de do do do, de da da da* – a witless refrain playing over and over again, an incredible waste of everyone's time; you might as well sing along as plug your ears.

Later on the night of the fight I was fast asleep in my room when three people crept in; one of them was Waller, but to this day I don't know who the others were.

'What's going on?' I said.

'Shut up and go back to sleep.' Waller's familiar Norwich burr.

Hands pushed me back. *What the fuck's going on? Am I going to be buggered by someone from East Anglia?* No, they were climbing out of the window. Bizarre . . .

It suddenly clicked: they were using my cell to gain access to Cherrington's next door, going out of my window and into his. I realised they were probably going to plunder whatever they could from his 'home': tobacco, biscuits, soap, maybe a Harold Robbins novel (all the rage in the prison system among the black population). I think I said 'don't' a couple of times, but these guys had done more burglaries than you or I have had hot dinners. They were in and out in a couple of minutes. I went back to sleep and in the morning I was confused; I could barely remember what had happened. It seemed like a dream.

I was on my way to breakfast when I was hailed by Tony Wright, an intelligent and decent black guy. He swiftly marked my card regarding the burglary: my cell window faced on to another building housing inmates, and Waller and his little crew had been seen on their night manoeuvres.

'People are going to want to know what happened. That's all I'm saying, Day.'

He was a good bloke and very nice about it. The three black guys who joined me in my room while I was relaxing after my powdered egg and tomatoes were not so nice.

'Who was it, Day? Talk fast.' They eyed me. They ranged in size from short to very tall. Daley, the little one, was the worst;

he looked like a pit bull. I knew I couldn't divulge anything – it would be over for me if I did. I was very scared.

'You know I can't say anything,' I said.

Green, the tall one, barely fitted into the room and was bent under a shelf, staring at a photo of the Teardrop Explodes I'd cut out of the *NME*. He seemed unimpressed.

'Day, talk fast,' said Spooner. He was only twenty-one but already had the world-weary manner of the old lag. He almost shouted this command and I flinched. I remember that expression, 'Talk fast'; it left me little choice.

Just then a shout of pain flew down the corridor; I recognised Waller's rising screams. Good old Waller, he'd confessed. My three guests were out in a flash. I stayed where I was. I don't think Waller got seriously hurt – he was probably punched and kicked on the floor for a bit, then they'd have got back the stolen goods plus any of his possessions worth having.

I saw Waller that lunchtime, limping and clutching a tin tray of pie and cabbage. He nodded. I imagine he was forced to pay out some of his wages, too, for that little trick. Waller was one of those people who continually made bad decisions.

A few weeks after the break-in fiasco, for absolutely no reason at all, he pushed in front of a thickset guy named Webb who had the squashed features of a boxer and the build of a baby rhino but was a thoroughly decent fellow, I found. He'd been caught for a smash-and-grab in Bromley: the window had sliced through his hand and he lost two pints of blood, forcing him to go to hospital rather than run off with his bounty.

'What shop was it?' I asked him.

'W.H. Smith,' he replied.

You don't push in front of people unless you want a fight: plenty of blacks pushed in front of me whenever Marsh was absent and I felt ashamed but did nothing. Webb swiftly challenged Waller to a ruck in the showers. It was very well organised – there were no screws around. Waller looked like one of Tyson's early challengers as he stood in front of Webb, nervously hopping as about twenty or so people looked on. Webb swiftly hammered Waller to the ground and head-butted him, breaking his nose. It made a sickening noise, muffled like a stone striking a tree. All the fight went out of Waller. We sat with him afterwards as his nose went blue and red and green. Marsh told him off: 'What're you fighting with another white bloke for? Webb is one of us.'

It was a good point well made. I went back to my room and tried to feel nothing.

On visit days in Hollesley Bay the plum job on offer was serving teas to the inmates and their guests. Prisoners would be given cigarettes by their families and friends. If you'd agreed it with them beforehand they'd pass the contraband to you over the counter, then you'd hide it and give it back later and get a percentage for your trouble. Williams was a really cool black guy (part of a pickpocket gang from Elephant and Castle). On my first stint doing the teas he asked if I'd stash some fags for him. Like a fool, I agreed, and he duly passed me forty Embassy Regal. I felt honoured. When he'd returned to his table the inmate doing the teas with me said, 'Where are you going to hide them?'

I presumed there'd be lots of places in the kitchen. He looked at me. 'You know the screws search the kitchen,' he said.

I started to look around, suddenly unnerved, tearing around the kitchen offering up more and more obscure hiding places. Each time I suggested somewhere he calmly informed me: 'No, they'll look there.'

Time was running out. I started pushing up the polystyrene ceiling tiles.

'First place they'll look,' he said.

My heart rate was through the roof. I wanted to call the whole thing off. The other inmate was shaking his head sadly. What a twat: I was so desperate to be accepted and look where it had got me. The visitors were leaving when I suddenly had a brainwave.

There was a huge metal barrel full of slops: an oily mess of all kinds of food and kitchen waste. I pushed the fags under the surface. *Good,* I thought, *the cellophane'll protect them.* We left the kitchen and the screws began their search.

I knew they wouldn't sift through the sloppy mess. An hour passed with no alarms – I was home free.

Later I returned to the kitchen, put my hands into the barrel and pulled out what was left of the contraband: the cigarettes were completely destroyed; my hands were covered in bits of tobacco and wet cardboard. I was terrified. I carried what was left of the soggy packets to my room, devastated.

Williams was waiting in his room with his pals, looking forward to a nice smoke of tailor-mades. I must have been crazy to think he'd accept my tobacco mush, but I made my way downstairs, knocked on his door and went in. Everyone was pleased to see me. They were packed in there like sardines, laughing and joking.

'Whatem, Day,' Williams said.

I pushed the mess into his hand and said, 'Sorry, they got a bit wet.' Then I tried to shuffle off.

'Day! What's this?'

'They got a bit wet,' I said again, trying to style it out.

He was quite reasonable, really. He made me pay him back so many fags a week at a not-unreasonable rate. I never did the teas again.

Visits were held on a Saturday. The inmates without visitors sat upstairs watching *Grandstand* – although they could peer through the windows to see what was going on in the dining hall, where the visits were held. The most important thing for inmates was food and visitors brought a fantastic array of nosh for their nearest and dearest. The West Indian mums brought chicken and rice, dumplings and patties and also cans of Coke, which rum would be surreptitiously poured into. It was like the Notting Hill Carnival sometimes and so it should have been. The English families' foodstuffs were more traditional and sandwich-based, though they also brought pies, pasties, biscuits and sweets. The amount of food was astonishing, but it always got eaten. You were constantly hungry in borstal – they never seemed to feed you enough. My mum came to see me in Hollesley Bay. I was depressed and didn't know what to say to her. The prison-issue denims I'd been given were much too big for me and I looked ridiculous. I remember at some stage I got up and fell over, and the chaps doing the teas laughed at me. Apparently my mum had phoned the borstal to ask if she could send some underwear to me and the screws had sniggered at her. She must have been upset. Her second husband told me about this years later, laughing at the memory.

The visit that sticks in my memory and was a constant source of residual anger for years was when my dad came to see me. By this time he'd married his new partner, Judy Hill. He arrived at the given time and the screw laughed and said, 'I didn't know you were so posh.' (Much like at school, I hadn't advertised the fact that I was middle class.) My dad had brought me three Hornblower books, a typical gift – three books in which I had absolutely no interest. I cannot think of a worse type of fiction and this summed up our relationship.

I was nervous. He looked well, if a bit unsure of himself. It must have been a nightmare for him, going there and having to deal with such an emotional situation. I wasn't thinking about that: I was starving. Around me the other inmates' tables groaned under the weight of their individual harvest festivals. I saw Williams helping himself to a huge bowl of chicken stew and rice, while on another table a boy with 'cut here' tattooed on his neck tucked into a whole Victoria sponge. I looked across the table and saw that Dad had brought a Tupperware container; it was quite small, and inside was a piece of chicken in aspic and a Mars bar. The chicken was cold and greasy. My mind drifted back to the hamburger incident of long ago. We made small talk about my plastering course: he was keen for me to learn a trade to insulate me from criminal behaviour. He didn't ask me about how I felt or if I was being bullied; he just looked around him occasionally.

After exactly twenty minutes of this he said, 'Well, I'm meeting some of Judy's friends in a neighbouring village so I must be off.' *Twenty minutes.* I stammered goodbye and he left me clutching the remains of the chicken. I was completely unprepared for this. I was so upset – stunned – and had no defence for it. I'd had so much I'd wanted to say to him and he'd just fucked off. I couldn't believe how selfish he was; he just couldn't give of himself.

I sloped back upstairs. Everyone in the TV room had witnessed his early departure. They were shocked, and asked why he'd gone so quickly. I made up a story, saying we'd had a row. I felt utterly desolate. I'd wanted to hug him and try to tell him how I felt. I sat there, a florid emotional bruise growing and discolouring in my mind. On the TV screen a man was rubbing chalk on his hands, about to lift a huge weight. Listless young men were draped over hard chairs biting their nails. I felt like a young girl in a Jane Austen novel. I was aware of the blood pumping in my ears. My depth of feeling was almost gothic.

Twenty minutes. That's not even an episode of *Only Fools and Horses*.

Before you're admitted back into society you're allowed two open visits then a week's home leave. On the open visits you go to a pub with your friends and family. On my first open visit both my parents came up to see me, which was odd because the old man struggles to admit my mum's existence even now (at my brother's wedding he was sat next to her and blanked her).

We went to a pub somewhere near the borstal. I had a pint of orange juice and lemonade and stuffed my face with something. At some point the old man asked me what I intended to do when I was released.

'Get a job,' I said, eyeing the dessert menu.

'A job doing what?' he enquired.

'Dunno,' I said, teenager to the last.

He sighed angrily and pulled some glossy brochures from his briefcase. I honestly thought they were holiday brochures but no, dear reader, they were brochures for the holy trinity: the army, the navy and the air force. I surprised myself by standing up and making a little speech.

'I have just spent the last year polishing floors, cleaning toilets and being pushed around by people. If you think I'm joining any of those you've got another think coming.' (Or words to that effect.)

He was furious and went off at me: high unemployment, riots, criminal record, etc. I just said, 'No way. No fucking way!' I was adamant.

They went home and I went back to Hollesley Bay feeling another strange mixture of emotions. I suppose the old man was doing what he thought best for me: pack me off to Aldershot and hopefully it'd make a man of me. I'd have had just enough time to complete my basic training before toddling off to the Falklands, where I could have covered myself in glory or shrapnel or both. At least he'd have been proud of me at last.

On my second open visit Mum came up with my elder brother, Rob. We went to a different pub and the atmosphere was a lot more jovial. I was on a sort of high: I was going home soon and the world was full of possibility. At some stage Mum gave me a tenner and I went into the snug and put the lot into a fruit machine. My brother later told me that Mum saw this through the hatch and started crying.

Of course I was unaware of her sadness. I was at work, nudging, holding, exchanging wins for features. It would have taken more than her tears to force me to step back. I was like an ancient stonemason toiling away at a huge monolith I would never finish. When I was playing machines people came and went, the fields grew lush then withered, rivers dried up, cities crumbled to dust but the boy played on.

Obviously I was not cured of my addictive nature: the prison system had overlooked that little foible. I'd seen an old friend and just popped over to say hello – it wasn't my fault he'd fleeced me. Besides, a fruit machine will never judge you; it doesn't care if you're a murderer, a rapist or just smelly, your money is always good. Roll up, roll up – welcome back, my friends, to the show that never ends . . .

I spent my home leave pissed out of my head, sitting around on scatter cushions smoking double-zero Moroccan hashish and polishing my prison stories. At least I didn't have to make anything up to get people's attention – you don't have to embroider jail tales, not to a middle-class audience anyway. The girls were horrified and the boys were impressed. 'Fucking hell,' they said. 'Fucking hell, that must have been heavy.' 'Yes it was,' I said. 'Yes it was.' 'You poor thing,' said the girls. 'You poor thing.' I was hoping one of the ladies would offer up her minge as a balm to my twitching, narrow heart. Having been wanking for about a year solidly, I now had a huge cock and tiny balls.

I had been circuit training three times a week and running three miles a day, so I was fit as a fiddle and willing, should any young lady be kind enough to invite me to her bedchamber, to pound away until I'd erased the stench of prison from my system. What sort of monsters did borstal produce? Immensely fit young men with enormous sex drives riddled with self-loathing and paranoia. That was before I'd started smoking the hashish, which was very strong. I didn't get any offers – perhaps I was too dangerous now, being an ex-con, a twisted loner, a crazy hobo with no home of his own. I was ready, though, ready for anything as long as it was free.

Borstal training was abolished at some stage. It didn't work: people kept coming back for more. When I was in its tender care the official tariff was six months to two years. If you consistently bucked the system, fought, didn't toe the line, you'd do the entire two years; if you were a model prisoner it was possible that you'd only do six months (although from what I was told no inmate had ever accomplished this).

You had three-monthly reviews and at each one you'd sit before a board of screws and would be given time back for good behaviour or have time added on for bad behaviour. I was told by one prison officer that the screws would have looked favourably on me had I stood up to the black inmates. What was that about? I know we were in Suffolk but come on. One inmate, Billy Ruzgar, a compact Turk from the Holloway Road whose nose betrayed his amateur boxing career and who took no shit from anyone, had knocked out a black inmate in the stables and was promptly given four weeks back at his last review board (he ended up being released on the same day as me). I got two weeks at each review, which was quite normal: not good, not bad.

At my last review three officers sat in front of me. One, whose name escapes me, said, 'All in all I think you're all right and I recommend two weeks' remission. *Yes,* I thought. The conch was then passed to Mr Pitt, who I'd hardly noticed during my stay. He was a small man, ex-Old Bill, sporty. What he said completely astounded me.

'I think you are one of the most devious individuals I have ever encountered and I cannot recommend any time back.' The odd thing was that, although initially hurt by his comments, I was filled with a sort of pride: to have him think that I'd actually had some sort of plan during my internment, that I'd been even remotely in control of my destiny, was something to be celebrated.

Devious individual . . . What was he referring to? I presumed he meant my friendship with one of the hardest people in the borstal but that was surely just common sense, being as how I had no aptitude for fighting.

Devious. I was proud of it. Sad but true.

Chapter Seven

The day I left borstal was a good day. It's hard to put that feeling into words: it's like you've passed some incredibly hard exam; there was a sense of achievement like nothing I'd ever experienced. It was sunny and I bounced out of bed, went through the last-day rituals. I gave my breakfast away and handed over all dry goods and luxury items (shampoo, pens, old copies of the *NME*). I refrained from the cruel banter meted out to new arrivals: 'Are you going home today, mate? No? Must be me then . . .' I remember someone saying that to me just after I arrived. It seemed like an age ago. A year with remand, I'd done – a year of my short sweet life whittled and wanked away into nothingness.

And now I was being hurled back into the great beyond clutching £37.50. I had nowhere to live and no one to meet me. There was no waiting Jag with prostitute, no bundle of tenners and bottle of Cutty Sark. I was free as a bird, as were the other inmates released with me.

I was due to be released at eleven o'clock alongside Waller, Marsh and Billy Ruzgar. Ruzgar was respected and revered in Hollesley Bay and was a thoroughly decent chap all round. He told me, 'You'll be all right, Day. You've got it up here,' and tapped his temple. I hoped so.

We'd all been on home leave for a week, allowed to live it up and make preparations for the rest of our lives. The one catch to home leave was that you had to return under your own steam to do five more days at the borstal if you had a job or twelve more if you didn't. (Of course every inmate who wasn't completely stupid returned with some sort of moody letter from a custard factory or pet shop confirming their employment there.) My dad had got me a start with a building firm who were working on his house, so I just did the five days. We were called down to the office amid much backslapping and hyperactivity. We were going home. At last I could lift my head up. I had said my goodbyes; there weren't that many people who meant anything to me but it was still an oddly touching collection of little ceremonies.

I didn't expect to see anyone again. I was absolutely certain I'd never go back to jail in any way shape or form – rather more certain than Waller, who was arrested by two uniformed plod as we got changed into our civvies.

'Steven John Waller . . .' The barbaric breath of officialdom rent the air. Waller shuffled forwards like a stunted monkey returning to his organ grinder.

'He was doing burglaries on home leave,' whispered Marsh.

Waller had turned yellow. As he was led away his whole body shrank. I was shocked and amazed by this turn of events: to go directly from one prison to another, to think you were going home to the pub and the telly and as much booze and sex as you would be allowed and then have it snatched away. They let him put his own clothes on. He was tying up his shoelaces, could taste the Harp lager and smell the sausage rolls; he was free! I was devastated for him – no one deserved that, did they? To be disappeared back into the system like a terrorist, more porridge, more roll-ups and more punch-ups – it was just so sad and pointless.

My two compadres were entirely unmoved by Waller's plight.

'Silly cunt,' said Ruzgar. 'You don't nick anything on home leave – the Old Bill have a list of people out on licence.'

'Mug,' Marsh added, turning and spitting on the desk, rebel to the last. I didn't doubt he would be back inside; his future was nailed on. I hope I was wrong.

The next thing I remember we were on the train drinking cans of bitter and sticking our heads out of the window, our pasty faces buffeted by the crazy wind of freedom.

We got off at Liverpool Street, where tradition dictated that we all had a drink in Dirty Dick's, a bar across from the station. Ruzgar had a rum and Coke, put his foot on the brass rail and looked good. Marsh ordered three pints of lager, drank one down in one, burped, passed me one and started on the next. I had some peanuts and eyed the door mournfully. I was desperate to leave, but Marsh had just started. Ruzgar shook hands with us both and stepped out into the sunshine. I said, 'Right, I must be getting off.' (Although as I was still in prison mode I probably said, 'Tony, I'm gonna do one.')

'Not yet,' said Marsh. 'Not yet.'

Marsh was pissed and wanted to get a haircut, so we descended some filthy steps to a barber's below the station. He took something out of his mouth. I realised then he had no front teeth: he gripped his pink dental plate between his forefinger and thumb, spittle dripping on to the tiled floor as he wagged it at me. 'You owe me,' he said. I could have done without this. He'd got very drunk very quickly. 'I looked after you.' *Could I just run off? Would he come to South East London and find me?* He made the barber shave all his hair off.

'I gotta call this bird. She's got a bar in her front room, Tia Maria, the lot. She's got an Alsatian; she lets it lick her out.'

'Hey – no trouble,' said the barber.

I was horrified by now. Marsh was lurching around in the chair muttering, 'Put me on a train. You owe me.'

After paying the barber, we squeezed into a phone booth where he insisted I listen in on a call to the girl who had sex with her dog. She couldn't understand him. I really wanted to return to my new life, away from this barbarian. I wanted to go home.

I poured him into a carriage and waved him off.

He leant out of the window. 'Give us a call. We'll go out with my brother – he's just done a three in Maidstone – he's a right laugh.'

I never saw him again. He'd served a purpose, but I can't say I really liked him. No, that's unfair: I liked parts of him; ours was a holiday romance and nothing more. I think about him a lot. I always thought I'd see him some day, thought he'd turn up demanding a cut of *The Fast Show*.

On my first night out of borstal I ended up in the Rose and Crown just below Greenwich Park. I had nowhere to stay that night. No offers of lodging had been forthcoming from any family members, so I'd been forced to squirm and ask my elder brother. He said, 'It's not convenient.' He was under pressure from his flatmate but still, I remember those exact words bouncing around in my skull: *It's not convenient*. I think that moment was very damaging for me in terms of my psyche: I really knew then that I was alone. In some ways he did me a favour. I think it was at that precise moment that Zeus looked down and said, 'Hey, let's give this kid a break.' And ten years later, when I first walked on to the raised floor in that Forest Hill pub and adjusted the microphone, he threw me a thunderbolt. The rest was up to me.

I had a burning desire to show my family I could succeed without their help, to show them I could be a contender. That nasty vindictive little flame burnt brightly for a long time, my little pilot light of rejection. (It doesn't burn any more; it was finally extinguished by my wife and my children and by Terry Hall from the Specials telling me that Tommy Cockles was the funniest thing ever.)

Luckily there was a guy called Rankine McFarlaine in the pub, a Kiwi chef who lived in New Cross. On hearing of my predicament he offered me a bed and a good few pints. I was so happy. I was out and I was drunk and I had somewhere to live.

Rankine was a hard-drinking, good-natured bloke, good-looking in a way, too, with olive skin and a wedge haircut that temporarily blinded him on occasion. One night he was riding his bike in the dark through South East London and his scarf caught in the front wheel. He was pulled into the bike and on to the road, chin first, and suffered multiple facial injuries. He spent a few nights in hospital. For some reason the police came and interviewed him, and on leaving they returned the bag he'd been carrying on the night of the accident. It was one of those plastic bags with a little catch at the top, and inside were forty red Marlboros and a thousand pounds' worth of Lebanese hashish wrapped in clingfilm like so much halva.

Who says the police are idiots? Not me.

Rankine wore a long coat from Flip and smoked like Bogey, his fag flipping up and down as he spoke. He always had a bit of puff on him but booze was his thing. Some nights he'd come home pissed and roust me from my bed, then put on funny jackets and such and shout at me. He wanted to be an actor; I think he had a history of street performing in various places. Some seventeen years later he appeared at Up the Creek as an open spot and Malcolm Hardee said it was the worst act he'd ever seen – which was saying something!

At the time I just wanted to sleep: like a lot of people who can be a pest when drunk, I behave like a maiden aunt when sober and expect others to do likewise. Rankine said I was institutionalised and that worried me a bit – but only a bit. He loved music and that first week I lived in his house I listened constantly to *Red* by Black Uhuru and *Fear of Music* by Talking Heads. We also got stuck into the Cramps, 'Green Fuz' and all that, but it was those two records that blew me away. They're still two of my favourite albums, both hard as nails and beguiling as a box of snake-charmers, and I return to them again and again. I felt I understood David Byrne's weird sideways worldview: it was like he was singing just for me. Both these albums *sounded so good.*

I really want to impart to you how much music meant to me during those trying times. Believe me: I LOVE MUSIC. And it kept me alive more than anything else did (apart from food, of course).

The only thing better than listening to music is dancing to it, and the only thing better than *that* is playing it – and I've done all three, with varying degrees of success, so I know! (Actually, listening to *Dark Side of the Moon* on the headphones is better than playing 'Stepping Stone' badly to a half-full pub.)

Rankine lived in a grimy house in Clifton Mews, round the back of the New Cross main drag and not far from Goldsmiths. Rough and ready it was then and probably still is. There was an Irish nightclub at the end of the road and pitched battles were fought at the weekends fuelled by bad religion and copious amounts of the black stuff.

Still, I had a room and a job: things were looking up.

I'd started with the local building firm my dad had set me up with. They were renovating his new house in Egerton Drive in Greenwich, where he lived with his new wife, Judy. Judy is a choral singer and all-round buoyant posh lady. I've come to know her well and she's a good woman: fearless, with bags of energy and positivity. She's brilliant for my dad as she forces him to get away from his books and to interact with people. They are still inseparable and you can't ask for more than that.

The boss of the firm was called Arthur. He was a master builder – the proper job – and could do it all: laying bricks, plumbing, advanced joinery . . . It was a shame the rest of his firm weren't as skilled or as industrious as him, because he might have retired a wealthy man. Unfortunately this was the eighties, though, the decade in which the cowboys hitched their horses to the British building boom and tore the arse out of it.

The trouble with Arthur was that he was a nice bloke. He couldn't separate the wheat from the chaff and was paying top wages to workshy twonks who spent most of their time in the pub. And then there was me, the idiot's idiot: I had as much aptitude for building work as Tony Blair does for telling the truth. Still, at that time there were worse cack-handed clowns than me, earning much more money and making bigger cock-ups than I could ever dream of.

I was set to work with Paddy – an Irishman, believe it or not. He was a painter by trade and was a hive of industry whenever Arthur was around: bashing buckets, hurling dustsheets about, holding brushes up to his rheumy eye. What a fine example of the working man he was; it made your heart swell with pride just to wash his brushes. As soon as Arthur was gone, hurrying to the next disaster, Paddy would slump. He'd rub his hands and step nearer the fan heater. 'Very cold today,' he'd say. 'Very cold. What a job dis is, all your life in empty rooms.' He had that morbid hopeless timbre to his voice, like Frazer in *Dad's Army*. 'All your life in empty rooms.'

Paddy wore a baggy set of white overalls and smoked a lot. He loved nothing better than sitting in the van telling me tales of his terrible misfortune and how he'd risen above it through sheer hard work and presence of mind. We may as well have been back in jail, the amount of work we did. As soon as Arthur arrived, Paddy would jog towards him like an injured donkey on Blackpool beach, desperate for a customer.

'Mornin', Arter. We haven't the undercoat yet, and the sand isn't here, and your man hasn't come back wid the key to the house . . .' And so the litany of excuses would pour out of him, a solemn hymn of negativity.

Arthur should have fired him but he was too kind: he knew Paddy's missus, and knew that Paddy depended on his goodness of heart. Besides, every now and then the excuses would run out and he'd be faced with a tin of paint and a flat surface and he'd actually do some work – although he'd soon come up against an insurmountable problem, like the brush being too small or too big.

'I haven't the right brush,' he'd say. 'I can't do the cutting in with dat brush. I'm away to the builders' merchants.' The builders' merchants which was, oddly enough, called the Prince of Wales. Where they gave you Guinness instead of paint.

For some reason he saw me as a threat, me and my £60 a week. He thought that sixty quid would somehow topple Arthur's feeble financial house of cards and we'd all be thrown on the dole – which would have been ironic, given that half the firm were on the dole anyway. Not me, though: I'd decided on a fresh start; no black economy for me. (That would come later, after I'd been ground down by Noel Edmonds and the New Romantics.)

He was a slippery little gnome, was Paddy. He wanted me out, which wasn't charitable – me just out of choky, a nervous fawn of a lad who just wanted to get on his feet.

'There's no work,' he would say, holding me with a plaintive, imploring stare. 'There's no work; after dis job I can't see where we'll all be.' He used to bang on about this magical building site somewhere over the rainbow, up town, where the labourers got £400 a week.

'Four hundred a week!' he'd say. 'Imagine what you could do with that. Why don't you get up there? See if you can get a start?'

'Why don't you get up there, Paddy?' I'd say. 'A skilled man like you – you could pull in a grand, surely.'

'Oh no, I work for Arter,' he'd admonish me, horrified at my lack of compassion. 'I couldn't leave Arter; he needs me.' This while pulling an Embassy Regal from his pocket without displaying the packet. That was Paddy all over: he thought he had to hide his fags from me even though I didn't smoke. It was ludicrous. I've no idea why he resented me. I was a grafter in those days, albeit with no initiative and absolutely no aptitude for the work at hand. I was only labouring, washing tools, knocking up muck (cement) and carrying heavy objects; I couldn't do any damage. (That came later.)

I think Paddy thought that Arthur knew how lazy he was and had put me with him to report back all his indiscretions, all his lost hours, his dreamy pints. I would have done no such thing even if I *had* been asked to, which I hadn't. I'd been educated by prison folk: don't grass on anyone, ever. I was bored by the whole process – I just needed money to live.

One day a Reliant Robin pulled up – a *Reliant Robin*! – and a man with a beard appeared from inside it. 'Hello, Simon,' said the red opening in the beard. 'I'm Pat.' He was about forty, wearing a parka that was too small for him and had a big gold earring that caught the sun as he bounded towards me. He looked very dodgy. There were lots of random bits of building stuff tied to the top of the Robin, and pipes sticking out the back.

'Oh Jesus, it's yer man,' said Paddy.

Pat shook my hand warmly. 'I live in Rochester,' he said. 'Me and Arthur go back years.' After a bit of chit-chat he suddenly piped up: 'Can I just say, Simon, that your father is a coward.' Paddy winced and studied my face. Pat continued: 'Your father accused me of stealing a reel of copper wire from Egerton Drive and when I found it in the loft he refused to apologise.' Paddy was frozen. Pat went on: 'Your father is a coward. I've never stolen anything in my life.'

I nearly burst out laughing. He had odd socks on and had some sort of skin complaint on his left shin.

'I was in the house and he accused me of stealing a lousy reel of copper wire. I'm no thief, am I, Paddy? Besides, I've got bundles of wire at home.'

'No,' said Paddy. 'It's an awful business.' I realised that Paddy was probably terrified I was going to leap at Pat and strangle him, force him somehow to eat his words. I found it all very amusing and interesting, though: I had enough residual bitterness towards my dad to enjoy hearing him being slagged off, albeit by this clown. To this day I've no idea who was in the wrong. I imagine Pat *did* nick the wire and then put it back and found it at the same time, but you can't deny that 'Your father is a coward' is a brilliant and emotive opening line coming from a man driving a Reliant Robin. It's one that will stay with me for ever.

My dad had banned Pat from the house. In fact he'd also sent two other workmen packing, mainly because their work wasn't up to scratch. Arthur was the only person allowed to work in the house, which was slowing up the job a bit. The thing was, most of Arthur's workforce was useless and my dad was a stickler. He'd trained as an architect and had eighteen books on the construction of Rome alone: he knew what he was on about. So I don't blame him.

Pat made Paddy look like Leonardo da Vinci. He was a cunt from Kent and that was it: there was no more to him. He didn't appear to have any trade as such – he'd just arrive at a job, have a cup of tea then fuck off. This was before mobile phones so it was a lot easier to skive. He'd appear every Friday lunchtime, draw a huge wedge of notes from Arthur then disappear back to Rochester, needing the early finish to miss the traffic.

'He's working on other jobs,' Arthur would say, staring after him faintly wounded. We'd all look at the ground. But who does care about the boss? Once you have his money in your paw you're away to the bath, to scrape the plaster from your knuckles and the sand from between your toes, to watch the little window steam up and dream your weekend dreams. I felt sorry for Arthur. I know he had problems at the bank, and he suffered from terrible arthritis; he'd once been a champion cyclist. Still, it was Friday: I was going down the pub.

So there I was, living in New Cross, working, drinking lager at night, smoking pot at weekends, full of shame and guilt, really. I thought everyone was watching to see if I pinched their purse or wallet. If I came into a room and someone had misplaced a tenner or a lump of puff, I'd freeze as they looked for it, sometimes actually blushing as they searched. Then such relief when they found it.

Arthur took a job miles away from good old Greenwich, right up at the top of the Finchley Road, near that garage where you turn off for Brent Cross and the M1. It was an enormous house with beautiful plasterwork in some of the rooms – sort of floral designs inlaid on to panels and beautiful ornate ceilings too – and there were two lovely marble fireplaces. We were working for an American called Max. He looked like Paul Simon via Joe Pesci and he talked like someone was coming to get him. He wore a fur coat and Arthur said when he was young he was so poor he had to share one pair of shoes with eight brothers and sisters; he had a nice pair of crocodile shoes on now, though. Max was a rare client in that he watched us working the whole time, standing twitching by the skip as I rolled up a barrow of soil or pacing upstairs as the plasterer got to work.

On our first day he showed me into a lovely downstairs room and told me to tear all the plaster down, all that fantastic craftsmanship. I was appalled. *You guttersnipe*, I thought. *You lowlife American heathen.* (I still had principles back then.) I must have learnt more from my dad than I had thought, because it bothered me, doing that, ripping out all that majesty. It summed up the eighties for me, that job, because at the end, after two months' work, Max fucked off back to New Yoik and knocked Arthur for the money: didn't pay him a penny. All that vandalism and for what?

When I was working there one day, jumping down the steps carrying a bag of rubble, I twisted my ankle really badly – it's never been the same since. It swelled up like a horse's head and I was sent home and confined to the sofa. Rankine, god bless him, went out to work and left me a giant steak and a bottle of gin. I was very touched by this and any acts of kindness at that time; I must have somehow felt I deserved it after my penal servitude. Hard on the outside and soft on the inside, I was then, like a boiled sweet – and just as cheap. I could live on a fiver a day and frequently did, but I was very alive. Very alive but to what?

Rankine slightly ruined his good-Samaritan act by returning drunk, putting on a fluffy pink jacket, donning a wig and saying, 'Let's do a play.' His girlfriend was embarrassed and dragged him into the bedroom, where he shouted and muttered, occasionally collapsing into giggles. At one point he took a knife from the kitchen drawer and it all got a bit melodramatic: he was gone, eyes rolling back in his head. Quite scary but, after prison, not really; I knew he was just drunk. He was a great bloke. I mean, who else offered me a roof?

We moved to Gosterwood Street, still in New Cross. It's just off Evelyn Street, in another solidly rough area. Next door to us was a man who was overfriendly and kept calling me 'Simon' even though he didn't know me. I swerve people who do that. (Americans are the worst culprits: 'Well, Simon, my real home is in Nevada . . .' No, no, no, no, fuck off! You're not on first-name terms with me – we're just standing at a bus stop.)

I hated being down in New Cross. All my mates still lived in Greenwich, with its nice park and Georgian terraces. I'd stay with three of them, Rupert Moy, Tom Broadbent and John Cooper, whenever I could, alternating between their gaffs, cadging a bed and talking late into the night, the tips of our joints glowing in the dark like fireflies. Both Tom and John lived in flats within their parents' homes and Rupert was in one of his dad's flats. We were all trying to hang on to our childhoods for as long as society would let us, stringing our adolescence out. Eating cheese on toast at two in the morning, the house carpeted in sleep, the central heating ticking and purring. John Cooper was good to me and so were his mum and dad, who let me live there on and off for ages and always fed me. They were both teachers and proper liberals. The house they lived in is worth about two and a half million quid now – can you imagine two teachers living in such splendour these days? Who says the middle classes have it easy? They've been rumped like everyone else.

On Saturdays we'd all get up early, smoke an enormous amount of dope and lie back down in our sweaty sleeping bags to watch

Tiswas. Lenny Henry was the king in those days; he did that Rasta character who just shouted 'OK' and drank condensed milk – excellent! He was the first character comedian who registered with me and I drank in all his performances. There is a time when a comedian is really enjoying his work and this shines through: everything is new and exciting and there's an extra bit of spice coming through, which the audience pick up on. Ricky Gervais in *The Office* is another good example: he's really having a laugh. The trick is to hang on to that feeling, which is nigh-on impossible.

When *Tiswas* ended we'd race down to Goddard's on the one-way system to eat double pie and mash with teas or cans of Coke. Of course, now and then John would say, 'You can't stay at my house for ever, Si,' and I'd feel vulnerable again and trundle back to Gosterwood Street thinking, *Woe is me*.

New Cross was rough, though. One night two black kids searched me for money as I was coming through the park at the end of the street. The little one – he was about twelve – just started going through my pockets, saying, 'Give me a poun' now. Give me a poun' now.' I'd had enough of angry black youths and their appalling grammar. Borstal now seemed a distant surreal memory, with all those black kids polishing floors and playing football in the warm Suffolk sunshine; it was like some weird film I'd starred in. But there'd been no stunt men and I'd got damaged during principal photography . . . The tall one stood back, laughing at my lack of resistance. 'Watch de young bwoy searchin' de long man,' he chuckled.

I felt really angry with myself for not attacking them. They were only young and I was fit and strong. I saw what to do: knee the little one in the chin and drive my fist into the big one's throat. I was shaking. Of course I turned the other cheek, though, and surrendered like a girl, standing meekly while they took my 76p. What was the point of borstal training if I couldn't defend myself? I added it to my resentment list.

* * *

We were working one day on Max's house and a couple of young Irish bricklayers turned up. I got in a conversation with them about the merits of the Jam *v.* the Style Council. I was still wounded by the Jam's demise – although I was a Paul Weller fan so it made no odds to me what he was wearing just as long as he kept on writing songs. We ended up going to the pub, all of us. It was a brilliant sunny day and we had that feeling of excitement you get when you're in a pub miles from your manor. The two Irish chaps kept buying me pints of draught Holstein and I repaid them by being funny: doing impressions, funny walks, the full pub package. I had seven pints and was slaughtered. We got back to the job and I was swaying about, not knowing what to do.

Someone with a finely developed sense of humour gave me an angle grinder and put me to work cutting through some pipes that were housed in a sort of dumb waiter.

Unbeknown to me the electrician had that day run his main cables right through the house, basement to attic. They started swaying with the vibration of the grinder, backwards and forwards, ever nearer the churning metal teeth. I grinded on, goggles steamed up, pissed out of my tiny mind. I'd never had a throbbing cutting machine in my hands before and felt like some sort of action hero; I was quite taken with myself at that point. Suddenly there was a loud bang and I found myself sitting in the other room looking at the radiator close-up. It was upside down and I was throbbing all over. Some people were concerned and others were laughing – it was a hell of a way to sober up.

They stood me up and gave me a nip of Haig (quality). Suddenly the electrician appeared. He was another Irishman, but not the whimsical, playful type from Cork; he was from Belfast, had black eyes and wore a V-neck jumper with no shirt, from which wispy black hair protruded. I'd sawn through £120 worth of cable, apparently.

'You English bastard,' he spat.

I had a headache now and my feet felt funny. I started to think about my supper. Very quickly – *very* quickly – he attacked me with a shovel. It struck me on the top of the arm; I didn't feel it, though – too much adrenaline. The boys from the other side of the border pulled him off. I was shaking. They sent me home, punch drunk. I had tuna pasta for my tea, then me and Rankine played pool all night in the New Cross Arms. That will never become a gastro pub.

Chapter Eight

I was a recreational cannabis smoker back then: it had yet to really get hold of me. This was before the days when I'd sit around looking at coffee-table books about pot, talking in hushed tones about temple balls and Thai sticks, eating dope cakes and imagining the dog was a wolf. I did love LSD, though – I was all for it. I'd always had a psychedelic bent and that has bled into my work. While puffing I'd always ramble off on one, doing monologues to whoever was on the sofa; acid just took you further out there for longer, as far as I was concerned.

Back in the late seventies my friends and I had got hold of some of the microdots that were nabbed as part of Operation Julie. We'd got them from a bloke called Toad who lived in Plumstead and they were the proper job, dirty little bits of mind-bending nonsense. How we laughed, throwing our hands at each other and spending too long in front of the mirror. The melting greenery, the Artex ceiling breathing and undulating, the muffled sounds from upstairs ('What the fuck *is* that?'), more laughter. The yellow-skin come-down, examining your filthy feet, the veins showing through. All good at the time: more please.

Magic mushrooms were all the rage when I came out of borstal and still largely under the radar – people didn't sell them then, you just handed them out and got odd. People made tea, put them in honey, biscuits, whatever. Fellas had their picking sites, which they guarded jealously. Morris Travellers and Citroens would rumble out of town early burly and return with chattering, muddy-footed youngsters clutching plastic bags full of cow shit and bits of grass. Picking them was such an adventure. Living in the inner city, the alternative lifestyle was a bit gloomy: grafting all day, rolling baggy joints after work, stealing out to the garage in the middle of the night, buying cheap chocolate and Smith's crisps; it wasn't like we were in Malibu watching the sun come up, with the Doors on the radio and green-eyed hippy chicks with perfect tits and giant pubic hair dancing in the surf.

Also mushies (as the crusties called them) were free.

One wet Sunday night in October we got the call. Boots went on, coats, hats, gloves; maps were studied, petrol money was discussed. It was on: the big push. We were going to Essex, to an unspecified rural area, to do a robbery and no one was going to be harmed. Let's roll . . .

A friend of Rankine's came with us. He worked at the Scala – nice bloke, trendy suit, quite old. I can't remember the outward journey. Rankine had refused to tell me exactly where we were going, adding to the mystery. When we got there I saw it was a field, a wet field. We got out with our bags and our torches (I used a broken lighter). I hate Essex. It's the worst of all the counties, East London with trees. The county sign as you drive in is three machetes. Says it all, really. All I could see were cow shit and the pylons above marching off somewhere over our bent heads. We were psychedelic prospectors looking for a strike.

'If you eat one somehow the others seem easier to find,' said Rankine's chum.

'Give us one, then,' I said. That seemed to bother him.

I ate the limp cold fungi, which tasted of cow shit and the broken dreams of a thousand earthworms. The moon was bright, almost boiling down on us. The cows turned away in disgust, bored stiff by our antics like Red Indians watching cowboys trying to hunt buffalo.

Just then I saw a swathe of the little perishers between cow pats. I grabbed at them: one in the mouth, one in the bag.

'It definitely works, your theory, Tony.' Jesus, I'd remembered his name – I never remember people's names. These mushrooms were bang on.

Suddenly all I could see were magic mushrooms, pulsing like jellyfish, twitching at me, over here, over there. I ate loads, like a fat kid picking strawberries; I couldn't get enough. I was roaring now, laughing and staggering about.

'I've got loads,' I said. 'I've got loads.' Tony was looking at me nervously.

We repaired to the car. Inside it looked like a spaceship and the leather seats stank – the smell was so strong! It wasn't the seats, though: it was the shit on our boots. I kept burping and laughing, burping and laughing. I could feel every organ in my stomach, feel everything flowing up and around. I was luminous.

'It really works, the eating thing. The finding-eating thing,' said Tony. I tried not to look at his teeth. They were trying to get out of his mouth and his face had turned into a distant skull-cave area, lit up from the inside somehow for the tourists.

'How many did you have?' Rankine asked him.

'I always have about seven; I feel that's enough,' Tony pondered.

'Really?' I said. 'I stopped counting at about a hundred and sixty. He looked at me and the skull-cave squirmed into a disapproving normal-face grimace then back into the London Dungeon cage-exhibit look of before.

'That's much too many,' he said. I suddenly realised he was Australian.

'Don't worry,' I said. 'You'll be all right.' I burst out laughing again, spraying snot everywhere. 'Sorry, sorry,' I said. I suddenly felt vulnerable.

Rankine put the mothership into gear. The wine gums on the floor were bothering me: they looked so colourful and clean among the filth; I thought someone should rescue them. I suddenly had a brilliant idea.

'Let's go to a country pub – log fire, real ale – c'mon, it'll be lovely.'

They seemed dubious, taking the incredible exploding man into a pub.

We pulled up outside a likely-looking contender.

'You go and check it out, Simon,' Rankine said. I hurled myself through the door and saw a log fire: yes!

There were two people dressed entirely in white standing in front of a swirling copper waterfall; they had red snarling faces. A copper waterfall – you don't see that every day. I had a good long look. The man spoke. He was a vision of whiteness: white V-neck, white shirt, white slacks. I saw the gold and the tattoos too late.

'Shut the door, mate – it's brass monkeys out there.'

I looked back at the door. The pub was completely empty and silent except for the hushed rushing sounds from the copper waterfall. The woman stepped before me.

'Do you want something?'

'A pint of bitter, please,' I said. My throat had swollen up, leaving a tiny gap to breathe.

'There's no one behind the jump, mate,' the man shot back aggressively. There's only one thing worse than imagined bad vibes when you're tripping and that's real bad vibes. I fled back to the spaceship.

When we got home Rankine pulled a chicken out of the oven. It pulsed like something from *Eraserhead*. I went and lay down and did some ceiling duty. Hours later, the sun came up. It was cold and I didn't have a single possession besides some clothes and whatever I was reading.

I got laid off by Arthur and signed on. Paddy's prediction had finally come true: der was no work. I'd left Rankine's house (hadn't paid the rent, I expect) and was homeless again so I gave the social security my dad's address. I got my dole cheque every Wednesday: £41 and some shrapnel. My dad was always out during the day so I'd collar the postie and he'd hand it over outside the door, which was kind of him.

On cashing my giro my mood would improve considerably. Standing in the post office I'd sift through various debts in my mind, working out who I could get away with not paying: the more disposable income a friend had the less likely it was that he'd be reimbursed (unless it was one of the Moys, who were careful with money and always made sure they got their fivers and tenners back). Friends on the dole had to be paid, obviously. Ideally there'd be a friend who I didn't owe anything to who would offer me a bed; I could swank round there with beer money and perhaps a small bit of hash.

My modus operandi was the same as it always had been. On pulling the cash from the post office I'd go straight to a café and have a massive fry-up, trying to avoid any establishments with fruit machines. I might get my hair cut, always leaving a tip, then I'd go and call on someone and spend the day doing nothing, trying to while away the hours until friends came back from work. If no one was in I'd find a machine (pub, chip shop, café) and lose my money every time. That night I'd be on the ponce again, albeit with a new haircut.

I continued to hop between my three friends' abodes, somehow keeping afloat. I was very randy, of course, but couldn't seem to hit any sort of stride with the ladies, just the odd one-night stand here and there. I'd been celibate for a year in jug so it didn't bother me too much.

Tom Broadbent was a good friend at that time. I made him laugh, though he eventually got sick of me staying at his house and smoking all his puff. Tom was very clever and went to Westminster then Bristol University. He lived in an enormous mansion at the bottom of Crooms Hill overlooking Greenwich

Park; it's one of the best houses in Greenwich, full of antiques and original features, and has to be seen to be believed. His family had been a big noise in the seventies and the house had been featured in *House & Garden* and other magazines. They'd also filmed *Sunday Bloody Sunday* with Glenda Jackson there; I think Tom got a walk-on as a young kid.

When his parents divorced his dad had moved to Chelsea, leaving his mum in charge of this huge property. His mum suffered from some form of mental illness (as did Tom at some point, but I think his problems were more about enormous cannabis intake). She'd dress up in Victorian garb and suddenly burst in when we were stoned and make us polish tables. Once when we were tripping she had us up on the roof looking for imaginary leaks. I think his mum's problems really upset Tom but he was at a loss as to what to do. Some time later, when he was going through some problems of his own, an evil lodger tried to conspire with his mum to get him sectioned. I paid lip service but was strictly out for myself in those days and couldn't really connect with other people's misfortunes. As long as someone gave me a bed I was happy.

Tom's mum was very bright and had apparently been a shining star at Cambridge, but, as happens to a lot of clever women, was left to bring up three kids and with no outlet for a fierce intelligence her superfine mind came undone. Is it only clever people who are prone to mental illness? I've known several people who've struggled with their thought processes – two of them very close friends of mine – and all of them were bright, original thinkers. Mind you, a lot of people have called me mad, both behind my back and to my face. I have at times struggled to live a normal life, certainly, but I've been on telly now so it doesn't matter as much. What's mad anyway? It's a lot harder to define these days when the pursuit of money and fame at all costs is considered normal – and how mad is that? In this country the attitude to mental illness is warped to say the least. If you twist your ankle in the street people will come to your aid, while if you're talking to yourself they'll walk on.

For me as a teenager it was not football hooliganism but mental illness that was the English disease. Six kids from our circle suffered from mental-health problems. Their breakdowns appeared to start between the ages of sixteen and eighteen and their decline was both horrible and fascinating to watch. The parents of all but one of these people had broken up. Whether amid shouting and screaming or resigned silence, the end result of a break-up is the same: sadness and fear in the kids' heads (albeit that this was largely internalised by the people I knew).

All my friends' breakdowns were either triggered or compounded by cannabis abuse. This was before the appearance of skunk, the hideous toxic hybrid that's currently in vogue among the puffing classes, but nonetheless the dope in those days was very strong. Back then it was still being smuggled in by enthusiasts – Mr Nice and suchlike – people who wanted to 'turn on' other people to a great high. Of course gangsters were involved too, and when they finally took over the quality naturally suffered, but until then one joint of double zero or fresh red Lebanese hashish would knock you sideways for hours. You had to have a strong mindset to withstand it. Even before it got out of hand for me we all smoked a lot; we were very cocky and reckless with it.

We played a game where one person would crouch down and take twenty enormous deep breaths, and on the last one someone else would stand in front of him or her and blow cannabis smoke down into his lungs (a 'blowback'). The first person would then have their ribcage squeezed by a large member of the gang – actually lifted off the floor, like the Heimlich manoeuvre gone wrong. You'd essentially pass out for ten seconds; it was crazy. Once we were doing it at a blues party in Peckham and even the rude boys nodding by the speakers were shocked and appalled by us. We thought we were so 'out there, baby'.

So, take a kid, seventeen, nice family, quite well-off, intelligent, no drama: life has been easy. All of a sudden his parents break up, he's shunted between parental homes – perhaps there are new partners on the scene too. No one likes a moody teenager; he has to find somewhere to live. Everyone keeps saying, 'What are you going to do with the rest of your life?' He's full of teenage angst, swirling sexual feelings, and everything is either euphoria or boredom. On the outside he's tough, rolling with it, but he misses his mum. He wants to go back to the Tintin era, the bonfire nights and watching *Grandstand* on TV. Instead he's sitting in a squat with other people like him, smashing his brain to bits with joint after joint of ultra-strong hashish. The others seem fine with it all, though, and if he displays a bit of weakness – if he ruminates on his lot, shows any fear – someone (me) will jump on it and mercilessly take the piss.

It's a blueprint for disaster: survival of the fittest and devil take the hindmost.

I remember days when we'd smoke and smoke in people's bedrooms, the sound of the Hoover banging against the door. '*When are you going to move out, Ben … ?*' Who wants to grow up? Responsibility: is there anything worse?

A guy I knew from Blackheath threw himself off a building. The last thing I'd heard about him was that he'd been seen drawing with crayons on the pavement and was asked what he was doing. 'I just have to finish this then I'm meeting Madonna for lunch,' he'd said, not even looking up. He was dead a few months later.

A close friend of mine during my early Blackheath days, someone who'd played on the Brooklands' cricket team with me, started talking nonsense – replacing words with numbers and laughing manically. He was a big blond guy and it was slightly comical to watch. His parents didn't think it was funny, however – they whisked him out of our little group and got him some treatment, thank god. He's right as ninepence now. I think he works in the City.

In that same group was a young mixed-race guy called Paul, quiet and thoughtful but he liked a laugh too. One day he followed a friend into a public toilet, stared at him for slightly too long then attacked him. He descended into madness very quickly; his mum had him sectioned and he wound up in Bexley mental home. We went to see him and it was like Bedlam with seventies haircuts. When he got upset they took him behind a curtain and whacked him out with something – the liquid cosh. It was horrible to witness. He sat there drooling while we told him what we had planned for the weekend. We were fucking sixteen years old! He later ended up in Broadmoor after attacking a male nurse.(Apparently, while he was in Britain's premier nuthouse, he was having a cup of tea and watching *Top of the Pops* one day when Madness came on with Seamus Beaghen, the guitarist from our band, Simon and the Virgins, playing keyboards in the back. 'That's my friend Seamus,' Paul piped up. 'Is it, son? Is it?' countered Ronnie Kray.) After he was released he'd return sporadically to the pub, gurning from the Largactil doled out by the good doctors. Everyone would go quiet and edge away from him; the girls were terrified. Imagine how he felt . . . Other nights he'd come into the pub shouting and screaming. It was very upsetting to see but what could we do? We took the Pink Floyd-Syd Barrett route: a bit of umming and erring and some head-in-the-sand work.

I puffed on, secretly glad I was only a lying, homeless petty thief.

Two other friends very close to me had major breakdowns and similar scenes occurred. One of them was on a return flight from Australia and thought he was piloting the plane. He tormented himself for twenty-odd hours. It sounds funny, but just try to imagine going through that stress and emotion. Horrible. The other dug his own grave in his back garden. He's fine now but he struggled for a long time, with both the madness itself and the stigma of it in his personal life.

It was a weird and turbulent period. I've spoken to other people and these were not isolated incidents: other groups of kids in other parts of the country went through the same thing.

All of us then were in dire need of comfort and security from our family units. Were we prisoners of our parents' sexual needs? Had they pressed on with their claustrophobic and bland marriages would we have been OK? I don't think so. At that age you're very much alone in your head in some ways: the teenager will always be a volatile wounded bird. But he doesn't need to feast on poison then have a blanket thrown over his cage.

Looking back on all this I know that it definitely upset me a great deal, especially when close friends had breakdowns, but there was also a tendency to snigger about it. This was obviously a defence mechanism, and you can be sure I was one of the people making the jokes. People would say, 'You can't say that!' and laugh anyway. And as a comedian the laugh is the important thing: we're like bankers in that way; it's all about the bottom line. Also I was a selfish pig hellbent on feathering (then destroying) my own nest. I had my own problems.

It's hard here to sum up what it was all about. Some of the kids moved back home, took their medication, stayed off so-called 'recreational' drugs (a bizarre phrase) and made a complete recovery, while others did the same and are still having regular breakdowns. Attitudes to mental illness are similar to attitudes to global warming: there's a small group of people working tirelessly to sort it out while everyone else just hopes for the best and tries not to think about it.

I once had an argument with a friend of mine who'd suffered mental-health problems. We were really shouting at each other and at one point he said, 'I have a piece of paper that says I'm sane – what have you got?' That shut me up.

My friendships with all these people belong in a past life and I don't want to intrude on them here. All I can say is gawd bless us all.

Of course at the time I wasn't making connections between our emotional problems and the fact that we were all stoned all the time – I was just getting stoned all the time. Tom's house became quite a gathering place for our extended dope-smoking family and I was always round there. There was a hip couple called Paul and Natasha; she was really sexy, a crazy blonde hippy chick with a very forceful personality and a dirty laugh. She was one of the boys, that's for sure. She said she didn't get on with other girls, found them boring. I've known a few girls who've said this and it's seemed like half the truth – often they were threatened by other girls themselves. Everybody fancied Natasha, though. She had a fantastic body, long legs, the lot – she was the forces' favourite and her boyfriend had a full-time job keeping her on the straight and narrow. She was very impulsive and seemed kind of experienced sexually.

Natasha had a sweet but confused dog called Woof that accompanied her everywhere. It was always sitting in rooms full of cannabis smoke and consequently was a bit jumpy and unpredictable. People would give it bits of dope cake too: not very responsible, I know, but we were off our heads. Sometimes when you were stoned it would start growling and keep you pinned in your chair for ages; dogs can smell fear.

Oddly enough Natasha wasn't the best-looking girl on the scene – that honour went to Tom's girlfriend, Rebecca Frayn, the playwright's daughter. She was absolutely stunning: she looked like a bunny girl, with big doe eyes and outstanding physical attributes. I couldn't believe how fantastic she was and I couldn't believe she went out with Tom. I was appalled, as was everyone else in our circle, nasty little small-minded people that we were; we all agreed that she only went out with him because of his house and his money. Of course, Tom did have a few quid and he was no Cary Grant, but he was sort of cool in a way and very confident and that's half the job. I couldn't possibly imagine going out with a girl like Rebecca Frayn. I was dumbfounded in her presence – I think I knocked her tea over once, which didn't help.

There were loads of stoners in our gang, all good middle-class chaps, not sure what they wanted out of life, happy to walk the Rizla paper and try not to leave a trace. We were crazy about dope in all its forms. It just became a way of life for me; I bought right into the counterculture. We had big coffee-table books full of colour pictures of various types of hash and toothless Moroccans holding up chillums with fuck-off mountains in the background. There were a few head shops about, where we'd buy hash pipes and giant Rizlas. Everyone's dream was to go to India and smoke the place to the ground and at various points everyone went (though not me, of course: lack of funds). I remember I made a tape for Tom when he went with 'Walking on Sunshine' by Rocker's Revenge on it and 'Don't You Want Me' by the Human League. He ran out of money and got a lot of offers for that tape but he wouldn't sell it – not for any sentimental reasons; he just liked it.

We were all crazy about music. That's all we did, listen to music. In those days the height of anyone's ambition was to have a flat and a stereo. That was it. Maybe a car I suppose, but stereo equipment was very, very important: your deck, your amp, your speakers; the holy trinity.

At some point Natasha and Paul came into some money and got a pukka flat in leafy Blackheath – and, more importantly, a wicked hi-fi system, with a Rega Planar 3 deck, a Nad amplifier and Jamo speakers. It was the dog's doughnut and sat there, black and serious, ready for action.

We started hanging out there a bit – with the money they really upped their hash consumption. We were listening to the Psychedelic Furs, Echo & the Bunnymen and the Teardrop Explodes. Plus some Motown and a bit of disco. The British bands we rated sounded a lot more menacing after six joints of hash oil or a few bongs. 'Forever Now' and 'Heaven Up Here' were particularly compelling, though really I was a Teardrop Explodes nut. I have a lot of time for Julian Cope, despite his crusty leanings; I think he's a proper English eccentric, to be filed alongside Vic Reeves and Viv Stanshall. His memoir is a cracker too. On that stereo everything sounded fantastic, but of course I wasn't allowed anywhere near the record player. Not old shaky – I'd have caused havoc. I was still treated like a child by some people from that little gang; they'd look down their noses at me and treat me like a leper.

There were various dealers around. I found the whole dealer thing very amusing: basically, everyone was stoned virtually all the time so everyone was paranoid virtually all the time. This meant it was all very strict and formal, and only certain people would be allowed to liaise with the dealer. No one else: they didn't want loads of skint teenagers cluttering up their flats and woe betide anyone who brought someone round unannounced; this would result in a severe reprimand. I was seen as a bit of a loose cannon and was always kept away from the dealers. Thinking about it now I presume it was the borstal thing, plus the fact that I was absolutely skint and also very clumsy. I also had a habit of being loud, which never went down well. Everyone was always whispering and watching unintelligible films directed by Robert Altman or Hal Ashby; it was all hush-hush.

We were so paranoid it was exhausting. I remember people screaming at me not to look out of the back of the car window in case we were followed by a milkman. We were convinced we were being watched and that our phones were tapped. One dealer had a telescope with which he'd survey the outside world, examining strange men at bus stops, swinging back round to watch the entrance to the Wimpy again. No one ever got busted, though, not that I remember. It was all quite small-scale apart from Dave the Scar. He was a proper dealer, and I think he found our little gang quite amusing or maybe he just fancied Natasha. I was allowed round his pad off Lee Road, for some reason; this must have been much later. He had a black silk shirt on and black Farahs and his walls were covered with weapons. He also had electronic scales, which to us back then were the coolest thing in the world. It was very quiet round his flat the first time I went there. The word was he'd just got out of prison after serving seven years for armed robbery. He had a whopping Mars bar that crawled down his face and he looked through us. It was too quiet; I had to break the silence before it took on a life of its own and strangled us.

'Are they nunchucks?' I said nonchalantly, pointing to a weapon I'd seen in *Enter the Dragon*.

'I ain't got the hang of them yet,' he said, leaping up like a cat. He gave us a demonstration. A lamp got broken and the whirling bits of wood were too close for comfort. I had visions of being found in a skip with no teeth. *Why did I say that?* We made our excuses and left.

Jenny was a single mum with two small kids. She didn't like me, I was told, so it was ages till I was allowed round there. She was very paranoid. We had to make sure we had one of the right people with us or we couldn't score. It was so tiresome, all this 'You can't go up there'/'She can't go up there'/'She'll go mad if I take you up there'. We only wanted a tiny bit of pot. When I was finally allowed into her presence I was disappointed to say the least. She was very short, had bug eyes and was wearing coloured tights – which are a worse fashion statement than white jeans, as far as I am concerned. She had her kids there and kept the pot in a baking tray. I noticed how disdainful of us the kids were; seeing their mum stoned upset them a bit, I suppose. One of our gang started sleeping with Jenny after that and we had better access to her gear.

Toad was more like it. He was like a character in a Steely Dan song. He looked Algerian, dressed like a failed conjuror and lived in a squat in Plumstead. It was him who sold us acid and his puff was outstanding – he had a contact on a farm in Morocco and a couple of girls who brought it back concealed in their bottoms. He spoke in a croaky voice and said things like 'The wind is a spirit' and 'What a mindfuck'. He had no problem with me going round there: I think one of his girls had done a bit of jail time so my reputation was unimportant. He sold me a lump of hash from a sweaty goose egg that he pulled from the fold of his jerkin thing. The dope was green and blue and black. One of his bitches made me a cup of tea; she had a vest on and I could see her long nipples. I tried not to imagine her shitting the egg out. I rolled a joint and offered it to him first, which was the correct behaviour. (There were loads of rules like this – if a dealer got upset on the phone and denied people entry we'd all examine how we'd behaved the last time we were there in case we'd caused offence in some way.)

'This is the first pressing, Simon. It's very strong,' he croaked – he really did speak like a toad. He gave me the joint back and I had a good few puffs on it before passing it on. It came back to me very quickly and I tore into it like a man about to become a father outside a hospital. I felt OK – quite euphoric, actually. I left and made my way to the bus stop. I sat down and then it hit me like a train. I flopped back against the bus shelter and tried to look normal. It was lunchtime and the road was quiet; my ears started ringing and a pigeon landed nearby. He looked great. I tried to stand up and felt sick. I was completely gone and it was all I could do to stay on the seat. People came and went, buses came and went, lunchtime became teatime, old people became schoolchildren. It was like a time machine. Fashions came and went, the trees lost their leaves, the sun raced across the sky. I got the bus in the end, but it seemed to take hours to get home.

Oddly enough, I saw Toad years later in the car park at Safeway's, driving a four-by-four and wearing a suit. His old man had pegged it, leaving him several properties abroad. He looked a bit put out when I called him Toad; I think he'd reverted to his proper name. Good luck to him, I say. He was a smashing fella.

Lenny looked exactly like Cheech from Cheech and Chong. He had a huge droopy moustache and lived briefly in a council flat off Blackheath Hill. He was principally a heroin dealer but he flogged us a bit of puff now and then. He was also an excellent raconteur and I, being interested in anybody who had something to say, went round there on my own occasionally just for a cup of tea. I was very interested in drug culture and used to grill him about his experiences. We got on all right, mainly because I never asked him for heroin. Apparently people were always coming round under the auspices of buying pot and then asking him for heroin. They were 'just curious', they'd tell him. That's how it starts, I suppose. There but for the grace of god go I. (I went the other way, though: I later sat beneath the skirts of the white lady and she fleeced me in more ways than one.) 'I don't want some twenty-year-old coming round here who's never had an aspirin having a seizure on me carpet, do I?' he'd growl. He sold heroin only to his regulars – 'proper junkies', he called them.

'It's all bollocks now. The media have got hold of it and it'll be a fucking big problem in years to come,' he once said, grimacing at his tea dregs. 'I remember when there were only about fourteen junkies in London and I was one of them; now every cunt wants to have a go,' he went on. 'In 1961 I used to go to a chemist in Chelsea and get me tackle and cocaine on prescription. Me and a few of the chaps were there one day and this cunt comes down from the BBC with a microphone – next thing it's all over the news and a load of silly birds start taking it. Fucking ruined it for everyone.'

So there you have it: it was the BBC who were responsible for the enormous growth in drug abuse and drug trafficking throughout Britain in the sixties and seventies. Can't they leave anything alone? Time and time again they mess things up. And they can't even make a good drama about it . . .

Chapter Nine

As well as my addictions to fruit machines and cannabis, my clumsiness remained a big issue. I was very, *very* clumsy. A therapist has told me it was a huge lack of confidence that led to this endless smashing of crockery. I was forever knocking cups of tea over on the rattan flooring or the armchairs; people would get very irate and scold me unmercifully. During my early adulthood it was an enormous problem. I was treated like someone with Parkinson's: people would step carefully around me; cups and plates would be put just out of reach. Every time I had a mishap I'd blush uncontrollably and apologise. I was forever tripping up, stubbing my toe, banging my head. I'd think myself from A to B without actually concentrating on the physical demands of the journey and consequently fell over all the time. I used to fall up the stairs a lot, though never down them (strange, that). I was always in a rush, always in a hurry – but where to?

There I was: no job, no plan, no money, no home but I still considered myself happy-go-lucky, footloose and fancy-free. I often woke up and rubbed my hands together at the prospect of the day, mainly if there was some sort of social event on – a party, say, or when I'd persuaded someone to take me to their country cottage. I was always arranging these weekends away, just to get out of London.

It was around this time that Tom inherited a house in Greenwich for his twenty-first birthday. A house! A *house*! We were all very jealous and got together in groups and muttered about his good fortune. This wasn't hard, as all we did was get together in groups and slag off whoever wasn't in the room: we spent more time slagging each other off than we did sleeping. That was really my job in those days, talking about people behind their backs; that and being entertaining.

I soon persuaded Tom to let me live in his house. He was a bit reluctant but I was signing on and I said I could get the dole to pay some rent. It was a little cottage in Circus Street. You entered through a small door and it opened out into a small living room, three little bedrooms upstairs, and a small kitchen adjoining the living area. The whole house was shaped like a wedge of cheese. It didn't get much light but what did I care: I plonked my duvet down on my little mattress and threw my clothes in the corner of the room – my own room, in a house! I was over the moon, Brian. I had no knick-knacks, no posters from shows at art galleries or of pop stars, not even a clock, just a few cassettes. But I had a room and that was enough.

Tom was renting the place to three of us. My two housemates were people I knew from the loose gang of people who didn't quite fit anywhere else.

Paul Reed was a good mate. We understood each other: he had addiction issues too, let's put it like that. He was average build, not bad-looking with thick brown hair; he smoked fifty fags a day, drank about seventy cans of Coke a week and had eight sugars in his coffee. Oh, he didn't fuck about, Reedy. Like me, he couldn't sit still; he was always tapping, drumming, legs shaking. Also like me he was hopelessly addicted to fruit machines. We got on like a house on fire. The first time I met Reedy he played me 'Joy and Pain' by Maze featuring Frankie Beverly and 'Southern Freeez'. Later, after ironing his bags, he taught me how to do a soul spin. He seemed shocked I was unaware of this move. He was a soul boy, really, and not a bad dancer but – like me – whenever he went to discos he'd get stuck in the foyer playing the fruit machine. He was a chef and was always working so he had a few quid; we'd go to pubs and play the machines for hours, laughing at our stupidity as we changed up his wages.

It was rumoured that Reedy had been an expert cat burglar in his youth, like Raffles except he drove a white Fiat Punto rather than a Bentley. When it all came on top he joined the army, did two years there and came home the conquering hero.

I was on a train with him once, travelling from Charing Cross to Greenwich, and we were in a single carriage with an old guy sitting opposite us, our knees practically touching his. Reedy and I had been talking away for about twenty minutes when he suddenly pointed at the man and said, 'Do you know who that is?' his finger inches from the man's nose. I didn't.

'That's my dad!' He shrieked with laughter. His dad didn't look up – he just carried on with his crossword as Paul laughed. He had a laugh like a gay jack-in-the-box being strangled. I sat there, Reedy's crazy laugh ricocheting round the carriage, while his father continued with his crossword and pretended to be oblivious. They hadn't spoken since Paul had stolen some money from the house. He'd made things worse by attempting to convince the family there'd been a burglary by breaking a window and knocking things over in the kitchen, then lying on the floor when his sister came home. I could really relate to this sort of behaviour, this everyday desperation brought on by one's own stupidity or addictive nature.

Reedy and I used to dine out in local restaurants. Midway through the main course he'd call the waiter over and produce a bit of glass from the moussaka and try to get out of paying. This was a new one to me: I used to just eat three-quarters of the meal and then bolt from the restaurant. Whenever someone wanted to go for a meal in Greenwich with me I had to say, 'Not there, no; that one's shit.' I had to go to Woolwich for a Chinese 'cause

I'd queered my pitch everywhere local. I got cornered once in the Mogul in Greenwich – the guy went and stood by the door. Luckily the toilet was upstairs and I jumped out of a first-floor window then hobbled off with a lamb rogan josh slopping about inside me.

My other housemate was a different kettle of fish altogether. Colin Powell was older than us, small, gentle and balding (and now sadly passed away). One or both of his parents had crushed the life out of him: he was frightened of his own shadow and was very bothered about his hair; he'd stroke the back of his head for ages, speaking softly about things being unfair in the big wide world. Everyone could see it wasn't growing back.

Putting Colin in that house with us two was like putting a koala bear in with two tigers. We ruined him, or what was left of him. With Paul having been in the army and me in borstal we knew how to liven people up. We tried to make a man of Colin but we failed: he got the piss taken out of him day and night but he clung on in there like a sloth in a monsoon. Of course, we didn't really bully him – just pointed out where he was going wrong.

Once when it was his turn to cook us dinner he served up scrambled eggs and carrots, which he got a severe dressing-down for. Another time, he brought home a cake, ate a bit in front of us then tried to wrap it back up, saying he was saving it for the weekend. He had no idea. He kept going back to his parents' house when the cupboard was bare, which we considered disloyal. He was a nice guy really but he was a bit like Neil in *The Young Ones*: you just wanted to squeeze his head. I had lots of arguments with him and his gentle hippy friends. I smoked a lot of pot but was in no way a hippy. I believed you had to work for a living and I had nothing against the police. There were so many people on that scene who thought the sky was going to fall on their heads – they wanted to smash the machine but only providing they could start in the afternoon. They sat around talking about police brutality and how awful the Sus law was while living with their mums and dads and having pots of tea brought up to them and their shoes polished.

They thought that listening to Steel Pulse and Linton Kwesi Johnson gave them some insight into the difficulties of being young and black in Britain today. We still didn't know many black people (it may as well have been the fifties), so all this was just posturing to me. Talk is cheap. My own political forays might have been just as tenuous but at least they'd involved action. Years beforehand a group of us had been on the National Front march in Lewisham in order to give the NF what for. We were about fifteen and must have looked like the Famous Five off to catch some pirates. There was a girl with us, Abigail Pockney (I'll never forget her name), and as we came alongside the NF – mainly Millwall thugs – she started chanting 'The National Front is a Nazi front' in her best Radio Four head-girl tones. How I hated being middle class in situations like this. A group of men – *men*, not fifteen-year-olds – broke off from the group and we shit ourselves. They chased us up Granville Park but when they cornered us they turned away in disgust as our puppy fat wobbled and they saw we were too young. One of us, Martin Dunsford, had sideburns, though, and this cost him dearly: he got a good hiding.

Someone who arrived on the scene around the time we lived in Tom's house was Kenny Harris. He came from East Greenwich and was in no way middle class. He had tattoos of girls' names on his upper body and would deliberately not eat in order to get more out of it. He was small and wiry with a hawkish profile and was very paranoid: he'd sometimes leave the room then burst back in to check we weren't talking about him. A lot of people thought he was sordid and common but I thought he was great. He was a lot older than us – nearly forty – and obviously enjoyed the respect we gave him. Shit, man: he could make a chillum out of a potato! He made me laugh and was a welcome change from the endless parade of wishy-washy weekend stoners who stumbled through our house.

He was tricky, though. He reminded me of Steerpike, the sneaky kitchen porter from *Gormenghast* – in fact he closely resembled the original Mervyn Peake illustration. I think he saw us as his ticket out of the ghetto. He lived with his aunt in a council flat and would often befriend people's mums, pay them compliments and offer to perform small tasks, hoping to get his foot in the door.

He was a major stoner and knew all kinds of nefarious types. He liked me, of course: as he put it (with reference to my stint in borstal), I'd 'seen both sides'. As I got to know him, though, he exerted a sort of hold on me and certain other people that was a bit sinister. (Much later, when I ended up living with him in Deptford, he'd take offence if I wanted to go out in the evenings, confronting me as I made my toilet and saying things like, 'There won't be no one down that pub,' and, 'What? You think they care about you?' These well-chosen remarks and the bounty on offer would often convince me to stay put and we'd drink stolen vintage port decanted through a coffee filter, listen to the Doors and play crib. He'd often fall asleep with his mouth open looking like he'd died, his skin like parchment, wheezing like a bronchial stoat.)

He was always talking about his mate Baz, who apparently had Marvin Hagler's upper body and had stuck a burning tyre on someone's neck. Kenny wasn't in the least bit violent, though: he was all talk. I knew some of the people he knew from East Greenwich – after all, I'd been visiting pubs there since I was sixteen – and they seemed a bit wary of him. One of them said he had water on the brain. His refusal to eat solid food often resulted in him passing out while standing up during smoking sessions. He'd crash to the floor and we'd revive him by slapping his face; he'd come to like a newborn chick, laughing and squeaking. 'That was a good hit, man,' he'd say, his feral face creasing.

He took downers, too. Apparently one Christmas he'd got hold of a big bag of DF118s and had a few nibbles while cooking Christmas dinner for his aunt. At some stage he overwhelmed himself and dropped the turkey; he was too out of it to pick it up and his aunt couldn't lift it. I felt sorry for him when he told this story – my parents never saw the state I was in and that was how I liked it. They had no idea: I'd rock up at Christmas freshly scrubbed with my hand out and tell them positive things about my life. Who knows what they thought? We didn't have those conversations.

Kenny taught us all how to make chillums from vegetables and how to skin-up joints in the wind and rain; he showed us pubs that did lock-ins and where we could cash stolen giros. He was expert in credit-card fraud as well, and gave us tips on girls and sexual performance. He once told me, 'You know when you have had a good bunk-up because you puke your guts up afterwards.' This I took with a pinch of salt because he seemed to puke his guts up quite a lot anyway. Also, as far as I could see, he never had any sex. He was a bit sleazy and often slipped into bad Jamaican patois when talking to girls.

I once saw him eyeing a girl across the carpet (we were nearly always lying on carpets in the eighties) and he said to me, 'There's going to be a likkle bit of natural juice coming out of my natural stalk tonight, Rasta.' He fell asleep soon after that. His fondness for patois meant Kenny had a tenuous relationship with the black community. He'd greet random West Indians with things like, 'Blood and fire, Rastaman,' or, 'Jah know my bredren.' Usually they'd stare at his red eyes and dry skin and move on, but some people loved it and asked for a spliff – to which Kenny would reply, 'No, man, check me later,' and walk off.

Deep down he was all right, really, a pussy cat. We had a proper laugh over and over again but after a while he lost his hold on us and he couldn't seem to operate without that.

* * *

In 1983 I went to Glastonbury with Kenny and Jake Reason, the slightly dopey younger brother of Barnaby Reason, a face from the Blackheath scene. Jake looked a bit like Barney from *The Simpsons*, though he didn't drink as much. He adored and worshipped Kenny mainly because Kenny took a fatherly interest in him and attempted to mould him into his idea of a young man. He poked and cuffed him incessantly and told him to stand up straight. Kenny's main concern was that Jake would get us arrested by being too loud. Because Kenny thought everyone he didn't know was a policeman (even at Glastonbury he saw them everywhere) Jake was being warned continually.

I was very excited about going to Glastonbury: it was as if I'd been training at NASA and had finally been given the news I was going to the moon. I was more than qualified for the job. I could strip down a filter cigarette, lightly toast the tobacco, mix it with hashish and poke it back into the cigarette so you'd never notice the difference. (Or so I thought; actually you probably would.) And of course I loved music too – although I wasn't sure that Kenny would let us waste money on a programme, so it could be hard to know who was on where at what time. We left in the middle of a hot June night lying down like illegal immigrants in a bright-yellow Post Office van driven by a friend.

Kenny was running the show, obviously. He had secured the lift and had sixty quid on him; I had eight pounds and Jake not much more. We were banking on getting in for free – this was long before fences and security guards, cash points and live TV coverage. The official Glastonbury website tells me there were only 30,000 people there that year and that it cost twelve quid to get in! Still, twelve quid was too much for our little posse. While we lay in the back of the van Kenny drummed into us the importance of obeying his commands on arrival. He told us that in order to get in we'd have to dodge the stewards who drove up and down the perimeter roads collaring ticketless people and taking them to the main gates where they'd be forced to pay the dreaded entrance fee.

We were stoned of course; we smoked continually all the way down the M3. This was not ideal preparation: to Kenny it was a military operation and any mistake would lead to certain death. His endless instructions had us on a knife edge – we may as well have been parachuting into Vietnam as heading to Pilton.

Our first problem arose when the van dropped us off miles from the festival because the guy was going to Cornwall and didn't want to go too far out of his way. We gave Jake the heaviest bag and tramped off into the night, but soon became disorientated because of the hash and the fact that we didn't know where the fuck we were. Jake was fat and began to wilt and plead with us to stop for a rest. Kenny spoke to him harshly and we moved on. I took the bag off him, though, and gave him my slightly lighter one. Kenny was bag-free: he had to mastermind the whole operation so he needed his arms to make those little movements like in army films. He drove on, his little body bent into the night, chastising us like huskies. At some point after hours of walking, constantly gaining and losing heart in equal measure, we came upon a wondrous sight: a glowing settlement, an oasis of tents and parked cars. Glastonbury, our mothership. Kenny was triumphant but somehow became even more alert and wired at this point. At any sound of a vehicle he hurled us into the hedge, screaming as if under mortar fire, 'They're fucking stewards, man! They'll take us to the gate! Get down, Jake, you cunt, get down . . . !'

It looked quite close but was in fact still miles away. We were knackered and unshaven with sweaty bollocks, like the Home Guard struggling towards Never Never Land. Kenny said over and over again, 'We mustn't get captured.' At this late stage our bodies and minds began to betray us: it was too far, too far to walk in our state; we were city folk not hikers; we had to get a lift.

We lay in the bushes trying to determine who was a steward and who wasn't, judging by the makes and models of the various cars speeding by. We needed a multicoloured bus or a

Land Rover full of crusties. Eventually we took our chances and staggered out in front of a car. The driver was a slightly aggressive mixed-race guy and all too late we saw his steward's badge: *fuck!* Kenny was furious. Jake would get it later – it was he who'd begged us to flag down a car. He was exhausted, poor lad. Kenny sat in the front and set to work on the steward, offering him a joint of primo Afghani black hash, which he refused. He was driving like a lunatic and seemed to be under the influence of some sort of amphetamine.

As Kenny had predicted, he did want to take us to the main gate. We were doomed. We couldn't afford to part with thirty-six quid; that was a nightmare scenario. I sat slumped in the back seat, my mind churning, like Bob Hoskins in the closing scene of *The Long Good Friday*.

Suddenly, as the car accelerated over a small hill, there was a huge bang and a terrible grinding noise came from the front of the car. The steward cursed, the engine died and we coasted to a stop, all bad metallic noises and smoke. It was four-thirty and nearly light; the soft dewy meadows lay left and right. There was a long silence in the car. I could hear Glastonbury pulsing, an indistinct hubbub. We could almost smell the patchouli oil. In the darkness Kenny spoke.

'I don't want to worry you, mate, but I think you've blown your head gasket.' He had. We all got out of the car. The steward seemed heartbroken and Kenny took over. 'You won't get that started, mate – you've fucked the engine, man.' Then we just walked off, like freed slaves.

As soon as we got over the hill we ran and ran, stumbling through hedges and copses, down dips. We were trying to beat the sun: once it came up we'd be spotted like rats on a squash court. Incredibly we found ourselves in the festival, pitched the tent somehow (with a lot of cursing at Jake) and had a chillum that smashed me to bits. Then we squeezed into the tent like so many Boy Scouts. Sleep comes down.

We woke up at about nine and quickly discovered that we were in a car park, very near the festival but not in it. Unbelievable. We had a go at Jake for a bit then strode off. We walked through a gate and we were in – we'd done it! We laughed and laughed, the Dream Team, the Three Amigos, the Wretch Pack; lock up your Rizlas, we're here . . .

It was a bright sunny morning and we soon found ourselves in the market area at the top of the hill. I could see the main stage down to my left, and behind that unmarked countryside rising away, trees and sheep. Thirty thousand people is about right for a festival; everything was in focus. Young bearded men swathed in blankets standing over fires, beautiful girls splashing water on their faces from washing-up bowls, dogs shouting at each other. Everyone was so easy and happy. I'd never seen the whole organic vegetarian-food thing up close before. I lived on Fray Bentos and Crispy Pancakes at that point. Pasty women with dreadlocks selling wholemeal tofu burgers, real coffee and crepes with bean sprouts? Vegetarian cheese? I thought cheese *was* vegetarian. We were in such good spirits. We'd got in for free and that thirty-six quid we'd saved was going to buy us some primo hash. Jake was keen to steam into something fried and finally Kenny relented. As Jake bit into his all-in-one breakfast-combo roll Kenny warned him about the dangers of spending money on food rather than drugs. It seems extraordinary to me now that we had a forty-year-old man who deliberately didn't eat to improve his chances of passing out in charge of our diets.

We sat in the sun and drank coffee and watched Glastonbury waking up. I felt truly elated. I saw a beautiful girl climb out of a sleeping bag and stretch herself up to the sun. There were girls all over the place in denim shorts and Laura Ashley dresses having bad-hair days, glitter on their faces, nipples everywhere. They even said hello. I was interrupted from my reverie by Kenny.

'Peter – Peter.' He'd seen someone he knew.

'Hello, Kenny,' said a man with a beard. Kenny gave him an abridged version of our journey and he laughed. 'Where are you staying?' Peter said. We didn't don't know yet. 'Come and stay with us; we're in our usual place.' He led us through the yawning masses like Moses, treading on hippies left, right and centre. He apologised to some people but not others; I think he was still pissed from the night before.

His camp was a roped-off area containing a smouldering fire surrounded by sofas and armchairs and five tents, in one of which food and drink was laid out buffet-style. I was astonished. The camp was directly facing the main stage on the middle of the hill – I could quite clearly see roadies plugging in cables and wheeling amps about. What a fantastic spot. We were introduced to everyone: a mixed bunch of thirty-somethings, some older. They all seemed to have proper jobs and had been coming to Glastonbury for years. One fat guy said he first came in 1975, when there were only 4,000 people. I think as first-timers we were a genuinely invigorating presence. Kenny and I were sparking off each other and they were a good audience. One of the guys promised to get us jobs backstage. I couldn't believe it: jobs backstage? I might get to meet Osibisa . . .

We put our tent up and wandered off to find some hash. There were people camping just to the left of the main stage, which would be impossible now due to the sheer weight of numbers: that area now is a vast dusty or muddy thoroughfare, depending on the weather. I watched Glastonbury on television this year and I don't understand how it has become so big – 170,000 people. How did the counterculture become the culture? In 1983 it was like a village fete that had got out of hand. We strolled down the hill and came upon a kind-looking hippy mixing some hash and tobacco in a little gold bowl. He had a little card propped up on one of his guy ropes: 'hand-pressed chocolate Moroccan hash'. We had a little chat. Kenny was slightly aggressive (he might have suspected that the guy was drugs squad) but the hippy seemed to find him amusing.

'Hey,' he said, 'why don't you take a piece and smoke it. If you like it come back and buy some.' I couldn't quite believe what he was saying. He was letting me and Kenny Harris walk away with his gear and hoping we'd come back. We did go back, though: it was spectacular hashish and we bought an eighth off him.

His behaviour set the tone for our whole festival: peace and love, man.

We wandered around in the bright sunshine. For obvious reasons I can't put events into the correct order, but I can recall the flavour of my weekend.

I saw a young French-Arab standing behind a table brandishing two hot knives that he'd heated on a gas ring. A grubby girl stood beside him tearing off tiny pieces of hash from a big lump and placing them on the table next to three plastic bottles cut in half. There was a queue. A man stepped up and grabbed a bottle. In one deft movement the kid scooped up a bit of hash and compressed it between the knives so it burnt, and the customer dragged as much as he could of the resulting smoke into his lungs via the bottle then reeled away. It cost a pound. The boy was like some strange chef, he moved at such speed. If you didn't get the bottle over the hash you'd miss out and he'd curse you in French while the girl smiled malevolently.

I saw a man in silver swimming trunks carrying Mexican magic mushrooms like a cigarette girl in a cinema. His body glistened with suntan oil and he wore flying goggles.

I saw a lot of people fall over after leaving the mulled-cider wagon.

I saw a girl naked from the waist down buying some watermelon.

I saw a bloke dressed as a soldier crawling along the ground.

Glastonbury changes at night, becomes more a land of confusion. The main problem is uneven ground and guy ropes: walking about in the dark you feel as if you're being toyed with by the gods – men in robes with beards pulling strings and laughing, perhaps high on all the smoke drifting up through the atmosphere. The earth seems to move beneath your feet; you suddenly find your pace and stride increasing right before you fall over. You crash into people and tents. 'Sorry, sorry, sorry . . .' the cry goes up – it's all you can hear.

Camping rules were more of a grey area back then. People bivouacked everywhere. Punters would arrive in the middle of the night and find a nice flat bit of grass, set up shop and awaken to the dreaded sounds of metallic crashing and inhumane stench that indicated close proximity to the bogs.

At night the fires were lit and the music swung and drifted about on the winds, snatches of recognised verses, bass lines, keyboard swirls, shouts . . .

Our enclosure was becoming a problem: people kept tripping over our rope fence. Most just got and up scratched their heads like Stan Laurel then swayed off like Charlie Chaplin. Women with weather-beaten faces and bare legs would shout, 'This is a free festival!' They got told (nicely) to fuck off.

Basically we'd created a South East London pub, complete with beer barrels, sarcasm and crisps. We had two sofas and numerous chairs and, as with most pubs of a certain kind, there was trouble if the wrong person came in. Old friends were greeted with pats on the back and joints, maybe a line of speed and a pint of ale. But those who displayed uncertainty or had the wrong hat on were dispatched into the night. We stayed there for three days. Occasionally people would disappear for a bath, or to see Judy Tzuke or Curtis Mayfield. At times our fireside looked like a sketch for a Hogarth engraving but to me it was heaven on earth. Kenny and I became head bouncers and if people were on the wrong drugs and started getting too out-there or aggressive we'd send them on their way. One guy arrived wearing a bright-green V-neck jumper over a butterfly-collar shirt, proper Oxford bags and platform shoes worn down to nothing. He was jabbering and frightening the kids. I said, 'Quick, follow me,' and ran off; he followed me like a rabbit. When he caught up with me some way off he looked into my eyes like a child enjoying a game, waiting for his next command. It really freaked me out: he looked about six. I gave him a hug and he looked at me again pleadingly. I left him on the hill in the dark and when I got back people were laughing: 'You're a funny cunt, Simon.'

I was evolving my comic style, but it was vastly different from the one I'd later use on stage: this was just my way of surviving.

All this stuff is old hat now, you can see it on telly, but my life was so narrow and uninspired at that point that I thought I was on another planet. I can't quite stomach Glastonbury now. I had too much fun in 1983 and it's impossible to top it. At that time just being there was the height of my ambition. When I later became a stand-up I did the comedy tent once, second from top of the bill, but somehow it didn't match up – like a meal from your childhood, it didn't taste as good.

We had a good few hits off the Arab kid and saluted his gear, which was excellent. There is a greater sting and clarity to a pure-hash high than you get when you mix it with tobacco. We'd joined a throng of people going somewhere when I suddenly noticed up ahead a guy we knew from Greenwich, Bob the Knob. Bob the Knob was a hash dealer who always, *always* wore very-short shorts with keys attached to them, a tight T-shirt and a denim jacket. He was a major doughnut and an all-round laughing stock who tried to be down with the kids. We only bought gear off him if we had to. At Glastonbury he was walking along selling his wares, shouting, 'Hash oil! Good weed!' at the top of his voice. We positioned ourselves twenty feet back in the crowd and punctuated his cries with, 'It's shit!' and, 'He's a copper!' He kept spinning round but he never caught us. We thought we were the funniest people in the world. In those days I used to laugh and laugh, rolling around on the floor; laughing was like an out-of-body experience. Where does that go? I still laugh, of course, but why am I not capable of that hysteria any more?

Obviously the hot knives had something to do with it. But if I had some pure hash now I'd have to go and lie down in a darkened room.

I was intrigued by the Lost Children tent. At some point I lost Kenny and Jake and wandered in out of curiosity. There were a few sensible grown-up people sitting behind tables being attacked from all sides by hysterical parents who'd lost Saffron or Eric. Most of them were off their heads, eyes bugging out; they flicked their arms around and argued with each other. It seemed to me that a lot of these kids had probably walked off and left their parents because they were so out of it and boring.

It turned out that actually watching bands at Glastonbury was way down the list for me, despite my previous concerns about being able to. The only person I remember seeing that year was King Sunny Adé. I had a backstage pass by then and watched the show from the side of the stage. His band had that lightness of touch that all great African musicians have. Lasers shot out across the crowd and the music was like a river – it just flowed on; all the songs seemed to blend into one symphony. African music is best experienced live. I was right inside it, bouncing; the music seemed to shimmer and glow, warming everyone. It was a long way from Dr Feelgood.

Someone had made the mistake of giving Kenny carte blanche to examine people's backstage passes. He upset a few people – including Fun Boy Three, for whom he kept offering to skin up.

I slept at some point and suddenly we were going home. We washed our filthy fingernails and tried to ignore our greasy jeans. We splashed water in our hair and pretended we weren't gutted. I had one last look at the stage: *did I really stand up there trying to look like a roadie?* All around were the smoky remnants of fires. People were looking downcast everywhere; some didn't seem to believe it was over. I had a last look at the trees and fields beyond. I had to go home: I had to sign on.

Chapter Ten

At this stage of my life I was twenty-one and hadn't yet been involved in any sort of serious relationship with a girl or woman. I'd had a year off in borstal, too. I'd lost my virginity when I was seventeen in disastrous circumstances. (The girl was drunk and fell asleep before we'd done anything of merit and proceeded to have a terrible nightmare about an abortion she'd recently had, crying out, 'My baby!' over and over again. I can't make any jokes out of that.)

I began to see more and more of Natasha, the cool girl with the flat in Blackheath. Her boyfriend, Paul, went to New York and we started knocking around. She was a right laugh and it was nice to spend time with a girl, rather than all the blokes I saw. One night she seduced me. I had such a low opinion of myself at that time it was a bit like the pizza-delivery boy being invited in for a shag by Cheryl Cole.

At this time in my life I was very inexperienced at sexy stuff. If I was with a lady who was prepared to do it with me, the first part (foreplay) would amount to me positioning my hand on an area and rubbing vigorously while staring into her eyes looking for some signal of joy or surrender. It was a lottery. I was not au fait with the details of women's bits and bobs and preferred to paw at the breast as an obvious focal point. If I was having full sex I'd fumble my way in and proceed to hurl myself up and down and in and out at great speed, again looking deep into my opponent's eyes for some sign of victory.

What do men hope to see when they look into their lover's eyes? Worship, lust, fire, a coquettish abandonment, the fox, the swan . . .

What do men imagine is in their own eyes? Triumph, animal beauty, glory, bravery, the lion, the bear and – at the crucial moment – a madman's calm.

What women probably see is the same look a dog gives you when it's having a shit.

Natasha and I had a big romance. This involved us having sex during all of our spare time. I was the cat who had got the cream. She'd come round, bonk me and go: no affection, no girly stuff. I thought, *This is great! I'm getting all the best parts of a relationship without having my flat cluttered up with bras and healthy food.* Of course I fell heavily in love. First love, too, so all the more weighty.

She never left her bloke and he grew to loathe me. I know that because, one, she told me; and two, he used to look at me with intense disgust whenever we encountered each other at social functions. When she realised we'd both stick around if not exactly tolerate each other she just kept us going as textbook lover and steady boyfriend. I was completely besotted with her to the point of believing everything she said. My close friends told me to end it but I was addicted to her. I used to listen for her car, sitting by the window like a junkie waiting for his fix. But of course even when she turned up it was never enough.

Natasha was obsessed with star signs; she did people's charts and everything. She was an Aries (the ram) and I was a Gemini (the twins); her boyfriend Paul was a Gemini too, which meant she went out with four people. You'd think that two might have been enough. Being obsessed with her I naturally became obsessed with star signs too. I was ready to believe anything good about myself (or bad, for that matter) – plus I was stoned a lot of the time, which encouraged my interest in anything otherworldly.

She was very keen to do my chart, which involved me having to ring my mum to find out exactly when I was born.

'I can't remember,' she said. 'It was years ago.'

'What a bitch,' said Natasha.

'Yeah, what a bitch!' I said, not really understanding why my mum was a bitch. My little ram instructed me not to give up and eventually Mother and I narrowed it down to a two-hour period, which was what the astrologer Linda Goodman said you needed.

I waited on tenterhooks to discover my fate. I kept ringing Natasha up to ask her about it but this was before mobiles so if Paul answered I had to hang up. As Natasha was a double agent she often called me from phone boxes, her mad dog yapping at people waiting to use the phone. She was always calling Paul from phone boxes, too, when I was on duty with her. 'I won't be a minute,' she'd say. 'Look after Woof.' I was not mad keen on the dog: besides the fact of him growling at you when you were stoned he used to come in the room and watch us having sex, as if waiting for an invite for a threesome.

Paul, not being an idiot, would usually work out she was with me so the calls would last about two hours, with me having to get change from the newsagent's while she denied charges and placated him.

She had a wicked temper. Her brother was a local hard man and had been the school bully at Brooklands Primary. She hit me over the head with a jug once; we'd had a row and I made the mistake of not running after her. It was giro day and she caught me strolling off to the Wimpy without a care in the world. She'd asked me to return to the house then got hysterical when I didn't say the right things. One thing led to another. The more angry she got the more calm I became and after a while she smacked me upside the head with said crockery. She wasn't a bad person, just a bit volatile and greedy for experience – like a lot of young people. Her mum was the head teacher of a local school and was crackers too, but in a good way. I got on well with her. She used to laugh and say, 'I'm worried my daughter's leading you up the garden path, Simon,' though we both knew I'd been round and round the garden several times, had a drink out of the bird bath and was now standing by the sundial waiting for a new rake.

When Natasha eventually did my chart it turned out I had the wrong rising sign, which meant I'd never amount to anything. I was crestfallen. 'Sorry, you seem to have all these blocks on you,' she said and left. She didn't have time to explain in detail; she had to be somewhere else. (I'd often ask her to tarry awhile but to no avail.) I shut the door with a heavy heart and heard the distinctive exhaust of the Citroen fade away. So that was me finished, then: it was written in the stars. We carried on the affair, though. I was still required to drop everything and bonk her at a moment's notice, like an unpaid gigolo. Somehow I never got bored of this. I must have loved her, or perhaps the uncertainty of it all kept me engaged.

I remained full of the star-sign thing. I later discovered I was born on the same day of the year as Bob Dylan, and at an early stage in my stand-up career I thought I might become the Bob Dylan of comedy. It didn't pan out that way, sadly. (I also share my birthday with Queen Victoria, though, and I do look a bit like her first thing in the morning.) I borrowed various star-sign books from Natasha and starting spreading the word to friends. 'Watch out,' I'd say to girls at a party, 'He's a Scorpio: you can't trust him.' 'Oh, she's a Pisces: very indecisive . . .' People would stare at me in disbelief.

Amazingly, many of my friends who didn't like Natasha turned out to have the wrong star sign so were written off as small-minded or jealous or worse. My love of astrology didn't win me any friends on any of the building sites I worked at, either. 'What star sign are you?' is never going to be a sensible opening gambit at eight in the morning to a man with a hangover, is it? I once informed an Irishman that the foreman was a Libra and basically a fair person; he fired the pair of us the next day.

All this interest in star signs worried me a bit. Was I a poof? Natasha certainly wore the trousers in our relationship. I had first been concerned about my sexuality during assembly at primary school. All the boys sat on their bums with their knees up and their arms wrapped round them; I, however, sat with my legs splayed out to the side like a Victorian girl at a picnic. Every now and then I'd pull my knees up and hold on for dear life but after a while my arse bones would begin to ache and I'd resume my feminine repose.

I moved on from Western astrology to Chinese astrology. While I was flattered by what various books had to say about the Gemini – quick-witted, sensitive and creative – they were no match for the plaudits heaped upon my Chinese sign, the tiger. It transpired that having been born in 1962 I was a water tiger: the only tiger that liked to swim. (I loved swimming! How weird is that?) The book I had could scarcely contain its admiration for my sign: bold, brave, charismatic, daring, feared and loved in equal measure and also the luckiest of all the Chinese animals. This pandered to an earlier ideal I had of myself – the person I'd been when I was in the band; the person I'd been when I scored the winning runs at school. 'Tigers never go unnoticed and love being the centre of attention.' *Yes!* 'They will be very rebellious and must act out some of their ideals and lash out at the wrongs of society.' *Petty crime, borstal – of course!*

Everything was making sense: I was a tiger, not a pussy cat. 'Tigers are romantic, passionate and playful.' *Rrrrrrreooow!* I looked at my fingernails and purred into my dirty mirror. No wonder Natasha had sex with me.

Whenever I met another girl Natasha would come round and tell me to pack it in immediately. I was so besotted with her I complied. She was always blowing me out, just not turning up. I was full of self-pity under the surface, so I suppose it was inevitable that I'd get involved in a scene like that. I sat around and mooned over her for too long. Looking out of the window, relentlessly listening to the underrated second Teardrop Explodes album. 'Oh, I could make a meal/Of this wonderful despair I feel/ But waking up I turn and face the wall . . .'

Poor me, pity poor me. I should have been having fun.

It did get boring after a while but still it dragged on. We'd had a laugh at first but we should have just been friends. I think she was waiting for me to blossom into something – but what, and when?

Slowly these jigsaw pieces of sadness were building a picture of a comedian and they were all vital in my apprenticeship; they're links in a chain that's still round my neck. I'll always be in debt to my past, however grim.

I was staying at John Cooper's house one night and was already in my sleeping bag, all joints put out and books tossed aside, when I felt a strange feeling as if something bad had happened – a kind of premonition, if you like. I leapt up.

'I've gotta go, John,' I said, hastily getting dressed. 'Something's happened; I can feel it.'

I ran down Hyde Vale, across Royal Hill, down Prior Street and I was home, my heart beating nine to the dozen. I let myself in and slowly walked up the short staircase to my garret, flung open the door and was met by a terrible sight: my room was completely bare, just the floor and the ceiling and the walls. Someone had stolen my life.

It was Tom, of course. Faced with no rent whatsoever from me for about three months, he'd stolen my clothes and bedding. I was incensed, and later relayed the story to anyone who could be bothered to listen. 'He took my clothes,' I'd say, dumbfounded. 'Everything I had.' The net worth was about £11 and I owed him several hundred quid so I left it at that and decided to move out. I owed him a lot of money but he got a duvet cover and some T-shirts and I used this as an excuse not to ever pay him back.

They say moving house is one of the most stressful things you can undertake, but not for me this time. I didn't need a removal van – I didn't even need a van. Normally I just had a big carrier bag and now I didn't even need that: I had absolutely nothing.

This was when I got billeted with Kenny Harris in Deptford. He had a council flat in someone else's name in Douglas Way, just off the High Street. I wasn't over the moon to be living in Deptford with Kenny, but beggars can't be choosers and all that. I hadn't made the connection between my not paying any rent and ending up in Deptford; I remained convinced that I'd been very hard done-by. Anyway, I think Kenny was lonely and he welcomed me with with open arms.

Kenny had a mate who did silver service in a director's dining room and pinched booze. We always had a bottle of vintage port on the go, which appealed to our love of opiates. We played cards and watched TV. Occasionally I'd be treated to a flying visit/ bunk-up from Natasha. Life was pretty dull. I wished I was back in Greenwich and Blackheath and frequently stayed there. My room in Deptford was horrible, just a mattress, no posters or knick-knacks again; it was really unloved. I remember I used to get spots and washed my face in TCP, which made my skin red.

At night Kenny would spend hours blending tobacco and hash to make powerful joints. He'd say, 'Man, that spliff is laced!' and laugh disproportionately.

The fridge was always full of nothing. I used to walk up and down Deptford High Street looking in shop windows, buying pies and sausages from Kennedy's and wondering what was going to happen next.

The one good thing about the flat was that it was a stone's throw from the new Albany Empire, a community centre that had risen from the ashes of the old Albany where I'd seen a lot of bands. Dire Straits had been something like the house band there before they were famous. There'd been an even mix of spellbinding reggae master-classes and pub rock: I saw Jah Shaka supporting the Ruts there, which was magnificent, and Nine Below Zero played there a lot; my old band had even played there once.

The new Albany had a fantastic sound system. We'd get in there and puff like mad – I didn't drink much then, just a few pints of lager like every other young blade. I'd discovered dancing by this time, though: I used to love it. There was no fruit machine in there, which was a bonus: I was unfettered and could dance, dance, dance. I always danced on my own; I really went into one, not caring if I looked silly. It gave me a sense of release. I'd fight my way over to the speakers and plot up, trying not to tread on people's feet. Now I don't trust young men who don't dance: for me it reveals a simple flaw in their personalities – either they're concerned about being seen as un-cool, or they simply cannot let go. (A lot of the superstar DJs won't dance. I used to check up on them in nightclubs after hours, and in Ibiza; I have all the information stored away. Although maybe this is similar to comics not laughing at other stand-ups because they're too busy analysing the person's set.)

I had been a child of the *NME*, which in its own way is as destructive as the sun – you can like this band but you can't like that one, etc. It never covered disco or soul and besides, if I want to like Simply Red I will.

In those days they played a lot of eighties disco, which I loved. I knew nothing about dance music. I'd listened to a bit of Gil Scott-Heron and Curtis Mayfield, white-middle-class heroes both, but I missed Slade and Led Zeppelin. Slade are my favourite band of all time: they had more fire than a lot of punk bands. I used to listen to them and smash up my bedroom. I did listen to a lot of the indie bands but a lot of that music was rubbish and it wasn't very independent either. But records like 'Love Come Down' by Sharon Redd and 'Nothing Going On But the Rent' by Gwen Guthrie knocked me out. Natasha and I also liked 'Love Wars' by Womack and Womack, a fantastic paean to domestic abuse and which I understood a bit better after she jugged me. There are too many good records to mention here. I started to become aware of the production at that point, Mantronix, Chic, the Sugar Hill Gang – those records sounded incredible, supersonic in fact.

Then, of course, seemingly out of nowhere came 'Blue Monday' by New Order, an indescribable mix of robotic joy and human sadness that came from the future and took over the planet. It wasn't an easy record to dance to but I had a good go. I danced like there was someone else inside me trying to get out, a little Mexican fella who'd burnt himself, maybe, or a Chinese acrobat.

My brother Robert had started out buying punk singles on different-coloured vinyl but was by now a fully fledged DJ who'd moved on to organising boat parties and one-off club nights. He was making quite a name for himself and started the Yow Club at the Albany with Glenn Tilbrook from Squeeze. I used to go and dance on my own there too. Elvis Costello came and DJed there once – the first record he played was '1999' by Prince, which was a white label that no one had heard before. He brought the house down. This was before dance music separated into multi-genres like techno and drum and bass and there was more emphasis on good songs. Rob was a classic DJ. He had an enormous record collection and would think nothing of buying a rare James Brown live album from Japan for fifty quid, thinking it contained a certain track, and then putting it aside when he drew a blank. He was obsessed, which is what you have to be: it's not a game. Now everyone is a DJ; it's become the job of choice for people who can't do anything else. It's a bit like TV presenting in the sense that anyone can do it, compiling playlists they've heard in Starbucks or have read on the back of a biscuit tin. Rob saw it as his job to educate people in music as well as to make them dance. A lot of DJs suffer a lot from the cool-sheepdog thing. But basically through Rob I heard every decent dance record there was, which helped me prepare for the Lucozade-soaked madness to come.

Robert went on to DJ at Shoom and Special Branch. He was

a true pioneer: C.J. Mackintosh said he got into DJing because of my brother – and he was behind 'Pump Up the Volume' with Dave Dorrell so it doesn't get much more seminal than that. Rob played a lot with Coldcut and those kinds of people. Later, when I was sweating around in the nineties, drinking water and licking mirrors, I met a lot DJs who were quite taken aback when I told them Rob Day was my brother.

Of course I didn't tell him at the time. I was just jealous: he was one of the cool people and I was living on luck, eating boil-in-the-bag cod with a middle-aged stoner and signing on.

Kenny was still collapsing now and then from lack of food and too much smoke. I was always bringing him round at social occasions, splashing water on him and dragging him to a chair so I could go off and dance. It was like having your nan with you.

There was an aggressive scumbag I used to see in the street near the Deptford flat, a pasty, rat-faced kid who was the sort to bash the milkman or a vending machine if it gave him the wrong chewing gum. Borstal had taught me to recognise troublesome cunts a mile off and he certainly fell into that category. He didn't appear to be very bright. For some reason he'd got it into his head that I was a policeman – he might have seen me near a police station or it could have been my big feet. I've been accused of being a member of the fuzz in a few druggy situations: I didn't go down very well in a crack house in New Cross once because they thought I was a one-man raid and I've raised similar suspicions in raves too. There was another bloke we used to go out with called Suicide Steve who really looked like a copper – he always had a little clearing round him when he was dancing.

I've also been in the middle of some house party, hands in the air, sky high, full of love for my fellow man and gurning like a farm-hand lottery winner, and someone's said, 'Are you the cab, mate?' then placed some poor fellow on my arm who's quite beyond walking or talking. 'He's going to Kennington, mate.' It's odd to dress up in your Friday-night clothes, take loads of drugs and still be confused with a policeman or cab driver. Didn't I look young and freaky and cool, windswept and interesting? No. I looked like someone who shouldn't have been there. It used to really make my friends laugh but of course I didn't see the funny side: I wanted to belong.

One night in the Albany we had smuggled a bottle of vodka in and were swigging it back along with strong lager. I decided to go back home to get some puff so headed out to the foyer; it was very brightly lit and people never really hung about there. Suddenly the rat kid from Deptford was upon me.

'You're Old Bill, mate.' It was a strange thing to say to someone. I told him I wasn't, but he said it again: 'You're Old Bill, mate.' I denied the charge again. It had gone quiet and people were looking over. A tall black guy appeared. He appeared to be his friend and pushed me back.

'I'm saying it now: you're Old Bill, mate. What're you going to do about it?' The vodka had given me a clean high and I wasn't scared. That's the thing with vodka: you don't know how drunk you are. He repeated himself, 'What're you going to do about it?' rolling his shoulders.

How many times have youths asked each other that question down the years? And how many times has it ended in violence? 'What're you going to do about it?' The most basic of challenges. You're left no room to manoeuvre.

He said it again: 'What're you going to do about it?'

I suddenly felt free. I thought, *This is it – you've been trained for this.* I said, 'I don't want any trouble, mate,' and turned away. Then I span back and nutted him on the bridge of the nose. It was an excellent connection; he was out, flat on his face. His rat mate started to skulk round the edges of the room, well away from me but verbally abusing me. It reminded me of a documentary about monkeys: he was baring his teeth and pointing but little else.

Two huge black bouncers crept towards me. 'C'mon, man,

let's go.' They were wary of me. I was wearing a huge leather coat. I suddenly felt scared by what I'd done; I'd shocked myself. The bouncers threw me out and shook their heads in disgust. The rat kid was giving me details of how I was going to be shot the next day. I told him I'd look forward to it.

An actor I knew appeared from behind a car. His name was George and he was literally five feet tall.

He offered to drive me home. *Great,* I thought, *a tiny actor!* By now the black kid was up and swaying around, gaining in confidence and threatening me with gunshot wounds. Another two Herberts joined them. Things were looking bad. Of course they were never going to shoot me: it was 1983. Or so I thought. The following month a guy threatened a bouncer with a pistol.

George had a trendy Citroen. I remember thinking, *I don't need a middle-class midget; I need back-up.* If I was to be aided by a small actor perhaps Gary Coleman from *Diff'rent Strokes* might hold better sway in the black community. The youths started kicking his car. He told them not to kick his car. I looked at him – he wasn't scared and seemed strangely calm.

The injured kid moved towards us brandishing a bottle. All of a sudden George pulled a pair of nunchucks from beneath the driver's seat and started to swirl them around like Bruce Lee. It was as magnificent as it was unexpected.

They ran off. It was a resounding victory for the middle classes. I exorcised some sort of ghost that night: I hadn't enjoyed being humiliated by the black kids in borstal – they'd really made my life a misery at times and I can't deny that when I nutted that kid I was hitting back at a lot of people I'd encountered in the prison system. Now, for some reason, I felt I'd closed a chapter of my life with that head-butt. It was the last time I had a fight, anyway, and the last time I saw nunchucks being employed by an Equity member outside the Far East.

* * *

The eighties went on around me. I was appalled by Wham! – by the mindless joy of it all, the terrible dancing, the naked ambition and doughnut pride of Spandau Ballet. I heard bands like Simple Minds talking about world domination and I didn't understand. I saw people drinking champagne and using mobile phones and it seemed like another country to the one I was living in.

People around me were growing up, starting to get proper jobs. Jake's brother got a job as a commodities dealer, just like that: one minute he was lying about with us drinking tea and smoking trees, the next it was suit and tie and fast car and he was gone, left us behind. We drank in the Rose and Crown at the bottom of Crooms Hill in Greenwich and each Christmas everyone would turn up and tell each other what was happening in their lives.

The girls I used to snog and drink parental sherry with were finishing university and getting jobs. People were buying flats. I was like a polar bear in the zoo, too long in the same environment, endlessly moving over the same patch of ground and the free fish weren't doing it for me any more. I felt self-conscious, as if all eyes were on me, judging me. Every day I grew a bit older and a bit more bitter – though I still saw myself as happy-go-lucky.

I had a one-night stand with a girl who was very promiscuous. She must have had quite low self-esteem because she said, 'Are you sure you want to do this?' I'd drunk four pints of Tennent's – at that moment I'd have slept with a camel. At one point she looked at me a bit too long and said, 'You've had a lot of really bad things happen to you but you never let it get you down, do you?' I laughed and felt really depressed.

In the morning the chemical nightmare that is a Tennent's hangover forced me to dramatically reassess my position. I got up at six and put on a pair of Marigolds and started to do the non-existent washing up.

'Come back to bed,' she said.

'No, must get on,' I said.

She left. She'd been there before.

My old friend Rupert Moy now lived in a flat owned by his dad. There were two gay guys living downstairs and they did a bunk, owing his old man a load of dough. He was sifting through their mail afterwards and found a letter from the council offering one of them a council flat in Greenwich.

He said, 'Why don't you go down there and impersonate the guy and get the flat? He's not coming back – they owe my dad thousands.'

I was knocking around with a chippie called Malcolm Stafford at that point, a lovely gentle guy who laughed at me a lot. If someone finds you very funny it's easier to knock around with them than with people who don't, but you have to get on with them as well. And me and Malcolm got on great – apart from when I slept with his bird and another time when I tried to cash one of his cheques (he was going to whack me then but I already had ten stitches in my eyebrow from a good-natured tequila brawl with friends, two bottles between four people, not good).

It was painfully simple to get our flat. We met a lady from the council who took us up there and showed us around (this didn't take long).

'Do you want it?' she said.

'Yes please.'

So she gave us the keys and we had our own flat, right slap-bang in Greenwich: you could see the river from the kitchen window and it was one minute from the *Cutty Sark*. It was a fantastic stroke of luck and I felt really happy for the first time in ages.

It was good to get away from Kenny. He was a bit crazy and his trying to imprison me in the evenings and, among other things, get me to clean the bath properly hadn't helped our relationship.

I now lived by the river. I'd become part of all those great songs – 'Take Me to the River', 'The River Man', 'Down by the River' . . . Best of all, whenever I heard Joe Strummer wail 'I live by the river' during 'London Calling' I thought of my little council flat.

We were on the top floor and from the living-room window you could just see a little bit of Greenwich Park, a tiny square like a little watercolour of my childhood. It brought me great comfort, that view.

Malcolm was a good carpenter and was always in work so he provided the financial backbone the flat needed. I'd never had anything in my name before and I wasn't about to start now. We put the gas and electric in Malcolm's name, kept the flat in the intended tenant's name (Jeremy Harrison), paid the rent in cash and we were away.

I had still put no thought into what I wanted to do for a living. I was labouring on building sites most of the time, which was fine in summer but a nightmare in winter. I started work for an Irish contractor called Mulvaney's based in North London. I'd crawl out of bed at six-thirty, ring a number and someone from the IRA would say, 'Where are you?'

'Greenwich,' I'd reply.

'There's no woirk,' would come the thick brogue. Back to bed for me.

After several days of this the voice said magically, 'Go the Bethnal Green tube; der building a McDonald's.'

I arrived for work at seven-thirty. I was being paid £18 a day but I later found out they charged the building firm £45 for my labours. I was probably worth closer to £18 than £45 but there you go. I was experimenting for the first time with signing on and working, and had therefore given myself a false name, Peter Jones. On my first morning the foreman kept shouting at this bloke Peter. I kept thinking, *Is he deaf?* then suddenly realising it was me and spinning round ready for action.

They put me in a cellar a foot deep in filthy water with an aqua vac and told me to get on with it. At lunchtime I went upstairs and no one spoke to me. I read the *Sun* and ate something. A huge Irishman appeared with a smirk on his face; his hands looked like they'd been soaking in bleach and he radiated strength and cruelty. He looked like one of those people who whipped bare-chested men in the bowels of slave ships. He spat on the floor. He was putting on a show and he loved it; he had an enormous amount of charisma. From a Sainsbury's carrier bag he pulled a cold pork chop wrapped in cling film. He tore off the wrapping and put the grey meat in his mouth, chewed for a while, surveying us all, then spat out the bone.

'Are we here to talk or work?' Our lunch break was over.

In the afternoon I started to make inroads on the water in the basement and the floor became visible. I saw a door lying flat near the wall and went over to it. I picked it up with some difficulty and realised it covered a hole in the floor, which was also full of water and which I then proceeded to fall into with the door crashing down on to my knees. I felt very sorry for myself: I was in a dark basement, soaking wet with damaged knees and to top it all off I was called Peter.

I spent the remainder of the day loading a van with a lot of roof tiles that were being stolen by the site manager.

That night my knee swelled up and I felt sad but very manly.

Downstairs from us there was a mixed-race single mum with two beautiful daughters – they were six and four, or something like that. In the mornings she'd send them up for cigarettes. She was called Linda Brown but Malcolm called her Brownie. She was a bit thick but all right really. The trouble was that every night – every single night – she'd drink strong lager, smoke weed and pass out. This would have been fine but for the fact that she played a pirate reggae station at full blast all night long. It wasn't so much the music that bothered me as the jingles, which comprised a Barry White-type voice repeating the name of the station over and over again. There was something about the frequency of the guy's voice that got right into my brain and rattled my teeth, a bit like a dog whistle but at the other end of the scale. Even worse, I was the only person listening. Malcolm slept like a log every night and it didn't seem to bother him, but I became obsessed. I'm a very light sleeper at the best of times and it became a problem. Labouring was hard enough *with* a full night's sleep.

I'd sometimes go down to remonstrate with Brownie but even if she did come to the door she'd refuse to turn the radio down. I realised I was overreacting but I couldn't help myself. I started drinking Scotch at night, nipping at a half-bottle on my mattress on the floor while the bass rumbled on through the night. That didn't work: the Scotch just made me feel violent and gave me a hangover. I moaned and moaned to Malcolm but he was quite Zen anyway and I think he found it funny that I got so wound-up.

I started to resemble Herbert Lom as Peter Sellers' boss in the Pink Panther films, eyes twitching, pallid skin. I used to dread going to bed at night even though I knew I'd blown it all out of proportion.

Or had I? One night, after banging on Linda's door and getting no response, I returned to the flat and heard a giggle from Malcolm's room. He was in bed with Brownie: he'd been knocking her off the whole time. It was extraordinary but I managed to see the funny side – and after that Malcolm persuaded her to keep it down for me. He sort of dated her for a while and had to put up with her crazy life. She had all sorts of nut-bags round her flat and he had to get rid of some of them. One night a bloke appeared who looked like Dennis Andries with the smallest penknife in the world; he threatened to stab Malcolm in the heart but we just laughed at him. He asked for a glass of water then left.

Malcolm moved out of our flat eventually, when he began seeing this other girl. I was on my own and I loved it: free from human contact I could really start living in my head much more, which I preferred. I could walk round the house pretending to be other people, I could vacuum or sort out cupboards in the nude, I could be very happy or very sad and really experience both in mono.

The flat had two bedrooms, a small living room, a tiny hall and a kitchen. With Malcolm gone I thought I'd better do the place up – he'd had some nice pieces of furniture, which were now gone, and the living room had a really threadbare carpet that didn't reach the walls so there were exposed carpet tacks all round the perimeter. There was a gas fire, a dining table and an armchair but my only possession of real merit was an Akai boogie-box, which was good and loud.

I painted the hall black all over, including the floor – I don't know why – but it looked shit. I had an old book of photos of the Cornish coastline taken in the fifties; I cut it up and pasted the pictures on the walls in the bog, from floor to midway up. I was very happy with this effect – all the landscapes were devoid of people and you could really drift off when you were having a pooh.

I'd started to amass some books and cassettes and saucepans and I even had a cafetière – was I becoming middle class again?

I immediately took steps to stop paying the rent. I stopped paying the utility bills too. I never seemed to have any money. The council seemed fine with my growing rent arrears – they just sent me the odd letter politely complaining. Most of the people I knew had rent arrears anyway. Sadly the flat wasn't in my name so I couldn't get the rent paid by the government. The electricity board came round, though, and forced me to have a new meter fitted, with a key to charge up in advance at the post office or a petrol station. You ended up paying 20 per cent more for your electrickery that way but it was either that or get cut off completely. It was really depressing when the key ran out: you'd have to find twelve quid before the lights would come back on, so I'd be down the garage on a Sunday night spending valuable beer money on such fripperies – not good. It was daylight robbery, that key. The meter went round as if I was running a power station. Some people used to drill into their meters to stop them dead or slow them down, but this was only possible providing no one saw your meter.

You never let officials of any kind into your house anyway. It was like being at war – there'd be a knock at the door and you'd freeze, sometimes not moving for ages. I lived like that for years, freezing like a statue in Music and Movement then softly creeping towards the door and putting an eye to the spy hole. All my friends knew to call out; anyone who didn't was treated as a foreign invader and rebuffed.

Living on my own gave me the chance to be a lot more eccentric. I was still labouring – Malcolm had got me a job with a building firm called Bell's who continued to offer me work now and then. They were based in Roehampton, though, which wasn't ideal as it used to take an hour and forty minutes to get to work every day so I'd be knackered before I'd started. However, I was very fit at this stage. I started doing pull-ups at work on the scaffolding, then every night I'd run upstairs to my flat and proudly note that I wasn't even out of breath. I started doing press-ups and sit-ups before bed, too.

At some point I started doing press-ups in the nude, admiring myself in the mirror. I can safely say that this was one of the weirdest times in my life. I became very independent, not seeing my friends much. On Fridays I'd catch the bus down to my brother's club in New Cross and dance all night to Coldcut or whoever was DJing. I'd be drinking lemonade and hardly speaking to anyone; people would stare at me and I thought they must be saying to themselves, 'Who's that guy? He's a really good dancer.' I really thought this. Of course, I did talk to some people, and I noticed girls and stuff, but I always danced on my own: that was very important to me.

I'd come home on the night bus, run up the stairs again and stare at myself in the mirror for what seemed like ages. I felt great for a while but I soon became depressed again: I dropped the fitness, stopped looking in the mirror. I don't know exactly when this period ended but it didn't last long.

I liked my little estate by the river and felt at home for the first time. In the late eighties my mate Max got me a job at the Blue Mantle in the Old Kent Road. This was a shop selling fireplaces, which were all the rage during the building boom going on at the time.

The shop was owned by Mick Godden, who was lanky, ginger and loved making money (legally). He employed my friend Max to run the shop with a guy called Mark Swan, who was what you'd call interesting or odd depending on your mindset. He was good-looking, always had a flash character car, and was very funny and clever. He used to wear a badge that said 'We are the people our parents warned us about', which I thought was very cool, and he burnt a £10 note once while people screamed at him to stop. The first time I saw him socially he took me to see *Eraserhead*; he was wearing a sixties dinner jacket with jeans and rolled a massive spliff of black hash. We smoked it then he said before we went in to the cinema, 'Oh, by the way, some people say this film's a bit disturbing.'

He was right: it was a bit upsetting, especially after the joint. I wonder if Lynchy knew everyone watched that film on drugs – you really didn't need to be. At least they haven't remade it with Will Ferrell.

The Old Kent Road is the exact opposite of the King's Road in the sense that you'd be hard pressed to remember any shop on it. The Thomas A'Beckett, the famous boxing pub, is the only real landmark – our shop was directly opposite it. Mick also owned a car site down the road and other properties; he loved a bargain and was one of those people who got a buzz out of not spending any money. He was a nice guy, though, and liked having us youngsters about the place. He loved sitting by the fire telling stories about the old days, too.

Being the Old Kent Road, there were more totters per square mile than anywhere else in the world. By totter I mean everyone from a fully fledged aged rag-and-bone man with a horse and cart and a bell to a Millwall thug with a van and light fingers. They brought the fires in, Mick bought them for peanuts, we cleaned them up with wire brushes, painted them with something called Zeebright and then flogged them for anything between two and five hundred quid. It wasn't a rip-off: you'd get a nice fireplace with new or antique tiles and a wooden surround for that. We shifted a hell of a lot and the shop was full of them – cast iron, cast iron, cast iron everywhere. In the winter they'd soak up and hold the cold and the shop would be freezing. I developed a Russian-style method of keeping warm that involved stamping our feet and shouting indiscriminately and very loudly, almost screaming; it was very invigorating and I'd recommend it to anyone working in a very cold environment.

I became expert not in anything to do with fireplaces but at coaxing Mick into strolling down memory lane, which meant we could drink tea rather than work. In fact I was and have always been a useless salesman. People were puzzled by this: 'You've got so much chat,' they'd say, 'that's all selling is.' The truth was I'd back off at the last moment. At the crucial point when you had to front the customer, to be hard and push them over the line, get them to open the cheque book, I'd bottle it, always.

Mick had a partner called Alan who reminded me of the gangster Eddie Richardson, although this was a romantic notion. He often came over to use the phone and could be heard remonstrating with an unknown person. Once I heard him say, 'I don't need some cunt with AIDS in his gums telling me that.' He was a bit scary, to say the least. Working in the Old Kent Road it helped to have someone like Alan on the firm; he must have known the right people. You can't earn as much as Mick did in an environment like that and not have someone around who can handle himself. Some of the totters were lethal. The infamous Millwall thug Harry the Dog also dabbled in interiors; he'd often arrive with a sack of tiles and hurl them at Max, shouting, 'Have a gander at that, son.' One day he actually grabbed Max's testicles in greeting, squeezed them really hard.

Of course a lot of the stuff that came in was stolen and we couldn't touch it. We didn't need to, anyway – there was so much good stuff coming through the door. I remember a horrid little short man bringing in a box of beautiful tiles depicting bucolic harvest-festival scenes. They were fantastic, reds, blues and gold, really detailed work; I think they were Belgian. He laid them on the floor and I realised it was a huge mural. Sadly there was one tile missing so Mick didn't buy them; I think they were stolen anyway, though god knows where from.

Mick Godden was a brilliant salesman. He'd alter his style depending on the person but he was most effective with our most commonplace punters, the young middle-class couples. The shop being dirty and located in the Old Kent Road gave him an advantage: this sort of customer was used to shopping in John Lewis or Habitat so they'd often enter the shop gingerly as if they expected to be slung on a meat hook and have their toes broken. They'd tiptoe in, amazed by all the fires, and Mick would look up from the safety of his chair by the fire but then ignore them. Silence. The clock ticked. They'd start to look around nervously, talking very quietly as if in church. Mick would carry on reading his paper.

Suddenly he'd frown and look up as if they were children come to collect a football they'd kicked over the fence. 'Can I help you?' His tone of voice indicated they'd already started wasting his time.

'We're looking for a fireplace,' the mice would venture. Mick would get up and approach them, acting as if they'd asked for a barley-sugar violin.

'What?' he'd say, his brow furrowing.

'We want a fireplace,' they'd stammer.

'Yes, I know that. How big's your opening?' They'd produce a piece of paper with the measurements on and he'd snatch it. 'Right, you can have that one, or this one would fit, or that one.' He'd look at them like they were idiots, just aggressive enough. It was precision stuff: too much and they might leave or ask why he was being rude. His standing there, not speaking, not saying anything, was forcing them to make a decision.

They'd twitter like birds. 'This one's nice . . .'

He always got the sale – it worked every time. I thought it was genius, to act as if such people were bothering you, keeping you from something important. Just taking their dough, time and time again. Mick had been taught by the best: he did his apprenticeship at Battersea funfair on the stalls – the hoopla, the shooting gallery, that kind of thing. He always told a story about a guy with a stall who'd watch people walking by, wait until they were nearly out of earshot and then shout, 'You flapped one on the gate.'

'What?' they'd say, pausing.

'You flapped one on the gate.'

They'd start walking back.

'You flapped one on the gate.'

They'd be intrigued: *what was this man saying?*

By now they'd be at his stall and he'd have them in the palm of his hand.

I found all this stuff fascinating: the power of personality over solid hard work, keeping your wits about you and your wits keeping you, the patter *v.* the hammer, the chat *v.* the chisel . . . And yet I couldn't sell things either, so that door seemed locked too.

I worked at the Blue Mantle for a couple of years, then they widened the road and it was knocked down. I think Mick still sells fires over the road in the old fire station. It's weird when a part of your life is paved over – it's like it never happened. It's a

Tesco now. I don't think any of the totters got jobs in there; it's hard to imagine Harry the Dog on the deli counter.

Some good came out of the Blue Mantle's demise, though. Max and Mark Swan started their own shop in Blackheath in a refurbished railway station owned by Jools Holland. It was called Helicon Mountain – I don't know why – and it was there that I first met the men who were to shape my life. They were the future: they were Vic Reeves and Bob Mortimer.

Chapter Eleven

At some point in the eighties Rupert Moy gave me a job working for his landscape-gardening firm. I took home £150 a week and in the summer it seemed like the best job in the world. The worst thing about my previous varied casual employment had been having to deal with all the other people I worked with: the carriage-clock men, people who got upset if I hung my coat on their peg or put the broom in the wrong place; they seemed to know I was passing through and was a waste of their time. I did meet some good people, mainly in the building game, people who loved life and wanted a laugh, but not many kindred spirits. But now I was working with one of my best mates, among friends.

Back at school Rupert and I had initially been drawn together by our shared disdain of being middle class. I remember clearly us both staggering home from Thomas Tallis and him saying to me, 'Just because your dad talks posh it doesn't mean you're posh yourself, does it?'

'No way,' I'd replied, delighted to have met my soulmate.

With a name like Rupert it had been hard for him to get any rep going at school. I think that's why he'd always been keen to highlight his fighting skills, which were maybe born partly of his frustration with being quite well-off; he reached puberty early, too, which gave him an advantage. When we left school and hung about together we started picking up working-class attributes: we wore donkey jackets and Fred Perrys and dropped our Hs. He got a job back then in the parks for Greenwich Council as well, so became officially working class. We'd go to the pub at six sharp and play pool, intent on beating each other: we were very competitive over the green baize and also with girls, though he beat me hands down most of the time there. The *Sun* would be rolled up and slapped on the knee during conversation as we drank light ales and smoked ten Bensons in the bookies', pontificating over Pat Eddery and Steve Cauthen's latest mounts. We watched the boxing obsessively and he became a devoted West Ham fan. We adopted choice slang words, sneered at posh people and generally kept it real as much as we could.

Now, with the gardening, I once again didn't display a great deal of aptitude – I never learnt the names of any flowers or how to do tree maintenance – but it was cosy driving round Blackheath and Greenwich and obviously I got to meet people in their gardens, which was good because I've always made a study of the human race. In fact I suppose none of my time in the doldrums was completely wasted because I was forever watching people, picking up mannerisms and character traits.

I still do this, of course, but it's not as easy. Money, with its taxi cabs and nice houses in good areas, can insulate you from interesting folk; the whole point of being wealthy, it seems, is to distance yourself from the crowd. You need to be skint to really see people. When you're poor you're thrown together with the human race so much more, on public transport, in different jobs, pubs and cafés. And prison is the best place in the world to observe your fellow man, although he behaves a lot differently under that much pressure.

I used to eat in cafés every day from when I left school until I earned enough to go to restaurants, and they're good places to watch people. Gambardella's in Blackheath Royal Standard was great. It had the original fifties interior, the chrome coffee machine and plastic bucket seats. The food was diabolical, though. Sausages like old toes, and soggy cabbage. What did I care? I was always starving. Pie, chips and beans cost 57p; in the early eighties I always had that. The place was run by two brothers. Sadly one of them died when I still went there – he had a heart attack, I believe. Naturally the other brother was very upset. The next time I went in there, though, a builder shouted out, 'Oi, I hope you ain't put your brother in this fucking pie.'

This sort of classic gallows humour was prevalent in South East London. The spiritual home of such discourse was Cold Blow Lane, home of Millwall. Something about being in that crowd gave people confidence: some very funny people would engage in a sort of call-and-response with each other there. I heard some shocking but funny remarks that were at once spiteful, fresh and original. It wasn't just about violence at the Den. There was even some football occasionally, too, especially when Teddy Sheringham was strolling about.

Another great café was Lil's Diner in East Greenwich, a tiny place full of church pews instead of seats where you could get meat and three veg boiled to fuck for 50p. It later became Charlie's Café, and was run by the ex-Charlton goalkeeper Charlie Wright. He was a loud, abrasive Scot who wasn't above threatening those customers he didn't like with violence. Great chips, though, and the Mother's Pride was fresh and had butter on it, which was rare in that sort of place.

Eating in cafés is fine if you're doing physical work all day but it's not a healthy diet. I used to see blokes who must be dead now, all those fry-ups and stodgy puddings. One bloke who used to go to a café I frequented would always have the same thing: two cheese and onion rolls. He'd press down on them to flatten them then pour salt into them for ten seconds. Everyone in the café would go quiet. Ten seconds!

Politics and football and last night's TV are the main topics of conversation in café society. And any women who walk past, of course.

On Fridays at Eden Garden Services we'd do garden maintenance, going from garden to garden mowing lawns for kind old ladies and retired gents. I was seduced by the greenery and felt myself becoming vaguely content: was this it? I had a flat and a fairly decent job, but was this me?

At work we'd always be in comedic mode, doing voices and skits, and we kept abreast of any new comedy on TV. I'd always loved comedy and my frequent stoned monologues and impressions of local people often had people howling with laughter. (Certainly Natasha had found me hysterical – that was one of the reasons she'd made me her favourite waste of time.) Gradually I'd begun to think about actually using this comic ability somehow, maybe even as a job. But how? I was petrified of making any kind of step towards this, be it via drama school, stand-up comedy or even charades. Working six days a week can be very taxing on the spirit. I was a garden labourer and that was it.

I hated the gardening in winter. It was horrible trying to dig up frozen ground; in autumn you just pick up wet leaves all day long for three months. But he did me a favour, Rupert, giving me that job – it was the first time I felt secure, the first time things didn't unravel immediately.

As I did with all my jobs I eventually ran it into the ground. I was never going to be or wanted to be a partner, plus in the cold weather I was very negative – I used to try to force Rupert to let me go home if it rained. I'd been there for a good few years just treading water when finally we fell out over a girl, Jessica. I fancied her and sort of thought there was something between us, but one day I went to work and discovered she'd been in the sack with him. I was furious and jealous in equal measure. He started seeing her for real and I huffed off and laid down my tools. (He ended up having kids with her, so it was obviously more serious than I'd thought.) We'd had great fun but suddenly fifteen years had gone by and I was in the same place, whereas he had a solid relationship, a successful business and a close family in which I was a sort of failed cuckoo.

I flounced around being hurt, drinking a lot and moaning, but it was clear he didn't need me back. I was twenty-nine, I had a flat in someone else's name, I still didn't have that many possessions and time was marching on. What now, Batman?

I had a safe little social life, though. I still had the same circle of friends and we went to the same pub in Greenwich every night and drank three or four pints of real ale. It was a Young's pub so Ram and Special was my tipple. I'd stopped smoking pot, really; I did it only occasionally now. It had become very boring and didn't really fit with the working vibe, plus I never liked the hippy connotations of cannabis. It all got too much when the crusty people came on the scene: I hated those clowns. As a youth cult they're the direct opposite of mods, with their long-term unemployment, dogs on strings and avoidance of soap. They put me right off puff for ever.

Though I didn't realise it at the time, Jessica was the catalyst for my stand-up career. I'd been working six-day weeks and knocking round with Rupert in my spare time too. Now Rupert's relationship with her suddenly meant I was free to be me.

I'd watched *The Young Ones* and loved it – apart from Mike, who I didn't think worked properly. It became what we now call water-cooler TV. (Back then I'd never even *seen* a water cooler, having never been in a proper office.) Everyone thought Rik Mayall was brilliant. He also did a character called Kevin Turvey, a strange manic Brummie, and was a nervous, wild performer who gave it everything. I was transfixed by him and started dreaming in earnest of performing myself. I began swimming and running regularly and generally feeling more optimistic. I came in one night and saw an interview with Eddie Murphy in which he said, 'People look in my eyes and see I am happy; I'm just doing what comes naturally.' I had been making people laugh since I was old enough to stand up and felt sure I could make anyone laugh if I put my mind to it. Could I do what he did?

Around this time I saw Eric Bogosian perform at the Albany Empire. He did a number of characters, including a black pimp, and was excellent. There was hardly anyone there but he really resonated with me. I walked home exhilarated. I remember thinking that's what I'd do if I did comedy: characters, not stand-up. The thought of being myself on stage was horrific; and the idea of talking about your life and feelings, or railing against the government, was ghastly.

Saturday Night Live appeared and Harry Enfield was upon us. Stavros was a massive breakthrough for character comedy on TV; he just stood there for five minutes and took you right into his world. Most young people at that time ate kebabs but who would have thought of doing a character based on the guy in the shop? Genius. I watched it every week. A few people in the quality press thought it was racist, but Harry became a hero to the doner dealers right through London – they loved it – and there can be no higher praise. Bugger-All Money was good too; it seemed so new and exciting.

I decided then that I wanted to be Harry Enfield, or something like him, but how? Being on TV seemed a world away from where I was (57 Rockfield House, Welland Street, to be exact). I was still the same skint idiot who put his train fare in the fruit machine and frequently went through the lost-sock bag at the launderette.

I remember going up town around this time and everyone drinking Mexican beer with a bit of lime stuck in it. I got my change on a saucer! It was like being in New York. I saw the same people at the same time in the same pub and drank the same beer . . .

I still saw my dad occasionally. I'd go round to his house and sit there feeling awkward; we didn't seem to know each other.

It was now thirteen years since I'd left home and I saw him so seldom that I never knew what to say. 'I find I'm using the bong less and less, Dad . . .' 'I owe the council twelve hundred quid. They think I'm a gay bloke called Jeremy, though, so if it comes on top I'll pretend I have AIDS.' I'd end up discussing one of his books or something he was interested in, it was easier that way.

Malcolm Hardee was what people call a character, but that's like saying Mohammed Ali was a boxer. He ran the Tunnel Club in a pub just outside the Blackwall Tunnel. He used to do a rude Punch and Judy show in the seventies and claimed to have invented alternative comedy; he was also the lynchpin of The Greatest Show on Legs, a comedy ensemble whose 'Balloon Dance' became a hit on late-night TV and elsewhere in Europe. It involved men covering up their private parts with balloons, which would get popped to music.

The Tunnel Club gave a showcase to all the emerging alternative stand-ups. Everyone played there: the Comic Strip people in various forms and guises, Jo Brand, Jeremy Hardy, Alexei Sayle. If you were funny, people laughed; if you weren't funny, you were subjected to verbal personal abuse the likes of which you'd probably never heard before. They were a tough crowd, hard but fair. The Millwall chaps got in there regularly – and, as I mentioned, generally weren't backwards in coming forwards. The quality of heckling was exceptional at the Tunnel and if you ask any of those pioneering stand-ups they'll tell you it was the best club to play, because if you stormed it there you knew you were on your way.

I'd started writing comedy in my head, though not on paper. Could I start out at the Tunnel Club? I reckoned I'd be slaughtered.

Being newly unemployed, I started hanging out at Max and Mark Swan's shop in Blackheath. Jim and Bob (or Vic Reeves and Bob Mortimer) had rented the upstairs office to write comedy.

When I met them the first thing that struck me was how well they dressed: three-button suits, Hush Puppies, shirts and ties; Bob wore the odd T-shirt for work but all round they were very smart. They smoked fags, were nice, polite, cocky in a charming way. They laughed all the time and you could tell they were on the way up. With their Darlington and Middlesbrough accents they were a breath of fresh air.

Jim had started a comedy show called *Vic Reeves' Big Night Out* in Deptford, by Goldsmiths. It was totally different to anything on the comedy circuit, a rambling shambles of odd artworks, catchphrases, bizarre almost psychedelic comic characters, all pinned together by his mock-cheesy-showman chutzpah. Jim had already done bits with Jonathan Ross on *The Last Resort* and had become pally with him. Ross was very helpful to a lot of aspiring comics (including me, some time later). Channel Four had been down and subsequently offered Jim and Bob a series: they were going to be stars.

Mark Swan told me straight out, 'You're funnier than them. You should do a stand-up show.'

It seemed like a great idea. The minute he said that I was off and running. I immediately told him of my various ideas and he joined up the dots for me: I'd start doing a character and he'd laugh and add some bits and his own ideas. For whatever reason, he believed in me – and that was what I needed. Left to my own devices I'd always give in to negative thoughts eventually and I'd never persist with my dreams.

Besides, what did I have to lose? I was unemployed, hungry and angry and I had issues with women and my parents. I was a natural.

We started writing together properly. I came up with a number of characters – Tommy Cockles, the music-hall character, for one; we both put a lot into that. I can't remember who had what idea, but Mark wrote lines of material that I performed unchanged. I also did a crusty called Smudge who was really a capitalist; it was a dig at all the weekend crusties with rich parents, who had drawers full of giros they didn't really need. Mark made me a wig with dreads he bought from a West Indian hairdressers and I had a rainbow-coloured jumper to wear.

One night I was lying in bed perfecting my Robert De Niro impression when an idea came to me. I jumped out of bed and wrote a sketch around an impersonation of De Niro in *Raging Bull*. It was the scene in which he remonstrates with Vicky, his wife, but I'd substituted her infidelity with her eating my sweets: 'I know what you been doin', Vicky: you been eatin' my sweets. The Mars bar, the Milky Way and the family bag of Revels . . .' (We had jazz playing in the background when I eventually performed this and to this day it's one of my favourite bits of work. It was sketches like this that set me apart from the observational comics of the day and eventually got my foot in the door with the TV people.) There was a sketch with *Brookside* directed by David Lynch, too, and another one where I detailed the chain-of-command in hashish dealing: starting out with a guy in a council flat right up to a gangster in an Essex mansion I did all five characters very fast. Mark was very good at getting me to work hard on all the technical stuff. My Attention-Deficit Disorder meant I was always trying to leave his flat and wander off, but he'd make me stay and rehearse everything over and over again.

At that time on the stand-up circuit there was nothing like my twenty minutes. It contained ten different characters and was fresh and funky, with the added desperation of someone with no safety net: if I failed at this it was all over for me.

I performed for the first time at the Rub-a-Dub club in Sydenham, at a sort of talent night being judged by Jim and Bob. I'd rehearsed in front of Swanny but nothing prepared me for my first gig. The feeling of fear was quite new, like a terrible illness; I felt I was on some horrible drug and couldn't speak to anyone. I walked around outside the pub and it was like waiting to fight someone after school. I thought that this was the most real thing I had ever done. It was like hyper-reality, too real.

I have no idea who I was in competition with but I know there were some experienced stand-ups. I was jumping in at the deep end. Mark had obviously worked out that if Jim and Bob liked me they could be very helpful. I can't remember much about the gig. I remember looking at the punters; there were people there I had to prove things to. Rupert was there with Jessica and naturally I wanted to stick it to them. And Natasha was there too, I believe. The stakes were high! I couldn't look at them. I went and stood in a little ruined garden at the back of the pub. It reminded me of the places I'd found during my old shit jobs, the places in which I'd loafed or drifted off. I remember looking around at the old broken furniture, smashed pots and torn posters and thinking, *This is it: this is your life right here; you've nowhere else to go. If you fuck this up it's over for you – you can't do anything else.* I knew I was good, though: I knew I had a strong, interesting set. But would they laugh?

I went on stage, did my set and everyone laughed. I smashed the place to pieces. People who knew me were shocked; I could see it in their faces. Best of all, Jim and Bob absolutely loved it – I could see Bob doubling up with laughter, holding on to the bar. It was like a dream, the best moment of my life at that point – of course it was. I felt alive at last. I'd had an extraordinary success after a little lifetime of failure and paranoia and boredom. I was the new kid in town. I was the bomb. I was a stand-up comic.

I went home in a cab and had this feeling of contentment and satisfaction like I'd never experienced before, a sort of Ready Brek glow but based on reality not a drug high. I'd done it: I shook up the world! I never had that particular feeling again. A part of me was fixed that night in Sydenham – a bit of ambition dropped away right there. I didn't ever want to conquer the world, really, but I wanted to show people what I was made of. That night something was put right inside me. Of course it helped that the gig was a success. There were people there who'd known me only as the 'bed and breakfast' man, the junior tramp, and showing them I could be something else felt magnificent. However juvenile it may seem, I'd proved to myself I could do it and that was half the reason I did it. I see other comics who have experienced much greater success than I have and there's still that desperation in their eyes, the desire to hold the room enthralled with their personality, to shout louder than everyone else. I'm not knocking it; I just don't have to do it myself any more, which is a relief. People often say to me, 'You should be much more famous than you are; you could have done this or that . . .' Well, how famous should I be? How high should I get before I have a rest and eat a boiled egg dipped in salt? I did stand-up comedy and that was the big step for me.

I behaved as if I was on happy pills for ages. I bounced around. Simple tasks became pleasures. I started to look people in the eye. When I bought a newspaper and a Twix the Indian newsagent made that transaction with a man on the way up. I still went to the launderette but I didn't slump by the spin dryer any more; I hopped about the place thinking up material. I went to a restaurant and had a starter and a main course . . . Suddenly I'd become a whole person. I became more confident with womankind; I sang in the bath; I offered people directions in the street; I smiled at children; I did a few more gigs and everyone laughed . . .

Soon after my first gig Jim invited me to *An Audience with Jackie Mason*, the squashed Jewish comic legend. This was before the whole cult-of-celebrity thing and there was no shame in sitting with loads of famous people in a studio. Besides, there were no Dean Gaffneys here. There was Bruce Forsyth, Tim Rice, Britt Ekland, Roger Moore – the old school, the sort of people who live in big houses by the Thames twenty-five minutes outside London. I sat just behind Ron Moody and had Cynthia Payne behind me; Jim was on my left and Pelé on my right (not really). Jackie Mason was awesome. He called Brucie a Nazi and blanked Lesley-Anne Down.

Jim wanted to ask a question. A nervous girl gave him a card that read, 'Have you got any advice for aspiring comics?' but he refused to ask that. He wanted to say, 'Jackie, what's the biggest of the big cats?' Or 'Jackie, what's the longest river in the world?' They said he couldn't, which was a shame. Later a man got up and asked Mason if he would have entertained people on their way to the gas chambers (and there they were thinking he'd have balked at Jim's cat question!). Jackie replied: 'That is a question you should not have asked because tonight we are doing a show about me, not Hitler.' Funny man.

On the night of my first gig I'd heard Jim say that I could go on tour with him and Bob. I'd thought he was joking but soon afterwards I got a call from the agent Phil McIntyre's people checking my availability. This was my dream come true: I'd got myself a national tour with the hottest comics in the country after just one gig! How was it that after staying in one place all my life I suddenly had the world come to me? Jim and Bob were from the industrial North East but had pitched up right on my doorstep and offered me a job. In another piece of strangery the snooker hall I'd played in for years had suddenly become a massive comedy club – thirty seconds from my front door. All very fortuitous, but I had put myself in the shop window. I felt the gods were smiling on me, maybe even laughing.

You could never say Mark Swan was a run-of-the-mill guy. During the time I knew him he did kung-fu, yoga and karate; he was a pagan, a white witch, and was one of the first people in East Greenwich to try a macrobiotic diet. He could also do backwards talking and smoking like the dwarf in *Twin Peaks*. He had an incredible collection of comics – a roomful, in fact – which he kept sacrosanct, and he had the exact same car as driven by John Thaw in *The Sweeney*, right down to the tissues in the back. He also had a police hat he'd put on to scare motorists and was one of the first people with one of those lasers that are banned at the football now. He was very open-minded and happy to talk about anything, however taboo. Some people couldn't handle him and thought he was weird. I felt a kinship because I sensed people had always thought I was a bit strange too. He was very funny and entertaining – eccentric, you might say – and nothing in this book does him justice, really. For a long time we had a great partnership: he was my co-writer, general cheerleader and assistant.

Everything was ticking along nicely. Jim and Bob drank in Camberwell and I started going down there and standing joshing in a circle with them and their mates. We were all excited about the tour. One night out of the blue Bob said to me, 'I hear Mark's joining you on stage, Tom.' (He always called me Tom after Tommy Cockles.)

'You what?' I said.

'That's what he told me, Tom – that you're doing a double-act.'

Bob loved a wind-up but I had a feeling he was serious. I rang Swanny from the pub phone and asked him what Bob was on about. I was annoyed: Mark had never been on stage and to wait until a big tour and with limited rehearsal time to try to become a double-act was crazy. I started to rant and rave but he cut me short. 'Come round,' he said.

I got to his council flat wound up and ran up the stairs two at a time. In my heart I knew I wasn't prepared to share the limelight with anyone else at this stage. Although hardly a seasoned performer myself, I knew, in some strange way, that I was a natural. I was going all the way, or certainly part of the way. I had a feeling that Mark, while clearly funny, couldn't perform under pressure, under the lights. My twenty minutes were totally solid and a lot of the people who worked with Vic Reeves were just pissing about. I knew I had the edge on everyone on the tour – besides Jim and Bob, of course.

When I arrived at Mark's flat he was standing with his elbow on the mantelpiece, wearing a kimono and smoking a giant cigar.

This was classic Swanny, a bit odd but you had to admire his front. I was taken aback but not distracted.

'Let me explain,' he said in a strange voice. 'I'm like an old murderer – I've done everything; nothing gives me a thrill any more. All my life I have been searching for something. This is it! This is something we can do.'

I was adamant. I wanted to know why he hadn't said anything before. 'The tour starts next week,' I said.

'What are we going to do? We can't just start doing funny.'

'Yes we can!' he snapped back. 'We can do it!' he kept saying.

'What?' I said. 'What are we going to do?'

He had no idea. He was delusional – he seemed to think we could just get on stage and riff off each other.

I was rock-hard with him. I could see the tops of the trees and I wasn't going to share the view with anyone else.

'No way,' I said. 'I'm a solo performer: I don't want a partner. Sorry.' The room fell quiet. I could hear kids playing outside. A van pulled away. I walked out, back along the river towards home. I wasn't surprised by my own ruthless behaviour; I felt calm. I had all the cards: I'd been on stage in Sydenham and won the talent night. I was real. I'd always been a self-serving cunt and now I was going to get paid for it.

A few years later, Mark appeared with Jim and Bob in a show at the Gilded Balloon in Edinburgh. He was given a classic Jim and Bob job: to climb out of a barrel and do King Poseidon singing Burl Ives or something. He was terribly nervous, they hadn't rehearsed the show properly and the crowd were drunk. The performance in general got quite a bad reaction, which was unusual at that time. After the show Jim had a pop at Mark for not doing his bit right and he was crushed; he never went on stage again. Our relationship was never the same after my refusal anyway. He was very controlling, Swanny; there was a slightly sinister side to him.

I once encountered him under the stage at one of Jim and Bob's early TV recordings. He said, 'Don't listen to them [Jim and Bob] – I'm the only person you need. I'll take care of everything.' He was deadly serious. At other times he said things like, 'I'm giving this three more months then I'm going into manufacturing.' He wanted to be my manager and somehow get half my earnings but that wasn't how it worked with stand-up and I still don't know what he expected from me. He'd turn up at meetings with dark glasses on and carrying an aluminium briefcase. I loved him but I think he thought we were going to make a lot of money very quickly. I didn't make any money until ten years later. Sadly we eventually fell out completely over forty quid, his cut of a *Barrymore* chat-show appearance.

We had a row on the phone and he said he'd kick my balls back up into my stomach, which still makes me laugh today. It was all sad and silly. But once he realised he couldn't control me the whole thing was dead in the water. It's a shame, because he got me started, but once he cut me off that was it. He wasn't the sort of person to make up – and anyway, we had no TV show where he could earn money as a writer or producer; I just did stand-up and he got nothing out of that. I wish him well, wherever he is. I miss him – he was genuinely different. Though he probably thinks I stabbed him in the heart and the back. Maybe I did.

Chapter Twelve

I'd done only about three gigs and now I was hitching my wagon to *Vic Reeves' Big Night Out*. It was scary but it suited me because I wasn't centre stage and I knew I'd be able to look and learn. Oddly enough I felt extremely comfortable in my new world. I'd always loved a challenge – it was just that up until now I'd always placed myself in completely dull and unchallenging situations. Since school the only places I'd been able to really compete were the pool table and the pub quiz. Now I felt ready to whip it.

We were a motley crew setting off on a wet autumnal morning. Jim had assembled a gang of creative people he'd befriended in South East London as well as others he'd grown up with. There was Fred, who played Les – the man who loved spirit levels but feared chives – a lovely bloke but too sensitive for the crazy cakewalk that is a showbusiness career. An old friend of theirs, John Irvine, did all Jim's music for the show and in the interval sometimes he performed odd songs. There was a bloke called Dorian who was an air-traffic controller and looked like a cartoon character you'd never want to read about. Bob and I had him under the cosh from the word go, but he was remarkably resilient: he just kept popping up like a blow-up doll at sea. Another guy called Mike used to shout out, 'Have you got any booze for baby?' He was all right, a good Yorkshire lad.

Everyone was OK really. (Apart from Dorian, who was a bit of a pest – you wanted to squash his head on occasion or take a stick to him.) They were all very nice people and had known Jim for years; they were his friends and all admired him greatly, as did I. It must have been amazing to watch Jim's crazy hallucinogenic dreams become reality, and be part of it. We were all Python-based really: that was our grounding. But Jim's talent and flair were outstanding. He's a brilliant painter, he's had a Number One hit record and designs his own clothes. He's a true British eccentric, right up there with Spike Milligan and Viv Stanshall. Together Bob and Jim influenced nineties comedy more than anyone I can think of and a lot of comics are in their debt: Harry Hill, the Mighty Boosh – even Ant and Dec (though of course they're not comics per se). Also Britain's biggest and boldest modern artist, Damien Hirst, took a few leaves from Reeves. A sheep cut in half? A shark suspended in a tank? They're just props from *Big Night Out* but with a bit of flannel for the art journos. (Complete rubbish or fact? Make up your own mind.) It's surely no coincidence that he went to college right opposite the venue where the original *Big Night Out* was performed. (Hang on, though: what if Jim wandered into Goldsmiths and saw Hirst's stuff? Hmm . . .)

It was a big tour, pretty much sold out. Most of the venues were standing only. When people talk about comedy being the new rock 'n' roll this was it. I wasn't prepared for the volume at the gigs: 1,000 people all standing singing, shouting catchphrases; it was bonkers. Full cans of beer were lobbed at Jim in Wales, and sausages and bacon were thrown throughout the tour because of Jim and Bob's meat fixation. It was a swirling maelstrom of loud music and shouted catchphrases. People would come and go on stage wearing strange wigs and hastily put-together costumes. It was such a laugh! I loved it, but I didn't love going on stage and doing my bit on my own in the interval – that was different. It would all go quiet. I was usually either ignored or heckled off immediately. Sometimes I did all right, but not often.

Apparently a young Johnny Vegas came to see the show somewhere and got into a row with a guy who was heckling me. It's always nice when you meet performers you love and they say they like your stuff. It keeps you going.

It was a valuable lesson for me, that tour. Afterwards it was hard to be scared of doing pub gigs – or any gigs, for that matter. When you have been screamed off stage by 800 Scousers you get a sense of perspective.

That first tour was quite rock 'n' roll. We had a police escort in Nottingham – young girls were screaming and trying to get into the ashtrays and stow away. There was a giant fat bloke who had clippings from local papers and a smudgy photo of me I'd never seen, which he was keen to show me. It was very funny, my fat fan and Jim and Bob's screaming girlies. What is rock 'n' roll anyway? All we threw into the swimming pool were Kit Kat wrappers.

Having now done quite a few tours it seems to me that this rock 'n' roll thing consists of a group of men sitting in a badly lit bar in a regional hotel with one grumpy barman who longs for his bed, talking into the night and drinking warm bottled lager under the influence of something that looks like cocaine but definitely isn't. (More likely it's a strange mix of household dust and baby laxative sold to you by the bus driver who claims to supply Guns N' Roses and Metallica.) Outside it starts to get light and you examine your greasy jeans and realise you feel ill. The net result of 200 quid's worth of powder is similar to the feeling you get after drinking four pints of Nescafé, except you feel randy, and you walk down the long corridor trying to block out the ghastly patterns of the carpet that upsets your fragile brain. You climb into fresh but unfamiliar sheets, then you're up and down weeing in the harshly lit bathroom like a mole with prostate trouble. The sun comes up and the phone rings and you ignore it. You want your mummy, but instead the cleaner barges in and looks at you as if you've interfered with her children. You crawl on to the bus and slump; other half-dead creatures join you. You have a Rennie and a fag, break out the Purdey's and the Tizer and move on . . .

At some point James Brown, then editor of the *NME*, appeared. He was a strange young man with a reedy Yorkshire voice, small and nerdy but blessed with enormous confidence and a complete understanding of the media – like a sort of indie Chris Evans. He told me of his plans to start a magazine for young people, with good writing, lots of music and no adverts for expensive shoes. I'd like to see a copy of the first edition of *Loaded* to see how it all began. It did become tiresome but he made a fortune and wedged himself firmly into our culture. I found him fascinating because he was so sure of himself. He was almost autistic in his disregard for people's feelings. When he spoke it was like a little paragraph that could be printed off and immediately put on the page.

When we were in Sheffield the Human League joined us for a couple of days too. It was great but weird to be suddenly sharing sandwiches backstage with creative people I had admired. The girls were there as well. I remember the blonde one having the brain of a rocking horse: she couldn't understand how I could be Tommy Cockles on stage and a young bloke off it. She kept saying, 'But you were old and now you're young. But you were old and now you're young . . .'

Phil Oakey was a prince, shy and kind. He made a point of saying he liked Tommy Cockles too, which was nice as I was (and still am now) desperate for any compliments. At one point James Brown took in the dressing room, with Phil Oakey sitting against the wall, his little tum peering over his waistband, Jim and Bob discussing the sitcom *Something Involving Twine*, me eating crisps. He said to me: 'But you lose your ability to be creative, to be funny, to write songs, to paint.' He pointed to Oakey sat on the floor with a slight potbelly. 'He's lost it.' He swung round to Jim and Bob. 'They'll lose it. You won't because you have no talent . . .' It was a good speech and I assumed he wasn't joking, though you could never tell – he'd just stare back at you like a grasshopper.

Brown has calmed down now. The only thing that remains of his desire for world domination is his hair, which still twists and turns and bobs and weaves.

We stopped the bus on Saddleworth Moor one day and I watched him and Jim talking, their minds fizzing and popping like two little men from outer space. I've always thought Jim has alien tendencies – there's something about the eyes. His brain is remarkable, like a pulsating egg-world full of ideas, pictures and facts; as a foodstuff he needs no gravy. This was the first time I'd seen Northerners up close and they were impressive examples of a redoubtable breed. They do creativity very well, having a dogged sensible undertow that keeps them from firing off into space. There's always something of the canal and the factory as well as the rocket and the grenade about their persons. They've whipped London for years: the Fall, Joy Division, New Order, the Happy Mondays, the Smiths, Oasis.

The tour wasn't very long, only about twenty dates, but it was a great experience for our young hero – and a chance to see a bit of Britain. We'd hop off the bus in various places up North and Jim would conduct odd and inaccurate lectures involving local landmarks and myths. It's true what they say about people being more friendly up North, though. A good example of this is found when shopping. We always went to the same shops: Our Price, Boots and Marks & Spencer. Music, toothpaste, pants and socks – that's all a young man needs on tour. When you wake up after drinking Hungarian wine and smoking Boar's Head roll-ups all night with the roadies, you need to put on a clean pair of pants and brush your teeth to feel half-normal. The further up the M1 you go the nicer the ladies are on the tills. In London they're surly and distracted, by the Midlands they're calling you 'darling' and smiling, and by the time you get to Newcastle they're packing your bags, touching your hands, leaning on your shoulder and saying things like, 'Don't he look like our Kenny, Sandra?' Or, 'He's got lovely eyes, ain't he, Moll.'

Of course it all ends in Scotland, when you're right back to square one. The tills are covered in frost and they frown at a £10 note: 'I have nae change, laddie . . .'

We did two tours in the end, the second of which was much longer. (You'll have to forgive me if I've confused certain events and got them mixed up: let's face it, it doesn't really matter.) I was determined not to get lost in Jim and Bob's wacky world; I kept my own style and my own characters intact. Between tours I was still doing my original twenty-minute routine that had won the talent night, but it involved costume changes and tapes and often didn't work – especially at festivals. I had a nightmare at Reading once, when Sean Hughes, fresh from winning the Perrier, found out I was getting more money than him and demanded to go on before me. He was one of the best stand-ups in the country at that point and he blew me off stage. He was the headliner but in effect had made *me* the headliner, me with my little twenty minutes. I was a novice compared to him and died on my arse. I mention this because in fact at all the hundreds of other gigs I've done I've been treated immaculately by everyone concerned. I've not found the worlds of either stand-up comedy or TV to be in any way cut-throat; I can't recall anyone else ever upsetting me properly – and I'm a bit of a girl's blouse, really. (I was pleased when Hughes got a clump from Jah Wobble on *Buzzcocks*. You don't have a pop at a legend! As a team captain on that show it's your job to make the other guests feel comfortable, not to make snide remarks. He probably learnt his lesson. I certainly hope so.)

While I'm having a whinge I must recount my father's return to the fray. I'd called him up proudly on a few occasions and asked him to come and see me perform. He finally agreed to come to a student gig somewhere in London. I was very keen to impress him and when I put the phone down I realised I was extra nervous. Prior to being on TV I never fared well in front of the student community, for some reason. Often they're a bit rowdy and out to make a name for themselves in front of each other and this didn't sit well with me as I had no handy put-downs.

The gig was in a nondescript hall on campus and the crowd were well-oiled. When I came on the Dad/student combo overpowered me and I was nervous as a kitten. I started swearing more than usual and it wasn't a good experience for anyone. I was gutted not to have smashed in front of my old man but figured he'd still be proud anyway. As the crowd filed out I found him inspecting a noticeboard by the door; I was a bit hyper and greeted him awkwardly. He looked at me sternly and said, 'I thought you said you didn't swear.' He was genuinely annoyed and I was dumbfounded. It took me right back to my childhood and I felt crushed. For all my new shoes, black cabs and better-looking birds, it seemed I was still a disappointment to him.

We went for a pint in the badly lit bar, with students pointing and cat-calling or giving me the thumbs-up. Dad just sat there: he didn't ask me anything about my material or my career or my life. Same old, same old. I thought of a subject he'd be interested in and started talking about it.

What had I expected from him? I must admit, I was amazed that he wasn't more positive, but he was who he was: old school. We get along great now. Perhaps it was me who needed to change . . .

As my performing continued Tommy Cockles, the music-hall Zelig, became increasingly popular and I dropped the other stuff from my set. By the second tour I was just doing Tommy, which made me much more comfortable. I'd never been happy being myself on stage – essentially I didn't know who I was and wasn't confident enough in myself to talk to the audience. Slowly but surely, Cockles was on the march.

Jim and Bob's comedy did split opinion – they were very much a Marmite affair. But they'd completely rejuvenated the British comedy scene and would soon come to dominate it. I thought they were outstanding and couldn't fault any aspect of their work. It was literate, sparky and never descended into knob gags. I was completely in awe of both of them equally; they were funny, clever, interesting and lively. Jim was the more open of the two and seemed the more ambitious, but Bob was the steel core in the partnership. He was a shrewd cookie and (make no mistake) was cute and very charming but also had a grubby perverted mind that I found refreshing. They seemed genuinely interested in me and my material. The strange thing was that on the bus when I said things that were meant to be funny they'd often remain stony-faced but at other times they'd burst out laughing at what I considered a normal remark. Their conversations on the bus were sometimes better than the gigs. They'd just ramble on about different mountain ranges or seabirds. Music was very important: they both loved prog rock but Free gave the tour its soundtrack. I once put on Steely Dan, with whom I'd become obsessed, but they wouldn't have it. (Neither of them seemed remotely interested in America in any form, although Elvis is a recurring theme in Jim's art.) We'd look at people in their cars and discuss their imagined lives. Jim and Bob had a love of language that chimed with me and we chattered happily up and down the motorways of old England.

There was no rivalry. I knew my place and wasn't expecting any sort of promotion. It was the same with *The Fast Show* later in my career. I'm quite happy playing second or third fiddle, which has annoyed various girlfriends and agents over the years. But that's just me: I'm a team player – albeit one who desperately wants to steal the show.

A good example of this happened when we were doing the second tour. A part of the show was called 'Novelty Island', where different odd and feeble acts performed and Bob playing

Graham Lister would come on at the end and vainly attempt to win. Throughout the tour I was placed on a plinth in a ginger wig behind the pen and introduced as 'Mike Cheeseman, the manager of the local town store'. Jim would harangue and abuse me, calling me a 'ginger get' and 'ginger fraud' – much as he later did with Jack Dee and Mark Lamarr.

It's quite weird to be abused in front of 1,000 people, albeit as make-believe. After a few nights I suddenly swivelled on my little podium and bellowed in full Jamaican patois: 'You chat fuckries to me, bloodclaat? You want my shoe, Reeves, you hugly-bugly fool?' Then I took my shoe off and threatened Jim with it. The audience went mad, and Bob was laughing too. We kept it in and it became a show highlight: I got to tell the ringmaster to shut up, which gets the audience on your side. Everyone was happy. People still come up and mention that bit to me. Of course, I tried other things that didn't work and I'd be rebuffed by the boys. I found it hard to fit in to their stuff sometimes. Paul Whitehouse is always saying, 'No one really used you properly, Day, until I came along,' and in a way he's right.

After the second tour finished we returned to London and I said my goodbyes and hopped off the bus. As soon as I went up to my flat and sat down I became me again, the old me: bored, insecure and skint. It felt like the tour had never happened; it existed in a fast-fading dream of which I could only remember certain scenes. I felt a bit flat, which is common in such situations. I had no work ethic to speak of so the pen didn't come out. In a way it was like being on the dole again. But I puffed up my chest and looked out at the little square of Greenwich Park through my window, remembering my glorious triumphs on the boards up and down Britain. I was still the hot new comic, was I not? All this had come from Jim and Bob: they'd told me again and again how good they thought I was and not to be discouraged by people not getting Tommy Cockles. They'd also said to expect some jealousy because I'd slithered up the pole so quickly. As far as I was concerned, if I was good enough for them I was good enough full-stop.

I returned to normality; I watched some televised sport, I expect, and ate some tuna pasta. What next? I didn't have an agent or anything booked up. I went down the pub and told everyone about the tour.

I ended up compèring at the Rub-a-Dub Club at the Amersham Arms in New Cross. I had to write new material each week, which is always good. I remember being quite ambitious then, with backing tapes and stuff. I did a thing about the difference between American and English soldiers' attitudes; for the British chap I played the *633 Squadron* theme music and was very gung-ho, while for the American I read a sad letter with something from *Nebraska* by Bruce Springsteen. I remember writing: 'I have sand in my shoes, sand in my ears, sand in my eyes – hell, I even have sand in my heart.' Not that funny, but real and that's what I was always looking for in characters. You must believe in them and their lives.

Comedy promoters started ringing me to offer gigs throughout London, cash in hand. I did everything that came my way. I'd either storm it or get silence, people talking among themselves – which was partly them not getting Tommy and partly because I wasn't experienced enough to turn gigs around. Certainly without Jim and Bob standing in the wings laughing I felt a bit more uneasy, but I was picking up valuable skills and understanding. And when I got big laughs early on Tommy took over and he never put a foot wrong. He was completely fearless.

The bottom line is that you try more stuff when you're starting out, push it more, and as time goes on you compromise and change things in order to help the audience, to encourage them to think slightly less. You get more laughs but you're challenging yourself and the audience a little less each time.

It might be surprising but when I started out I wanted to be Lenny Bruce. I wanted to confront issues. Bob gave me a very sage piece of advice. I remember we were sitting on the tour bus, and he was dressed in a slightly stained brown three-button suit, undone to expose a 'Meat is Murder' T-shirt, and he was smoking, as usual. He was always thinking about work, Bob; he was quite down on his and Jim's output sometimes and always thought they'd be 'found out', as he put it. He said to me, 'If you want to get on TV, Tom, put a ginger wig on.'

If someone had said that to Lenny Bruce he'd have told them where to get off, but I've appeared in *Holby*, *EastEnders* and *Heartbeat* now and when I got my own TV series, the flawed but wonderful comedy-drama *Grass*, I wore a ginger wig. So I feel that by taking Bob's advice I have, in the long run, been proved right.

My act now comprised twenty minutes' Tommy Cockles, music-hall legend. Tommy wore a blazer and cravat and checked trousers with comedy glasses, and was based on one of those people you see on documentaries about dead entertainers – among the famous faces there's always one bloke you don't recognise who appears to have known the deceased better than everyone else and will use the person's first name a lot and be slightly bitter.

I had the idea of mixing up real events and adding surreal elements, placing Tommy with anyone from the Gurkhas to Brian Jones from the Rolling Stones working on a Buck Western steam press (Swanny's line) or having him accidently take China-white heroin. He was an idiot who spoke from a position of authority, and he ended up in the soup like Norman Wisdom or George Formby would have. It was surreal but quiet; you had to listen. Besides the obvious ones I suppose my influences were Pete and Dud's surreal rambles and Ivor Cutler; I'd also seen *Norbert Smith – A Life*, Harry Enfield's spoof documentary, which was the most brilliant thing I'd ever seen, world-class comedy.

I had two comedy fall-backs – pushing my glasses up the bridge of my nose or saying, 'Eerrrr!' – and of course my catch-phrase, 'They really were marvellous times.'

In those days I was about the only person doing a character on the comedy circuit; the only other was John Shuttleworth, Graham Fellows' excellent amateur-keyboard enthusiast. People in some of the venues were confused: they thought it was real, that I was just some old fool in the wrong venue, and they'd boo me off. I'd never come out of character and when confronted with people heckling or talking over me I'd reprimand them feebly: 'Keep the noise down, please,' or, 'If you don't pack it in I shall go . . .' Of course they'd just say, 'Fuck off, then.'

The truth is I'm not a fearless live performer and that comment was inviting an early bath. For Tommy to work you needed complete quiet; it was very gentle, with no swearing or big punch lines. Before TV exposure every gig was touch and go and it depended on how open-minded the audience was. The alternative-comedy circuit had settled down into something quite straightforward – it had to, in a way, because in places like Jongleurs you couldn't get away with too much oddity unless you were already a big name. Apart from Jim and Bob there wasn't much weird stuff about. They remained very good to me. Bob would say, 'It all goes over their heads, Tom – it's too clever. These people live in Putney.' Whether or not this was true it had the required effect on my ego. I did sometimes wish I had a more basic act that would go down better in some of the more rowdy venues, though.

I was earning money here and there for gigs but I was still skint all the time. Jim and Bob started filming their first TV series and I did a few tiny bits in that, which was all very exciting. I had a proper job at last and people started treating me with a bit more respect. I had a clean slate with people I met now; they didn't know me as someone who used to cadge drinks or use other people's razors.

It was a measure of how far I'd come as a performer that when I entered the *Time Out* New Act of the Year in 1991 I thought I had a good chance of winning it. Held at the Hackney Empire, this was the second-most prestigious British comedy award for new acts (after the Perrier) and all the past winners had gone on to have good careers.

My on-stage persona was in marked contrast to my real self. My mood swung more than Glenn Miller – up and down like a bride's nightie, I was. There were times when I thought I could conquer the world and others when I was sure I was the same old idiot everyone used to know. I still felt depressed and empty sometimes but, having assumed I'd never make anything of myself, I was largely happy in the main part. Most of my friends hated their jobs and I loved mine. The Ready Brek glow was still there. At the Empire I would appear as a music-hall act, which was obviously an enormous advantage. Tommy was still largely unknown but I felt the time was right and I had a good feeling about the contest. Regardless of how insecure I may appear here, I had no doubts about Tommy Cockles: I knew he was a solid original act and that given the right audience I could get good results.

I took a little gang of my old mates from Greenwich with me – Max and Dan Joseph came, and Mark Swan must have been there. I was nervous but confident. The Hackney Empire is a lovely venue, with a sloping stage, gilded boxes, faded red plush seats – exactly the sort of place Tommy where would have performed, so I felt I had an edge right away and was ready for action. I wandered around with a pint looking at the pictures of old music-hall acts on the walls. Suddenly I noticed Harry Hill lurking in the stalls. This was before he had become the Harry Hill you know and love; I don't think he had the collars but he had the brothel creepers. I knew him vaguely and thought his act was OK. He told a lot of jokes. (From little acorns!) We'd done a gig together in Manchester, where he didn't get paid and I did. He did very well that night and I died, which should have made him happy, but we were all skint then and he moaned a bit.

However, I moaned a lot more in the morning after having slept on a carpet in a student residence soaked in bong water.

He came over. 'Do you think you have a chance?' he said, hopping from one foot to another.

'Yeah. Maybe,' I said. I didn't know what he was getting at.

'Think you might win?' he said, hopping again like he needed the loo.

'I think I could,' I replied more slowly, measuring him a little.

'No – my man's going to win easy,' he said. 'Alistair –' he pointed over at Alistair McGowan – 'he's very, very good.'

I was due on stage in twenty minutes and this was a diabolical move for the cheeky doctor to pull on me. I was incensed at the time, but I thought, *Alistair fucking McGowan – is that all you've got? Alistair fucking McGowan . . .*

I have to thank Harold because he really got me going. I was very angry. Like a lot of people who are good at teasing and verbally bullying people I'm very sensitive. I thought, *I'll have you, you pair of cunts!*

To say I stormed it would be doing me a gross disservice. As I stood in the wings I realised all my comedy pals had stood in the same place: Tommy Trinder, Flanagan and Allen, Dan Leno, Charlie Chaplin. They were all around me, brushing off my dandruff, lighting my fag, straightening my cravat. 'Go on, Tommy, show 'em how it's done,' they said.

I felt great on stage. I'd got the act down to a fine art and the audience really went for it. It was a great pleasure to be playing a theatre with plush seating and proper acoustics after all the shouting and beer spray of the *Big Night Out* tour; I'm a confidence player and I felt good from start to finish. And, like a preacher in a church lit by stained-glass windows, my manifesto was given added credence by my surroundings. It felt like my show; I flung the good word down and rolled out my carpet of dreams for all to see. With Tommy live, the better reaction I received the slower and more like an old man I spoke. I was pausing and sighing – and at one point I clutched my chest and then said, 'Oh it's all right, it's only my lung collapsing.'

It was an ad lib but they went for it. I started an imaginary conversation with someone in the wings. I hadn't done this sort of thing before, though, and tried not to get too carried away. I walked off stage to cheers and applause.

Neither of my parents were there – not interested – nor any of my family. It didn't matter: I was a self-made man now; I'd reinvented myself, from riches to rags to riches. I'd played the three-card trick on myself and won.

They announced I'd emerged victorious. As a wind-up someone had told me that the prize was £500 and I bounded up on stage to collect my award thinking, *A cheque for 500 quid!* I actually asked Roland Muldoon for the money on stage and he laughed. I was momentarily put out because I'd already spent the money, but my enormous bloated ego soon crushed such vulgar thoughts. The results were me first, McGowan second and Kevin Eldon third. Both those guys are excellent comic actors and I'm still proud to have had my little victory. I'm like a little boy: I love winning things. (Though it was a long time ago now, so perhaps I should move on . . .) I think Kevin is finally getting the respect he deserves, as he's been ever present in all that is good about TV comedy.

After the show I was accosted by a handsome couple, Juliet Blake and Trevor Hopkins, who basically offered me a TV contract. It was all getting a bit silly. I accepted in principle and our gang drove back through the Blackwall Tunnel laughing triumphantly.

'Let's get some coke,' I said.

'No, let's not get some coke,' they all said.

I think part of me was determined to become a coke head. I was still a sucker for all that nonsense: John Belushi, marble tabletops, loose women – bring it on. I'm an idiot and must always learn the hard way.

These were my real friends, people I'd known for years and years, and they knew better. After that night I saw them less and less. I was a star now, a big, bright, mysterious burning star, and there were other people who wanted to be in my orbit.

I was offered a weekly slot as Tommy Cockles on a show called *Paramount City*, a returning late-night comedy show on BBC1. Arthur Smith had compèred the first series but he was replaced by Curtis and Ishmael, a black double-act, for the second.

Janet Street-Porter was executive producer and I think she wanted the show to be a bit multiracial and modern. We had a live audience and she frequently got the black audience members to sit up the front; she also got Curtis and Ishmael to wear African robes one night, which was a bit strong, I thought. It was quite surreal to have loads of young black guys shouting, 'G'wan, Tommy! Respec' da Cockleman!'

I have to say, I love Janet. There has never been a woman like her in TV and there never will be again. The men at the BBC couldn't handle her: they had no point of reference and she terrified them. Men in power are much more comfortable with someone who's going to flirt and appear interested in them. The BBC is full of attractive women who sit on desks swinging their legs and widening their eyes when you talk to them – there are also a lot of fat birds there who do all the work.

Paramount City was twinned with *Comedy Central*, a show that went out in America. Denis Leary hosted that and would do his links in between Curtis and Ishmael. We had a mix of American and English stand-ups. Thinking back now I have no idea whether they showed Tommy to the American audience (probably not), but they must have shown some of the English comics and the band we had each week – EMF, anyone?

I thought Denis Leary was brilliant. His show *No Cure for Cancer* came off the back of *Paramount City* and he really tore it up live. He was bold, charismatic and quite near the mark. A lot of people say he ripped off Bill Hicks but I don't see that – I later supported Bill Hicks a number of times and worked with Leary for eight weeks and they were different. Hicks was more laid-back and thoughtful; still brilliant, but he's been deified to such an extent it's hard to judge him properly.

Leary had it all for me. I'd say that he and Jerry Sadowitz were two of my favourite acts. Sadowitz was fantastic. He terrified people, he was so miserable and angry. I saw him spit on someone once and say, 'Did you like that, you cunt? I have AIDS, too.' It was a long way from Ben Elton.

I got paid £800 a week for *Paramount City* – a fortune to me. I was used to getting 150 quid a week when I was gardening so now I was rich. And I was on BBC1! I told my parents, of course, and random girls too.

Each week different British comics would come on the show and tell me how funny I was. There was a different American comic on each week as well. Norm MacDonald, Steven Wright, Charles Fleischer – all kinds of people – and they too told me how funny I was. Man, was I funny! At this stage I really began to believe I was the cat's whiskers, the dog's bollocks, the ship's biscuit and the monkey's paw all rolled into one. Because I'd travelled so far so quickly, I began to think, *How far can I go? I could be Peter Sellers, couldn't I?*

I think a lot of performers experience this feeling. If you've dreamt of something all or part of your life and it comes true, you go a bit mad. No one dreams of vaguely working in show-business, presenting a Brit Award or doing *The Bill*: they dream of winning an Oscar.

The show was filmed in the Windmill Theatre and I'd invite people for a drink afterwards in the tiny upstairs bar, an even mix of mates and girls I wanted to impress. One night Paul Raymond appeared with bodyguards. He leant towards me and proffered his gnarly paw, holding me in his baleful gaze: 'I think you're the best thing on the show, young man. I don't understand all the others.'

It was hard to be humble. One of the porn industry's greats – our very own Hugh Hefner – had given me the nod. He didn't send over a busty bird but you can't have it all. I was now an uptown guy: how long before I was having drinks with Michael Caine and Shakira in the Connaught before dinner at the Ivy? How long before I won Rear of the Year and Philip Treacy started making hats for me? I'd gone from skulking through South East London looking for money in the street to being the toast of Soho. I spent my wages in an orgy of black cabs, overpriced designer shirts and corked wine. My ego had grown along with my wages. I was very judgemental about other comics on the show, and slagged off anyone who I thought wasn't up to scratch. I'd only been working a year and a half! I remember watching Lee Evans and saying to a friend, 'It's entertaining but he won't get anywhere with that physical stuff.' If I thought someone was good I'd say, 'You're brilliant, very funny,' thinking they must have been very excited to get the thumbs-up from me.

I had arrived, but I'd soon have to leave again. Though maybe not just yet.

Chapter Thirteen

My love life was looking up enormously. I had the option to start going out with an attractive, intelligent and stable girl or to push on with a series of one-night stands with slightly damaged and odd but sexy women. Being still full of self-loathing I chose the latter and got some predictable results.

I had a thing with a ginger girl who worked with handicapped children. She wanted me to talk like Tommy Cockles in bed, which was strange. I refused. He's not really a sexy man, is he? Though I suppose it was better than a lad asking me to wank him off dressed as Competitive Dad . . .

There was a beautiful mixed-race girl who I'd known vaguely from the neighbourhood, and who had a boyfriend, stopping me in the street and talking to me for way too long. The boyfriend was standing there and I felt a bit bad for him as she could scarcely conceal her attraction to me. It was weird: what was she attracted to? A couple of days later I was in the flat; it was midday and there was a knock at the door. It was her, all embarrassed and gushing – in the middle of the day. A booty call! I hardly knew her. I felt powerful and wise and manly all at once. 'I just thought I'd come round and see how you were,' she said. She was so embarrassed. It was strange, like she couldn't help herself, and all because I'd dressed up as a sixty-year-old man and talked about the Gurkhas.

I was so surprised I didn't even invite her in properly – we just stood about not knowing what to say to each other, although I still felt immensely cool. At one point she reached out and touched me on the chest and I felt like David Essex for a few seconds. It was all new to me, this. She left soon after that.

I was in a wine bar in Deptford and another girl, who'd been to my primary school and was incredibly pretty, broke down and started crying as a prerequisite for a snog. She'd just returned from Hong Kong and had obviously heard about my change in fortunes. I was happy with all this stuff, don't get me wrong, and took advantage of it as much as possible, but with her it felt too false and weird. She'd just got off the plane and I hadn't seen her since Mud were in the charts.

The following night I had a date with her but I chose to spend the evening with Paul Reed playing fruit machines. She was furious and swept into my flat wearing silver trousers and not a little eyeliner. She was so pretty. I felt I was in a bad eighties film. 'No one has ever done that to me before,' she said. We were strangers, though – how could she be so angry? I think the fact that I'd been trying to nudge bells and lemons on to win-lines with someone who used to be in the army was the reason she was so incandescent. Of course I loved all the fuss really; it made me feel like I was someone special.

Comic legend Malcolm Hardee had closed down the Tunnel and opened his new comedy club, Up the Creek, in the old snooker hall. It was bizarre: the very place where I had wasted vast tracts of my time had become my own personal comedy club. I always found snooker nights a bit depressing. The break of sixteen, the bad lager, the £5 wager, the boat people endlessly playing the fruit machine . . . But all that was a distant memory; it was now London's greatest comedy club – Malcolm said so. I'd played there a few times and done very well. By this point, with Tommy being on TV, I got a much better reception everywhere. People were in on the joke now and it seemed too easy sometimes. One night I was sitting at the Creek watching some comedy when Malcolm approached me and began to mutter a sort of comedy CV at me, claiming to have managed Rik Mayall, Harry Enfield and Alexei Sayle. He twirled his fag and whispered conspiratorially at me. I suddenly realised he was asking me if I wanted him to become my agent, and without a second thought I agreed. Malcolm Hardee, the man who stole Freddie Mercury's birthday cake, my agent? Why not? What a great place to start.

I've met people in comedy who think of Malcolm Hardee as a joke, as someone who wipes his arse on the curtains and gets his knob out at funerals, a clown, a ne'er-do-well. Yes, he was obsessed with exhibiting his giant balls, but that was the whole point of him. He treated his genitals like distorted gifts to the nation: he displayed them at any time, day or night, like a woman puts her washing on the line. Sober or drunk, they were just there. Often I'd be watching telly with him and he'd idly start playing with his knob. One of his sketches finished with him being naked and, like a stripper, he'd hang about in the nude talking to people for ages afterwards. But comedy is now so serious they have stand-up courses at university: it's a career choice for people who aren't funny. Malcolm was hilarious, gentle, obscene, loyal, stupid, childish, polite, timid and magnificent. Above all he was friends with everyone he met. Everyone at once understood him and was on his side. Malcolm had a knack (and this became clearer to me later, at his funeral) of making people believe they were his best friend. Loads of people I've spoken to thought of him this way; it made them feel special, the Hardee seal of approval. He wasn't picky about who he stamped it with, either: he loved hanging around with complete cunts. (He knew some truly awful people – he'd have loved David Brent; in real life they'd have been great mates.) But the only people I've heard slag him off are higher-ups in the comedy game, and you can't trust them anyway.

He was covered in spots and covered in glory. He liked soup, good curry and rum and Coke; on Mondays he ate chocolates and watched *The Bill*, but every other night he was out and about with a wildly differing selection of men and women. Everyone knew Malcolm – everyone. He had many catchphrases, including: 'Oi oi!'; 'Knob out!'; 'Dear personal friend of mine . . .' (whether he or she); 'My face is my passport'; 'Rice is for poofs'; 'I've seen them all come and go' (my personal favourite); 'I remember when this was all fields'; and 'Cor, he was shit' (in reference to an act).

He hated being on his own and loved to spend the whole day with you from dawn to dusk; provided you had no problem with pubs and the bookies' you'd have a good day. He was also enormously popular with the opposite sex and confounded other men's expectations again and again with his swordsmanship. Younger, better-looking comics would stare aghast as he wandered off into the night with another attractive woman – turning back, twitching and shrugging his shoulders. You'd be standing with him and he'd point to a lady, anyone from a well-known comic actress to a young punk chick or an old lady, and say, 'I fucked her.' You'd look at the woman in question and sometimes she'd know what he'd said and squirm slightly. It was difficult to tell whether he was telling the truth; with Malcolm anything was possible.

Way before *The X Factor* started humiliating people with mental problems Malcolm pushed the deluded and disturbed on to the stage. He'd deliberately book terrible open spots, people who weren't right in the head, and sit chuckling as they performed. There's a tape of him doing a gong show above a pub in Birmingham that features two of the most tragic acts I have seen: a man mumbling and wearing a cowboy suit who ends the show by shooting himself in the foot; and a large lady spinning and dancing in a nylon catsuit. You have to see it to believe it. He also pushed the following acts into the spotlight: Mr Methane (a farting man in a catsuit); Eddie Shit (a man who sang pop songs and replaced key words with 'shit'); Rockin' Gorby (a Gorbachev lookalike who sang); Chris Luby (an ex-army depressive who made aircraft and marching-band noises); and the Bastard Son of Tommy Cooper (a tiny Welsh self-harmer and contortionist). There were many more but you get the picture. Let's not be snobbish about these acts: at some point every one of them stormed Up the Creek and I'd rather see a speciality act than some kid in a T-shirt who wants to be Russell Howard. Though to be fair Eddie Shit did pale after the first four times you'd seen him.

When Malcolm died in 2005 a huge hole was left in the fabric of South East London. He was the father of alternative comedy and, more importantly, a father figure to scores of stand-up comedians who were kept going by his patronage. Put simply, if Malcolm thought you were funny, nothing else mattered. His funeral was an incredible affair – every decent stand-up of modern times was there and a few shit ones too. (Let's not forget the shit ones: it was Malcolm's encouragement of bad acts that gave confidence to the good ones.) To see so many comedians, people expert in hiding emotions, all openly weeping was incredibly moving. In death he became the Lady Diana of the comedy world; the people's Mr Punch had passed away and no one was laughing.

I was off the booze at Malcolm's funeral and didn't go to the piss-up afterwards. He'd been my close friend for fifteen years. I'd lived with him, toured with him and slept with him (he had a habit of climbing into your bed when pissed), and he was my best mate and my dad rolled into one. How could someone be a great influence and a terrible influence at exactly the same time? I cried my eyes out when he died, the first time I have truly cried for another human being. After I got married I'd seen less and less of him: you couldn't really fit Malcolm into married life. He'd behaved like a big kid at my wedding, urinating openly, eating cocaine and stealing purses. I'd expected that, as by then I'd become part of the establishment. At one point he'd heckled my father-in-law, looking at me as though I'd join in and call it all off.

In death to me he's become an almost biblical figure. I'm not sure if we've witnessed the passing of some kind of vagabond saint: the ragged clothes, the humble demeanour, the pustules and boils upon his back – did he flay himself alone in his simple room? He never spoke of religion and yet to this day he's still worshipped. It's a deification of sorts. Butchers, bakers, candlestick-makers, he was and is the people's champion. He rose from the great river and sank beneath its eddying currents. Long live the real king of comedy.

At this stage of my life I was on the brink of change with my drug use. I was about to progress from taking cocaine 'recreationally' to becoming a full-on coke monkey – all I needed was more money and I was going to really punish my brain and body. Cocaine held no fears for me. I'd done plenty of acid as a teenager and downers mixed with booze a good few times, so what was there to be scared of really?

I had no dependants and I was a TV comedian – I was meant to do coke, wasn't I? If I got hold of a hundred quid I would always buy a gram for fifty or sixty; if I got hold of forty quid I'd buy half a gram and have ten left over for beer. I was a simple soul. I didn't take it every day: I binged twice a week, sometimes a few of us round three gram sometimes just me with a gram. If I was out and about I dished it out.

I became a regular uptight ghostly fixture in the pubs and clubs of South East London, pubs in which I used to play the fruit machines and lose all my money. Not any more. Now I had plenty of cash, though it must have seemed to the bar staff that I had a terribly weak bladder too. I was always popping in and out of the loo. Each time I returned I'd ask for a drink in a slightly more serious manner – because that's the worst thing about coke: it stops you laughing. People began to come up to me and ask for it. Some of them I knew well and I didn't mind, I'd give them a line. Others were cheeky strangers who got rebuffed. It's a strange world, the sniffing, the facial tics, your heightened sexuality (often completely at odds with the girl you're attempting to upend), then there's the running out, the searching for the dealer, the grinding of the teeth, the second-to-last line/watery-pooh combo, the saving of the last line for when you get home, the rushing into the house and chopping it out before you've taken off your coat and then the grim realisation that you have no more and must toss and turn all night or down some thick green medicinal Night Nurse to aid your restless kip. Honestly, madam, what a fucking palaver and all in the name of a good time. And bear in mind that this was before I had a problem with it!

I met *Cold Feet* and *Fast Show* star John Thomson at a gig in Birmingham. He saw me doing Tommy and we hit it off straight away. We shared a few obsessions, namely Christopher Walken, video games and alcohol. John and I quickly became good friends. Largely because of work he decided to move down from Manchester and plot up in South East London. At first he lived in New Cross with Zoë Ball but eventually, after having the TV stolen four times in four weeks, he moved up to Blackheath Village. John always did a lot of voiceovers so he had plenty of cash, and he was very generous with everyone – especially me. With my *Paramount City* contract finished stand-up was providing my only income. I was earning OK money but hurled it away as soon as I got it. I took great pleasure in splashing money about among the people who'd known me as a poverty-stricken layabout; in the pub I was like an Arab – everyone got a drink.

John was mad about toys, joke shops, clowns and film memorabilia. He had a globe that told your fortune, talking robots and a fantastic collection of eighties action movies on video cassette.

We both loved film and spent hours watching vids, doing the accents and stuff. I would have loved to have done a double-act with John but we were both people who needed a nuts-and-bolts man to write down all the ideas and push us forward. We were too similar, really: we just wanted to have a laugh and our careers were doing OK. By this time I'd met Jonathan Ross through Jim and Bob and there was talk about doing a sitcom with his production company, Channel X, featuring Tommy Cockles. Mark Swan and I wrote a script and he was going to pitch to the then boss of BBC2, Alan Yentob.

In those days I was very headstrong and arrogant regarding work. After *Paramount City* Janet Street-Porter arranged a meeting with a view to offering me some sort of deal, but I was told by Jonathan and his Channel X companion Mike Bolland (the original Shrek) to hold out for the sitcom. I spent the night before the meeting at a friend's house in Lewisham taking violently strong cocaine. My friend was a criminal and people kept arriving, each one with eyes deader and more fishlike than the last. I was quite paranoid despite knowing the guy whose party it was. I suppose I thought it was big and clever to cultivate friendships with members of the underworld, though I have a genuine interest in crime and punishment having experienced it first-hand.

Of course I never talked about borstal to these guys – they were the real thing, and when they went down it was for years. I'd been on BBC1, though: I was in show business. There's a link between the entertainment industry and the criminal fraternity, a love of late nights and glamour; both sets of people get paid too much for doing too little. You could trace our friendship and that party right back to Sam Giancana and Frank Sinatra. (They never put a horse's head in Alan Yentob's bed, though, and Vegas is a bit more glamorous than Lewisham.)

I went to the meeting with Janet Street-Porter, hungover and with an attitude. She promptly offered me a slot on *Def II* – a magazine programme that showed on BBC2 at six-thirty, after *Star Trek* – doing Tommy Cockles. She said they'd build sets around me to complement the stories, so I could do what I liked. I refused: what a prat! I can safely say that was the biggest mistake of my career, turning down a TV series. We didn't get the sitcom. I don't blame Jonathan Ross, though: he was young and gung-ho; if he'd thought it through he might have told me to accept Janet's offer.

Much later I met Janet at Jim/Vic Reeves' wedding and we talked about it. She said, 'I knew you wouldn't get a sitcom – no one knew who the fuck you were!' I can laugh now, but only because of *The Fast Show*. On these small things a man's fate twists and turns in the breeze . . .

I had now settled into my vocation as stand-up comedian, which to the general public might seem a fascinating and terrifying way to earn a living but was the only thing I'd ever done with any success. I'd taken to it like a duck to water. I realise now how lucky I was having Jim and Bob squire me around and promote me, because I jumped up the ladder very fast, but I still had a decade of gigs in front of me, each one slightly different from the last. I've lost count of the number of people who've said to me, 'I don't know how you do that: I could never, ever, do stand-up comedy.' I always say, 'I've done worse things, more scary things; besides, I had no choice.' And I didn't: I was desperate.

Stand-up comedy is scary. The actual show is normally fine once you're up there, but waiting to do the show is the worst thing. Even now if I have a gig it sits in my mind all day like a spider. No matter what I do or however I entertain myself it nags away at the mind. You have to do it; it won't go away. All those people looking at you . . . Will you be shit? Will they be pissed and shout at you? Most of the time everything's fine but occasionally things go wrong: you have a bad gig and then the inquest starts, the examining of circumstances, the key points where you lost the audience, the excuses. Personally I'm terrible at dealing with the audience. I treat the whole thing as a theatre show and I don't encourage heckling, while some people live off the audience and get better laughs interacting with them than they do with their written material. It's true that if you're doing a twenty-minute spot and do ten minutes of it with the audience you can pick out your best stuff for the last ten. I regret never having learnt to deal with the punters, but up until 2009 I'd only ever performed live as a character so I never did the whole 'Where are you from?' thing. Also, when I started out I wanted to distance myself from what I considered observational stand-up comedy. I've had my moments with hecklers – put them down, arrested their development – but I see other comics and marvel at their ability to control a room.

Being a character further defended my ego from attack: if Tommy had a bad gig it wasn't me being booed – it was a character, someone else. I say that but it didn't change how I felt, of course; I felt terrible. I used to hate having a bad gig – it really did me in – but luckily I've had them very rarely. And later on the success of *The Fast Show* meant people came to see me and *wanted* to listen, though that's still not to say I was Chris Rock every night. (*No, really, you were ...*) Whenever I did a bit of TV during my early career I'd behave like a lottery winner, spending money left, right and centre; then, when the TV stopped, I'd be thrown back on to the rocks of stand-up, travelling the nation, my guts churning at the prospect of entertaining the good people of Hull or Aldershot or Dundee.

I used to find it depressing sometimes, gigging on my own, clutching my little bag containing Tommy's glasses and cravat, killing time at Euston before the train came, arriving at an empty venue, the smell of stale beer and fags. I'd be on my own all day – often I'd even stay on my own after the gig. Perhaps I should have connected more with the audience instead of the caretaker bloke at the venue (keys on belt, roll-ups, fire-prevention expertise). But my black mood was always replaced by a feeling of relief and a small sense of triumph when I'd done it again, they'd all laughed, everything was all right and I was a worthwhile person: and now for some interesting bottled lager and a curry, perhaps, or a conversation with a fat fan.

I didn't ever go out and comb the audience for available women. Plenty of stand-ups do – some check out their options before they go on stage, squinting from behind the curtain or (if they're unknown) just wandering about the room. I was single then so I didn't miss my home life so much: how can you miss an empty flat? All you're missing is the freedom to be on your own again, the freedom of not having to do a gig again, to walk around listening to REM or Laurel Aitken, to pay bills late or watch some televised sport.

I never wrote new material for Tommy, or very seldom did. I didn't do him justice in that way. He stagnated, and often in gigs I just went through the motions. Now I write every day. I have a wife and kids to support and other clichés, but in the early days I didn't give a fuck about building a career – I just did what I was offered or what Malcolm booked for me. I realise now that in this game you get out exactly what you put in, but back then I thought I'd be carried along on a cloud of moderate success for ever. Often when left to my own devices I'd drift into indolence: look out of the window, walk about my neighbourhood, ring people up and go for uninspiring drinks – anything but write comedy. But I'm an addict and addiction is a disease of negative thinking, so that's one excuse.

Now I write like a demon. (I'm going to bring this book in right on time!) That's what the threat of poverty plus the added responsibility of kids does to your brain. In this game you wake up one morning and you are yesterday's news. I've been yesterday's news for quite some time now and it's OK – in fact I'm not sure if I was ever today's news.

People always say I haven't changed but I'm sure I have somehow. I still feel the same inside but my children are a blessed relief, as children won't allow you to mire yourself in self-obsession. I have no time for endless personal analysis – children will not tolerate procrastination or opting out of reality; they bite you and poke you in the eyes. This makes things very simple. My kids are my life now and that is it. I still retain an essential selfishness, though, which nourishes me through sleep deprivation, nappy changing, toy overflow and general noise and disobedience problems.

Having been on telly and experienced first-hand its ego- and wallet-healing properties, I wanted to get back as soon as possible. I did a few little bits as Tommy here and there on some more chat shows. I did *Barrymore* and a really pointless *Pebble Mill at One* with Alan Titchmarsh, who kept turning to the audience and saying, 'I'm completely lost – are you?' ruining the joke. He seemed to possess the intellect and wherewithal of a sock puppet – a sock puppet without anyone's hand in it. His enormous success is a depressing indicator of how daytime TV has become night-time TV: people like him planting bulbs, or cooks cooking meat in different ways, now get the millions of viewers comedy used to get. It's sad that a chummy, tousle-haired, mush-brained young man who does brass rubbing or keeps sparrows in his wellies is now a far better bet for ratings than an original comedy show. People worrying what Nigella would say if they didn't have crème fraiche on their treacle tart, or sitting in a shed with Monty Don? Fuck off: it's just not good enough.

I carried on gigging, a lot of it with Malcolm Hardee – it was always more fun that way. Among other things we did a few Edinburghs. It's a beautiful city but I never got it. A comedy festival is a strange thing to be part of: comics don't do festive because they're too busy watching everybody – they're always on their toes, a bit wary to really let go – and that atmosphere is stifling. You take all those comedians, with their bent dreams and their needy bar-side manners, and put them all in one place, all in one pub, and the vibe is not cool, brother. Add a few grams of Scottish cocaine and people really get twitchy.

Young people come up from university. Firm friends each do a solo show: one guy sells out, while the other plays to tumbleweeds and the catcalls of a few Norwegian drunks. His friend is proclaimed a genius and he, in his head, is proclaimed a failure over and over again. All that pain is forced into the atmosphere of the bar and bears down on you; there's too much tension everywhere. A comedian can work a room but what happens when everyone in that room is working the room? There's no real dialogue, everyone finishing each other's sentences, shaded responses to false points well made. Not for me.

The only point of going to Edinburgh was to do well at *Late and Live*, the late show at the Gilded Balloon. I always stormed it for some reason, even though my proper shows were often lacklustre. I suppose you want the respect of your peers – I did anyway. And Tommy always kept his end up.

The year I remember was the year I invited a girl up. I'd first met her at the Ministry of Sound at three in the morning. She was tall and olive-skinned, wore all black with biker boots, and had a slightly cruel mouth and a suspicious manner. Sexy, you'd say, but unhappy – a very common combination. We went back to my mate's council flat in Tanner's Hill, Deptford (classy), as for some reason I was between abodes. She spent a lot of time in the cab telling me not to get the wrong idea: she didn't intend to sleep with me, do any heavy petting or even have a hug. We got back. I took another E; she drank a half-bottle of Bison vodka and fell asleep. I watched over her sleeping form, gurning quietly – all you could hear was the creaking of my teeth and the low thump of my heart and the bass from the stereo. It was effortlessly romantic. When she awoke we went to the pub and she started boozing again. She kept saying things like, 'You're not very good-looking, are you?' or 'There's nothing happening here, you know.' I'd smile amiably and pot a red, thinking, *I will make you love me*. I love a challenge. She was like one of those hunted, raised-by-wolves people; she'd stare at you a bit too long, narrowing her eyes. She was aggressive, serious and emotionally broken. As I said: perfect girlfriend material.

Aaaaaaaaargh! Up the Creek Comes to Edinburgh was the title of Malcolm's show. All the 'a's meant it was the first thing in the programme. Malcolm always had little endearing schemes like that, of which he was immensely proud.

He'd put together a top-class variety bill: Boothby Graffoe, a solid comic who did comedy songs that were actually quite good (I got on very well with him, which was all that mattered); and Terri Rogers, a sixty-year-old ventriloquist act. She was five feet tall and looked like a pug, more dead than alive; she was always covered in white powder with bright-red lipstick like cold veal and tomatoes (that's Graham Greene). She had that thing that a lot of performers of her generation had, a sort of regal demeanour: they believed themselves to be involved in a higher calling, treading the boards. She loved Tommy, of course – he reminded her of the old days. The shows were fun and we had a laugh. Terri's show was actually very good, too. She had a foul-mouthed puppet; I can't remember his name but he had that trademark sinister face crucial to any vent act. She'd remonstrate with him like a maiden aunt and he'd just say, 'Fuck off.' It was different. Malcolm was good at discovering old speciality acts that went well on the alternative circuit.

The best thing about doing the festival is staying in these fantastic mansion flats full of antiquities, with beautiful huge rooms, sandstone spiral staircases and old copies of the *Lady*. It was a real treat. Though how the four of us (not counting the lunatic woman I'd invited) were supposed to live together I had no idea. Terri ate only fried food and bags of crisps. She'd put twelve sausages (cheap ones) in a pan with cold oil and leave them heating slowly for an hour, until they started weeping, then she'd approach me in the splendid drawing room and stand by the fireplace with a straight back, alternately chewing a sausage butty and smoking while talking to me about the business. I was normally hungover and it was hard work. Boothby found it very amusing that she had taken such a shine to me; she thought he was below her somehow.

Malcolm would be in his dressing gown in bed with a broad-shouldered Scottish woman playing crib.

After a few days Terri started picking up on my coolness towards her. She'd approach me, begin a conversation and then shriek, 'You hate me!' and retire to her room. I felt I was in some weird Victorian comic strip.

Then the girl I'd invited arrived. She spent her first hour there repeating her mantra: the 'No sex for Simon, not ever' routine. She was very aggressive when laying down this stuff and I was under no illusions: it was going to be tough to get my oats, but I was going to try. Malcolm walked past me, said, 'Mad,' and went out.

So the girl was here, drinking a lot. Later she came to the show and slept through it, her snores strangely complementing Tommy's quiet ruminations. I was angry under my blazer, though: there were lots of girls who would have given their eye teeth to be in her shoes – row D, seat 16 of the Pleasance Theatre – and she was asleep! It's amazing what men will put up with for the faintest whiff of a promise of a chance of not much.

That night we slept in the same bed: brilliant. *Yes! Yes! Yes!* I brushed my teeth nervously, practised holding my stomach in then climbed into bed. She was unconscious, breathing heavily with her mouth open like a fish. I was enormously turned on by this and looked down on her like Zeus: she was totally in my power. I lifted her arm. It was very heavy and I let it fall. *If an arm falls in the bedroom and no one is there to hear it does that mean I won't get my end away?* She was out for the count. I went and slept in the other room.

The next night I squired her around the hip hang-outs of the festival, getting lots of winks of approval. One bloke said, 'You lucky bastard.' If only they knew . . . It was like dating Sleeping Beauty except she wouldn't wake up. That night was much the same as the first but this time Boothby and I had to drag her in to a spare room because she fell asleep on the floor of the drawing room. Terri was appalled. We smashed her head into a vase by accident. She didn't wake up, but we were trying not to laugh. This was more fun than sex, I realised, and I decided to give up. Boothby and I smoked some Scottish hash and went to bed. I'd backed the wrong horse but Terri was a bit too old really.

On the third night I had a really good chat with the girl and felt I was getting somewhere; I was almost getting to know her. When she started to get more and more upset I suddenly realised she was trying to tell me something really horrible about something that had happened – abuse I think. I was terrified. We sat very close on hard chairs in the kitchen, the strip light buzzing. The door opened slowly and Malcolm appeared, very drunk and wearing a dressing gown. He approached her from behind, cupping his cock and balls, twitching and shrugging. I always took the shrugging to mean: 'It's nothing; it's only my knob.'

The girl was crying. I leapt up and pushed Malcolm out of the room. She didn't notice anything, being covered in her all-consuming misery. She went to bed and I cooked an enormous breakfast and ate it in the moonlight. It hadn't panned out exactly as I hoped, but what can you do? I've always been attracted to women like Sleepy but why? I'm not like that – they are not kindred spirits. Why put yourself through all that grief? Why not go out with a nice lady bus driver? Later on, in therapy, I was told I *was* one of those people.

I think it's important to have at least one destructive relationship, though (I have had two fuck-off ones) so that when you meet someone half sensible you can snap it up (which is what I did eventually, but that was a long way off).

Chapter Fourteen

Chris Luby was one of Malcolm's discoveries, a fifty-year-old RAF fanatic with a moustache and khakis. He was a strange man, obsessed with all things military. I think he'd been in the army and got thrown out or had flat feet or something. I may be doing him a disservice here: he was the antithesis of the standard waspish middle-class stand-up, and he carried with him a whiff of the parade ground and bunk-room torment.

He was very morose in his cups, though. We did a mini-tour of the Midlands, two nights. The first show was in Leicester, where we'd been told the venue manager would put us up for the night. On arrival I was horrified to see that said venue manager was a crusty. He smiled at me, rolling a cigarette. Drum tobacco and dreadlocks: not my favourite combo. I felt depressed.

Luby started the show with a parade-ground sergeant major and ended with Spitfires and Lancaster bombers over the Channel. It was very loud and always went well, but it was so odd as an act – a man impersonating aircraft. I did Tommy, which went OK. The audience filtered out of the venue. The crusty was a bit stinky. Luby bought a crate of beer; his eyes had gone. It was going to be a long night. The crusty drove us deeper and deeper into the slums of Leicester while Luby spat in my ear. He was very happy, then he started talking about his wife and seemed less happy.

Yes, it was a squat. We drank warm beer and Luby started shouting at the crusty: 'You're an ugly bastard!' The crusty thought it was hilarious. After an hour of barrack-room bawling I suggested we retired before Luby began square-bashing in earnest. Luby refused, looking at me in disgust. I was so defeated I couldn't even drink any more. Eventually Luby and I repaired to a room with a broken window, dusty warped floorboards and peeling wallpaper – all that was missing was the child's doll with empty eye-sockets. The cold night air rushed in to greet us and blew Luby's pointless drivel all around. It wasn't his fault he was who he was, but it was three in the morning and we had to go to Birmingham together in the morning. He began to get undressed. When he was down to his brown underpants his legs were muscly and shiny white in the pale light. Suddenly he pitched forward and started snoring, bent over like a man prone and ready for some terrible sexual punishment. He farted loud and long and it smelt of dead dinner ladies. He was snoring and farting at the same time, cramped in his crazy yoga position. I noticed some dark stain on my blanket. I lay back and thought of England.

The next day, he started drinking on the train. His eyes went again. When we got to Brum I told him I had some friends to meet in the shopping centre; he looked at me like a little boy, crushed. I skated off nonetheless. Unfortunately he found me on my own in a Wimpy an hour later nursing a quarter pounder with cheese. I told him my friends were ill. He seemed very pleased to have linked up again and informed me there was an airfield nearby we could visit. Reluctantly I followed him, my head hung low. Actually it wasn't that bad, though: he really came alive there, almost jumping up and down, pointing out different aircraft and marvelling at the hangar dimensions. That night we stayed in a Travelodge and it felt like Claridge's. I slept the sleep of the dead.

We parted company at Charing Cross. As my train pulled out he saluted me from the platform. He did it really well, juddering his hand by his head and snapping his heels together. I nearly cried. I felt deep love for him: somehow we'd bonded without me knowing. I was puzzled, too. Perhaps people like Luby were meant to die under fire. He'd been born at the wrong time, and been denied his chance to participate in mortal combat, and now he was forced to walk the earth like a zombie Biggles without a plane. Whatever happens I will never forget his snore-fart combo. *Present arse! At ease!*

I was in Up the Creek one night when Malcolm suddenly materialised at my side very excited. He leant towards my ear like a ticket tout: 'There's a bloke downstairs wants to give you five grand to make an album.' The combination of his childlike glee and his constant bursts of laughter quickly confirmed that this was no wind-up and we scampered down from the upstairs bar like two schoolboys after one bag of chips.

I was greeted at the bar by a tall, dark and handsome stranger with fantastic hair and expensive clothes. My expert knowledge of pop trivia informed me that this was none other than Mark Fox, the bongo player in Haircut 100. He now worked for East West Records as an A&R man and very much wanted me to do a comedy album for them. Malcolm kept guffawing every time he mentioned the money, turning to strangers in the bar and pointing at Mark Fox as if he was an idiot. There were times I wished Malcolm behaved a bit more like Swifty Lazar but I'd made my bed and had to lie in it.

I was no stranger to the comedy album – Pete and Dud and Ivor Cutler were my all-time heroes and as a young lad I'd discovered the Peter Sellers LP *Songs for Swingin' Sellers* in my dad's record collection and been captivated by it. I particularly liked a skit involving a theatre producer auditioning a series of hopeless musical acts. The producer (Sellers) was very close to the mike and his agonised and bored sighs were laid over the screeching and wailing of the acts in the background. It was very intimate and brought you right into his world, that album. Hearing it was a revelation to me and it influenced me a great deal when I came to perform Tommy Cockles. You don't need to shout – that's what I got from it. If you spoke softly people could still hear you. I also had all the Monty Python records, which were hilarious. Monty Python laid the ground for all the comedy written and performed by my generation. Without them where would we be?

Malcolm insisted that we hire a lawyer to go over my contract with East West. It turned out I got five grand up front and five grand on completion of the album. I have no idea if the lawyer was real or not, as I never met or entered into any correspondence with him. I know I got three grand after various deductions and spent it on an Audio Lab amplifier, a Marantz CD player and a set of speakers. With my home complete I spent the next few months buying up all my favourite albums on CD and lying on the floor listening to them.

Mark Swan was still on the scene at this point and we set about writing a Tommy Cockles comedy album. We were set to record with a guy who had produced Tears for Fears – a nice chap, and up for it, but also very busy doing other projects. The sketch I remember was Tommy in the trenches. It started with him playing cards in a British trench; at some point, and under heavy fire, he hurled himself up and on to the battlefield, then sprinted across it killing everything in his path before jumping down into the German trench and dispatching all their soldiers. I was very keen to get this sketch just right. I had the German soldiers playing cards and recorded three different voices, which were mixed together. It sounded amazing. We had mortar fire and machine guns. It was very exciting but a slow process: the combination of me procrastinating, the producers doing other projects and the studio not being near my house caused the project to drag its feet. The best part of the whole thing was going up to the East West offices in Kensington. Mark Fox's PA was called Hannah and was very attractive. She had a long body honed by hours of karate and sensible eating and was a bit like a Bond girl but lived in King's Cross not Chelsea. I fell a bit in love with the idea of her and the idea of me and her. She was the kept woman of a famous married rock star who was also a karate expert, and I never came on too strong with her in case he suddenly came smashing through the window and beat the shit out of me. All the same she laughed in all the right places during conversation (which was when I stopped talking). I had no experience of this kind of girl: they were beyond my sphere of experience. They knew what was what and who was who. I really fancied her.

The trouble with all my relationships at this time was marrying up the two people I was – the 'before' and 'after' versions of me: the funny, interesting, dynamic man on the way up I'd appear to be during courtship, and the whining, selfish depressive I could be once in a relationship. I would be very agreeable on early dates and then could be very disagreeable once betrothed. Where was the interesting, interested boyfriend of yore? What ails him? Look, there he is, watching *Midweek Sports Special* and eating curry in bed, moaning about his lack of career opportunities.

He sighs, he groans, he laments his lot . . . But wait – what's this? He's on the TV screen, wearing a hat. He leaps from the bed, intensely serious, studying his fizzog. 'Listen to this bit,' he says, turning back to study your face. He looks young now, and so alive he illuminates the room. 'Ssshhh!' he shouts. 'Ssshhh!' He's not on for long, but it seems to be long enough: the moaning man has been quite forgotten and has been replaced by a happy child. He gets out his pen out and starts to write something down. Afterwards he lies in bed talking about himself for an hour and a half.

I was an emotional cripple then, still smarting over all the injustices I had suffered. The dangerous thing was that I was now successful and could use that fact as a weapon in my relationships. I thought being on TV gave me some sort of 'Get out of jail free' card in terms of responsibility. All my favourite comics were bad at real life: Tony Hancock, Peter Sellers, Peter Cook, errr, Peter Glaze . . . I think then I thought that it was a trade-off – that you got to be funny and be on TV but you suffered in your private life. It wasn't until much later that I realised all the stuff that had happened to me was largely my fault.

The comedy album never got finished. The producer was taken off the project by the boss of East West in Spain in order to produce an album of flamenco music for his son. They paid me off, though, so I didn't care.

In 1993 I finally parted company with Malcolm. I'd been fiercely protective of him while he managed me, though other acts were constantly telling me to stay away from him. Finally his relentless desire to fuck about and not be professional began to get tiresome. We once went to a number of production companies with an idea and after trekking round Soho I asked him which one he thought would be best for us.

'Channel X,' he said.

'Why?' I replied.

'They're on the ground floor,' he shot back.

Of course I loved being not professional too. I wanted to be the wild card, the maverick danger man, but I also knew inside I wanted to act as well as do gigs and Malcolm couldn't get me any work in that field. When I left his stewardship he was upset and informed me quietly that he'd charged VAT on every gig he booked for me and put it in his pocket. I was sort of confused and a bit hurt by this, but I knew he didn't mean anything by it. Besides, he'd robbed the government, not me.

I signed up with John Thomson's agent, Jan Murphy, a motherly lady who had offices in Beak Street. John had won the Perrier Comedy Award the previous year in tandem with Steve Coogan, though it was – at least in the media – seen very much as Steve's victory. John was sort of his unglamorous assistant, not really allowed to show what he could do. At that time the Perrier was a big deal: if you won it you were assured TV fame and untold riches (well, a TV pilot anyway). Now the award is about as much use as a chocolate fireguard, and changing the name of it didn't help.

John was bitter about being overlooked. Coogan was correctly judged to be a fantastic talent and someone who would go all the way to the top. He had Armando Iannucci and Patrick Marber in his camp, not forgetting Peter Baynham too. Go and look at their CVs on Wikipedia and you'll see they're all clever, focused people, high achievers, to put it mildly.

John needed to make the next step but he didn't have them, he had me – 'Hooray! Can I borrow a tenner . . . ?' He kept moaning about no one knowing he'd won the Perrier.

'Don't worry,' I said. 'We'll do a show at Edinburgh that'll knock Coogan's effort into a cocked hat.'

'It'll have to be good,' he ruminated. 'After all, I am a Perrier Award winner.'

'Don't worry,' I said.

I'd met Caroline Aherne on the comedy circuit. She did a character called Sister Mary Immaculate (a nun, of course) and had appeared on *Paramount City* alongside me too. She was good friends with both John and Steve Coogan and those three were the Manchester comedy scene. We got on well. We both wanted to do characters on telly. She really made me laugh and always took the piss in a fond and knowing manner – and I love girls who take the piss. (Although that was then: if you see me in the street now and shout, 'Oi baldy, lay off the pies!' you might get short shrift.)

Somehow John and I roped in Caroline to join us. She was a bit reluctant but we badgered her. To me she was always the most talented performer and writer of our generation – Mrs Merton was brilliant, so warm and clever she was irresistible, and *The Royle Family* was a radical bit of television (though few people at the BBC understood it and it was a miracle it was broadcast at all).

We booked the Assembly Rooms for two weeks during the festival, then John and I sat down and began to write the show in earnest.

A typical day's work went as follows . . . We'd convene in John's house at around ten in the morning after a good night's sleep. Unfortunately at the time only three nights out of seven involved such a good sleep; the other four were spent bending over mirrors, talking loudly to each other about ourselves with occasional drifts into self-pity over parental slights or self-respect issues, watching obscure Christopher Walken films and playing *ToeJam & Earl* on the Sega. We both were gifted character comedians but had no discipline. I wanted to write, though, and eventually did. John, on the other hand, wanted people to write for him. Together we got on too well to actually do any work. John made me laugh like no other person I'd ever met and I returned the favour. Ideas would be thrown up: 'Genius!' one of us would cry. 'Let's write it down.' But often we didn't have a pen, let alone a piece of paper.

Twenty minutes later we'd find ourselves eating crisps and watching *The Dead Zone*, with John perfectly mimicking Walken's weird voice. This went on and on: different films, different-flavoured crisps. Other times we'd go out to obscure pubs at lunchtime, point at people and imagine their lives. The result was the same: no work. As Edinburgh approached we started getting nervous. Caroline refused to come down to the Big Smoke to work. We slagged her off for a bit, using her absence as an excuse to do even less work.

It was strange for me to be hanging out in New Cross reborn as a successful person. I'd walked the very streets outside John's door in the freezing cold, penniless and pointless, sitting in cafés making the *Sun* last an hour then handing it back to its owner, playing fruit machines, every penny goes.

Eventually we decided to go up to Manchester and thrash the show out with Caroline, who very kindly put us up at her modest home. It was like the 1950s in the suburb where she lived: all the tradesmen who came to the door greeted her by her first name and immaculately dressed old people sat around on benches laughing. Everyone was so friendly and it was a marked change from New Cross, I can tell you.

It soon became apparent that Caroline was as nervous as we were about the show. I don't think she wanted to do it at all – and I don't think this was just because John and I hadn't yet done any work. Comics often struggle to work as a team because the roles are blurred. Who's the drummer? Who's the guitarist? Basically we're all singers and we all know best. That's why when a comic gets a team of nuts-and-bolts people around them – people who defer to the giant ego – he or she can really fly. We bickered and argued but still had fun. Caroline was very house-proud and at some stage I pissed on the floor of the downstairs toilet and didn't wipe it up. This didn't help matters. She and I got on very well, though, despite her enormous Bristols, which I must say were very distracting.

One day she was sitting on her sofa and turned to me. 'I'm going to do a show one day with a family just watching telly, not doing anything,' she said. 'And I'm going to get Bob and Sheila from *Brookside* to be in it.' You could tell with her that it was going to happen – it was something about the set of her jaw. She was someone to be taken seriously. Why does Manchester produce so many gifted people? Compare it to Liverpool or Leeds or London for that matter and in terms of music and comedy the Mancunians are like the Ancient Greeks.

I came up with a sketch called 'Have a dance' in which I played a light-entertainment host called Dave Nice who would invite ordinary members of the public to 'come on down and have a dance . . .' For instance: 'Let's meet Sarah Bidewell! Sarah lives over a pet shop in Bootle; she likes watching documentaries about plants, staring into the middle distance and keeping tabs on the local immigrant population. Sarah loves cats and is a chocoholic. Sarah, come on down and have a dance!' Then John or Caroline would do silly dancing. Quite a simple premise but way before its time.

We were to open with a spoof musical number, a sort of piss-take of 'Meet the gang 'cause the boys are here'. It was pretty funny but took a lot of rehearsing and Caroline was reluctant to say the least. In the end we arrived in Jockland without a show: we hadn't properly rehearsed the first half and had given up on the second, deciding instead to perform our established characters.

The first night was sold out and the atmosphere backstage very tense. I think we all knew we were in big trouble but what could we do? The show must go on and all that. We had called the show *Do You Like Us?* Which, looking back, was inviting disaster.

I had a crawling, sick feeling in my stomach. There were backstage people wandering around with headsets like Captain Scarlet; they seemed to be the only professional people present.

Our agent Jan Murphy was in the audience with her assistant and partner, John Wood, a mildly paranoid and caustic homosexual from Scotland. He wore glasses with red frames and questionable jackets but he was rock hard on the phone and took little shit from anyone.

Tommo and I took the stage and began the song. People were chuckling. I saw Jan and John sat in the third row looking expectant, their faces an exact indicator of what was happening inside our stomachs.

Caroline's cue came and went, then she appeared, started singing, forgot the words and ran away – she really did, she ran offstage! John and I fell apart and started mumbling, then stopped singing altogether. The tape played on and the audience went quiet. I stared at Jan and John Wood, who looked terrified. Just as the venue fell into complete silence John started clapping along to the music, his palms beating out a hollow echo of despair. People peered at him as if he was in the show. I think he tried to sing along too. We were certainly showing Steve Coogan the way to do it.

John Thomson and I left the stage. So now we were all backstage and there was no one onstage. Who was meant to be onstage? The crowd started talking. What next? We were all frozen in terror. The show was sold out – *sold out*! I think we did 'Have a dance' next, which went OK, albeit with people not knowing their lines. Again we came off and the stage was left empty again, giving the audience another chance to voice their amazement at the shambles laid out before them.

The rest of the show veered between car crash, earthquake and flood. When it was all over we sat backstage like puppies pulled from a sack in the canal, shivering and silent. And first into the dressing room? Yes, you got it: Steve Coogan.

This crushing mess was no one's fault but our own. We'd behaved like kids on a school journey going kayaking without a kayak expert and no kayak; we ended up in the river and it was cold. Did I learn anything from this? Sort of. I knew then that I needed someone to help me get my ideas on paper and in focus. Mark Swan would never have allowed that shambles to occur but he was long gone. Where was my half-man, half-desk person? I'd have to wait a bit longer to really shine.

Chapter Fifteen

In 1993 Jonathan Ross's production company, Channel X, embarked on the glorious folly that was *Saturday Zoo*, a music and comedy show to be broadcast on Channel Four at ten o'clock sharp on Saturday nights. Jonathan was hosting and there was to be a big-name guest every week; during the run these included Danny DeVito, Christopher Walken and Jean-Claude Van Damme (big enough for you?). Channel X also hired a fantastic array of comic talent to appear, among whom were Steve Coogan, Rebecca Front, Patrick Marber, me, John Thomson, Rowland Rivron, Kevin Day, Graham Fellows and Mark Thomas – plus Denis Leary, who appeared in filmed segments. Among the writers were David Quantick and Geoff Deane. Various script editors came and went, including Steve Punt and an old bloke who'd worked with Peter Cook and Dudley Moore. Addison Cresswell, the *enfant terrible* of comedy agents, withdrew his acts on the grounds that *Saturday Zoo* was a 'chicken with its head cut off' show. He was probably right.

All the comics were paid £1,000 a week regardless of whether or not they appeared. Appearing one week didn't necessarily mean you'd appear the next, and some performers who couldn't get a look in just gave up after a while and took the money. Sketches were written, ideas thrown up and characters discussed in a mess of egos, backbiting, pure joy and general tomfoolery.

The only lasting thing to come out of it was Coogan's character Paul Calf, which was rightly seen as brilliant and became an instant classic. Calf appeared every other week over the ten-week run, while other characters came and went. The producer was a chubby-cheeked Kenton Allen, who later became a hugely successful comedy producer. On *Saturday Zoo*, however, he tried to please all the people all the time and came unstuck. He was under a lot of pressure – not just from a stream of fame-hungry comedians but also from Channel Four, who weren't getting the ratings they'd hoped for. Allen really was the man in the middle and by the end of the series his leopard-skin waistcoat was looking a bit threadbare.

I, on the other hand, was having the time of my life. And I couldn't believe my luck: by some mysterious quirk of admin, John and I got paid double for the first two weeks – two grand a week! When someone noticed the error John Wood, who dealt with financial matters at Jan Murphy's office, put his foot down with Channel X: 'It's your mistake,' he said. He told them that if they were very nice he'd relent and accept the normal fee for the rest of the run, but we were keeping the extra for that first fortnight.

The show was an hour long and live – yes, *live*. It was scary: if you fucked up you couldn't go back and do it again; if you swore or overran you were in trouble. Handsome devil and all-round muso Sean Rowley was in charge of booking the bands and he did us all proud. Among others we had Stereo MCs, Suzanne Vega and PM Dawn (and they were weird, man). Rowley wore a fur coat with drainpipes and loafers but I didn't let that put me off. He was the man who later founded Guilty Pleasures, a truly broad musical church where nothing is naff, and our shared love of music led to a firm friendship that continues to this day. We were always the blokes putting on Medicine Head singles and obscure David Crosby albums back at people's houses. In those relatively early house-music days people would get very upset, pushing us aside and putting the nodding-dog music back on, terrified of losing face. I once said that Julian Cope was much more important to British pop music than Elvis in front of a group of ravers who'd metamorphosed from rockabillies. I was only joking but my point didn't go down very well either way, I can assure you; it was only the E flowing through their veins that saved me from getting a black eye.

The comic line-up fell into three camps: focused, talented and hard-working (Steve Coogan, Patrick Marber and Rebecca Front); unfocused, talented and soft-working (me and John Thomson); and unfocused (Rowland Rivron). (By the way, if you want to see Rowland at his best try to find his *Set of Six* series – it's absolutely brilliant, one of my favourite shows ever.)

I was by this stage of my life using cocaine regularly. I'd also started taking ecstasy and sweating in darkened rooms drinking water. I was a weekend raver and I loved it: being able to dance on your own all night and hug strangers – what's not to like? Here was a drug that actually did what it said on the tin, if only for a limited period.

I remember at one production meeting a sketch was discussed in which Patrick Marber was to appear as a raver. I spoke up immediately, my argument being that Marber couldn't portray an E monkey when he'd never taken the drug. John kept telling me to be quiet but I wouldn't have it. As the meeting broke up I piped up again: 'I took three Es last Thursday night – why can't I play the part?' I was deadly serious: to me comedy characters have to be based in strict reality; that was my point, however stupidly I put it. I knew Marber wouldn't play the part properly and he didn't – he was awful. I kept going on about it but people didn't get what I was on about. (I don't think he'll be suing me over these remarks: he's since gone on to bigger and better things.)

Throughout my career people have misjudged my deep seriousness about comedy in general. I've been written off as a chump, as someone who doesn't know what he's doing. I suppose I was a bit all over the place in those days. One day the political stand-up Mark Thomas was working in one room, looking at me and John through the window in another. We were looking back at him. I kept saying to John, 'He's a bit of a weirdo, isn't he?'

'Don't look,' said John. 'He's watching us.'

Later on Mark came up to John and said, 'Simon is mad, isn't he? Quietly mad.'

Obviously it's anecdotes like this that will push this book right to the top of the bestsellers lists worldwide ... I was certainly very up at this stage, though. I was finally having a laugh and a career at the same time: I was mad for it and it was mad for me.

I was single at the time and living in a room in a large house in Blackheath. The owners were artists and there was a tree in the living room that formed part of the building's structure. There was ornate carving everywhere, and trompe-l'oeil panels; it was amazing. A bit damp but you can't have it all. My tiny space at the top of the house did me fine.

Obviously my main plan during the course of *Saturday Zoo* was to appear as a series of groundbreaking, hilarious comedy characters, the only trouble being that I had no one to help me achieve this. My old sparring partner Mark Swan was incommunicado. I was on my own.

In addition to performing as much as possible Patrick Marber wrote, directed and fine-tuned Steve's performance as Paul Calf. They were sticklers, the pair of them, who left nothing to chance and the results were there for all to see. I, meanwhile, was busy befriending Jonathan Ross – going back to his house, smoking fags and forcing him to play Steely Dan at three in the morning. I was totally captivated by Ross. This was still the early nineties, remember, and before celebrity had become a derided, hollow boat in which anyone could sail provided they debased themselves in some way. Famous people were still fairly exotic and respected, and Ross was the boy-king. Intelligent and charismatic, he'd met a lot of famous people and had funny little stories about some of them. Thinking about it now I realise he never slagged anyone off – he was always positive about everyone – unlike me, who would coat people off at the drop of a hat.

It was all quite close-knit; he didn't have folk back from the pub. He was and is, basically, a family man, and his mum was always there and his father-in-law too. It wasn't very rock 'n' roll – we just played charades and stuff. (I was horrified when I went through his CDs one night and found mainly Disney and musical-theatre compilations. Now I have kids of my own I realise why, but at the time I thought he might be a homosexualist on the side.) I look back on that time as being really exciting and fun: I was getting paid to dress up and piss about, I met loads of new people, everyone told me I was funny and at the end of the night we fell into cabs and went home.

Part of me was desperate to hang out in nice houses in nice areas with people who were going somewhere. I'd been skint for so long I thought I'd had my chips, yet here I was hanging out with various top bananas. Of course, at the end of the night I'd return to my little room in Blackheath and think, *I'm earning a fortune – why haven't I rented a proper flat with a garden and a dishwasher? Why haven't I got a little mortgage together? Why do I claim to like living in this room? It's fucking tiny! Where's my car? Where's my accountant?* I didn't even own a telly and yet earlier in the evening I'd been helping Jean-Claude Van Damme use the fag machine, laughing with Danny DeVito as he said something I couldn't quite understand and drinking herbal tea with Suzanne Vega. I'd look around and think, *You're still a fuck-up: don't kid yourself; don't get any ideas.* Then, after my comedown was over, I'd be cock of the walk once again.

Halfway through the series I finally persuaded a girl named Camilla Deaken to go out with me. I'd seen her around in various clubs. She worked for the *Face* and was very pretty and clever and laughed a lot. Initially she'd been reluctant to make a go of it with me, preferring the more conventionally good-looking type of blokes, but I won her over in the end. She was very solid as a person, and loyal; I think I sensed those qualities early doors and clung on. We got on very well and had a great laugh. It worked out nicely because she also got on very well with Jonathan Ross's wife, Jane, so we'd spend quite a lot of time hanging out with them. (In fact we all went on holiday together to Miami, but that's another story.)

Camilla knew a lot of North London faces on the club scene and I started to listen to house music in earnest. We went to the Milk Bar in Soho a lot, and to various warehouse dos and Full Circle out past Heathrow.

I used to enjoy that scene. She had some really funny friends, proper characters who really made me laugh – John Howard, Dave Vickers, Sean Rolfe and her two best mates, Lesley and Sarah, who thought I was a postman. There was also Nicky Holloway, the pirate king of the Balearics, who made the most bunged-up, pug-ugly clubber feel like Cary Grant. He looked like someone who'd been thrown out of a helicopter by Mexican drug dealers: he had a voice like wet gravel and a face like a Peruvian shoe-shine boy who never ate his veg. Holloway started and finished more night-clubs than all the rest of them put together and was a stone-cold classic, the twisted, mangled mirror image of Tony Blackburn seen through a murky pool. He was a technicolour cartoon character among cardboard cut-outs, a Tasmanian devil crossed with the Artful Dodger. Someone should sign him up to write his memoirs – he has seen it all, done it all and spoilt it all, just like me.

Before E arrived I'd go to clubs and try to have a laugh but I found it all a bit dressy and cold: people would spend three hours getting ready, limp into the club, go and do their hair then stand still by the wall for the rest of the night. Also there was always a chance of a punch-up if you trod on someone's foot, which I was apt to do. (Back in Deptford I once trod on an alleged Yardie's toe but was luckily with some people from Jah Shaka's sound system who smoothed things out.) I've knocked over a lot of drinks, spilt amyl nitrate, dropped Es, smashed into people and fallen head over heels a few times during my clubbing days. I've never spilt any cocaine, though: that always found its way into my giant hooter, thenceforth up and onwards into my tiny mind.

Camilla tried to help me become a rounded human being but that conversion was a long way off. We took E and thought we were the funniest people in the world. In those days coke had yet to really take hold of the scene and people were just very nice to each other. Clubs, pills, dancing, laughing, shouting, 'Let's have it!' and 'Come on!' I was the life and soul of the party, a combination of Wayne Sleep, Lurch and Guru Josh. Then we'd all pile back somewhere and carry on too long. I'd still venture up and try to play Peter Gabriel records, which caused a few problems, but on the whole it was a great time to be a druggy.

The Friday night would be fantastic, with everyone really up and euphoric; Saturday would be more hard work but still OK – we'd be in a serious house party somewhere, dancing a bit sluggishly. Of course you could go home and sleep but that was for straight people, lightweights. We'd all go back to someone's house and be given a warm jumper and a cup of tea, though, and lie there hugging for ages. (Occasionally the male part of any such sandwich might get a bit fruity and be manoeuvred away on to the rug.) By the Sunday we'd be skanky druggy people fit for fuck all, with dead eyes and listless sweaty limbs and confused, lonely and feeble thought processes. *This is the end, beautiful friend* . . . Well, until next week anyway.

Sadly, over time the E vibe gave way to the coke vibe, which involved people going off on their own and masturbating themselves to death rather than having fun in a group. But such is life and – more importantly – such is cocaine. It's the worst drug ever: stupid, boring, relentless, dangerous and expensive (a lot like Simon Cowell, in a way).

I'd always be one of the last men standing anyway, licking mirrors, finishing up the booze, helping myself to leftover pills. I'd sit in Camilla's basement flat with the headphones on doing lines and drinking anything going, a night owl who was none too wise. Outside the foxes would be roaming about the bins and the postmen would be getting up while I ploughed on by the light of a little angle-poise lamp. From a distance through the window I might have resembled a master craftsmen – a jeweller or a goldsmith – such was my concentration; but no, I was just a man approaching thirty-five surrounded by drug paraphernalia and overflowing ashtrays, rolling Charlie spliffs and snorting Es, terrified to call it a night and have to deal with who I really was: a proper drug addict. It makes me shiver to remember it. It was OK, though, I thought: I was on telly and people envied me . . .

But in truth my druggy lifestyle was sometimes getting in the way of other stuff. Christopher Walken was a big hero of mine – for me he was the outstanding actor of his generation, a very compelling presence and he had the odd-bod moves and crazy intonation in his speech. I loved him. Unfortunately, the week he was on the show I'd spent the Friday sniffing and was too hungover to come in to the studio on the Saturday to meet him. You'd think that that might have taught me something, lying in bed in my garret watching *Match of the Day*, utterly bereft, while he was with the rest of the cast. Ho hum.

Kylie also made an appearance. Having signed to Deconstruction Records she was busy reinventing herself and had just released 'Confide in Me'. I looked her up in my star-sign books and discovered that her Western sign was Gemini and her Chinese sign was the Monkey. Very interesting: the Monkey was one of the few signs that did not gel with the Tiger. *We will see, my pretty!* The week she was on I wasn't appearing on the show but was in the studio. After a big line of coke I thought I'd go and introduce myself. She was standing in the middle of the empty studio, a tiny blonde waif with the arse of an African sprinter. As I moved towards her she looked at me nervously. The cocaine hit my brain and I felt mightily discouraged but inched closer nonetheless, trying to look nonchalant. The trouble was she was standing right in the middle of the studio floor, like a mermaid on a rock in the middle of a big pond, and it seemed to take half an hour to reach her. I edged in like a young Rigsby, twitching. On reaching her orbit I launched into conversation: 'You're a Gemini Monkey . . .' I realised how absurd this sounded the second the words came out.

She was lost for words, as was your hero. She was no taller than a chimp certainly but infinitely more attractive and the cocaine had frozen every charming bon mot on my lips. We shrank like ants in the huge studio space. Time was running out. 'That's good. Right . . .' she replied nervously.

I walked quickly away.

John Thomson and I had appeared throughout the series as Bruce Urquart and Larry Wize, two gay Hollywood reporters (they're probably on YouTube by now). A lot of performers are obsessed with playing Americans at the start of their careers – I'm not sure why. Maybe it's in the vain hope of being summoned to Hollywood. Certainly it was always very important to me to be able to do a wide range of accents properly, although this doesn't guarantee that you'll be asked to play a wide range of characters by directors and producers. In the acting game you're mainly asked to play a watered-down version of your finest hour.

The other thing of merit I did on *Saturday Zoo* was a character called Ice Pick, a white rapper with rich parents who lived in Notting Hill. I wrote the whole thing myself, word for word. It went out one week with Jonathan interviewing me live in the studio, as he did most characters. I was very proud of that skit – I think it was probably the best character I ever did up and at that point (without blowing my own trumpet) no one had yet spoken in that strange hybrid language of West Indian/Asian/Cockney that's so prevalent in character comedy now.

I had big plans for Ice Pick but for lots of reasons he never appeared on the show again. There was a mass of other performers trying to get their stuff on but I'd made an enemy of Jonathan's partner, Mike Bolland (or Shrek), who'd told me that all my characters were 'like mental patients'. I'd fronted him about this. 'What's wrong with that?' I said. 'Would you like to have a psychiatrist examine all my characters to see if they're mentally competent before they're allowed on air?'

He was just being childish. He knew I needed hard work and a certain amount of encouragement and he didn't think I was worth it. He cheesed round Coogan hoping for the jackpot but the Coogmeister never made a programme for Channel X. After *Saturday Zoo* Coogan set up his own production company, made some superb comedy and drove fast cars a lot.

After the show finished I carried on hanging out with Jonathan for a while, but I began to feel weird going round there: he was working on other things and I was back in South East London spending my time wondering if I was ever going to be in TV again. And now that I'd got the distraction of live weekly telly out of the way I started clubbing in earnest. I was out every weekend and spent the weekdays recovering – it's a full-time job getting off your nut, you know.

In fact my TV career was just beginning: I didn't know it yet but I was about to star in one of the most loved and celebrated TV shows of recent years. Me and my wooden furry teeth, my sweaty bollocks and my big red sore nose. I had barely started, but any day now I'd be coming to a small screen near you.

Paul Whitehouse and Charlie Higson had been asked to be involved in *Saturday Zoo* but were too busy. At some point Paul had come down to Greenwich and seen me do Tommy Cockles. I was shocked and overjoyed to receive his congratulations after the show, as he was one of my comic heroes – as far as I was concerned he and Harry Enfield set the bar in character comedy and the rest of us lay flat on the mat gazing up in awe.

I'd first worked with Charlie on Jim and Bob's *Big Night Out* – he was I think script editing or something and, like me, performing small parts. One week we played men in dinner suits who walked on and off the stage; there were four of us, but I can't remember who the other two were. Charlie took charge and arranged us carefully, pulling us back into line if we got out of step. The whole thing took thirty seconds and was largely pointless (we didn't even speak) but he behaved as if we were Gurkhas doing a twenty-one-gun salute for the Queen. I studied him for the rest of the day after that. He was bossy, patronising and meticulous but was absolutely focused on making the show as funny as possible.

One day in late 1993 Jan Murphy informed me that Paul and Charlie wanted a discussion with me about a show they were putting together. When I met them (in what seemed to be a wood-panelled Swiss pizza place in the heart of Soho) they told me they wanted me to be part of a team who'd perform characters in short sketches; anything I wanted to write would be welcome. The show had been commissioned and they were just putting together the team. It was like being asked to go on a bank job in a country with no police force and I ate my pizza with gusto.

We all met in a rehearsal room some time later, an assembled cast of comedy talent waiting to perform:

Paul Whitehouse (*the king*): our fearless leader. He'd learnt his trade with Harry Enfield and was now ready to become British champion. Enormously talented, bombastic, tough, canny and direct – and, above all, he had the ability to bring out the best in his men. A natural leader. Later went bonkers.

Charlie Higson (*the kingmaker*): the engine of *The Fast Show*. Conceited, diligent, sensible and kind, he was in control of the brakes, too, which is very important when dealing with such a varied group of machines.

Mark Williams: a proper comic actor. Very good physically, but didn't posses the acerbic snide wit of the stand-up comic; he had more of an open Midlands charm and a good heart. Later went bonkers.

Caroline Aherne: very funny – a genuine one-off and definitely the best female comedian of her generation. A pleasure to work with. Later went bonkers.

John Thomson: another trained actor. Round of body and head, he had a childishness that came over in his performances and he'd always bring some old-school Northern warmth to any sketch he was in. He came up with potentially the greatest character of all time, the Silky-Bra Kid – 'The silky bras are on me . . . !' Later went bonkers.

Arabella Weir: another proper actor. Spiky, clever and insecure, she came up with one of the most enduring catchphrases of *The Fast Show*, 'Does my bum look big in this?' Did not go bonkers later.

And me, Simon William Day: described by Paul Whitehouse as someone who can come up with a piece of comedy genius 'just like that' but who can also forget a piece of comedy genius 'just like that'. Favourite colour – blue; favourite food – chips; dream dinner-party guests – Brian Clough, Captain Beefheart, Mike Read, Coco Chanel, Grace Kelly and Walter Matthau. Already bonkers.

The first thing I wrote for the first series was Billy Bleach, the pub know-all. He was based on people I had seen in pubs in South East London. I wrote it in Camilla's basement (I doubt her family will get a blue plaque). I knew it was funny and I knew people would recognise the character. The bit when Billy helped the fat bloke with the fruit machine was of course based on my years as a spin doctor, helping people win on machines. I was very happy with this character and I did very well with it live; he later got his own spin-off show too. The character I first performed on the first day of filming was Andy the Affair Man, a guy who deluded himself that everybody wanted to sleep with him.

I had no experience of moving and talking at the same time: I'd been standing still for all my other TV work. Here you had to hit your mark (a piece of tape on the floor) and then deliver your line. It sounds easy but it isn't, especially when you're already nervous. I kept missing the mark. I did so the whole morning, and this in turn caused me to forget my lines as well, but the finished result was not too bad and I came up with a variation of the character while we were filming (I'm Not Gay) and some lines in the other bits as well.

One of Charlie and Paul's strengths as producers was that they'd always let you change lines and come up with ideas while you were filming. They'd incorporate your stuff into the day's shoot, sometimes even scrapping stuff of their own if they thought yours was better. Sadly very few people in this industry do this: everyone thinks they know best and most of them don't know their arse from their elbow.

Paul and Charlie were generally very complimentary about my work, but Paul was not above severely admonishing you in front of the whole cast and crew if you didn't know your lines or had been on the piss. 'Oi! You're a bloody disgrace missing the target from there – you want bloody shooting!' Occasionally he'd get his facts wrong or go too far, but if you want to win things you have to put up with that.

In my book he was and is the best character comedian of all time, after Peter Sellers, and to watch him laying down his rhymes was inspirational to all of us.

For the first series Arch Dyson directed the studio stuff and John Birkin directed everything on location. Birkin has some kind of blue blood (he's in *Debrett's*) and was very fastidious; he was always getting the camera track back out ten minutes before wrap, which infuriated the crew but he wanted it to look right. I enjoyed the location filming enormously, mainly because everybody got on with one another and we could sit around in strange hotel bars laughing, drinking bottled beer and eating terrible club sandwiches. As a group we gelled very well right up until the last tour in 2001, by which time egos were outsized, people had other careers and it all got a bit fractious.

Paul and Charlie were our bosses and that was the end of it – that's why it worked so well. Rather like Donald Fagen and Walter Becker of Steely Dan, they knew exactly what the show was and they hired the best people to do their stuff. And we were not allowed into the edit to influence their decisions, just as Donald Fagen wouldn't have allowed Jeff Skunk Baxter to tell them where and when his guitar solo should be. The result was three fantastic shows (or albums in the case of Steely Dan).

But Paul and Charlie were getting more than session musicians: we were all gifted character actors and all control freaks too, just like them. Each actor turned up with their part written, knowing what they wanted to wear and how the set might look. Whether it was Arabella's No Offence woman, or my Dave Angel, Caroline's Checkout Girl or Mark's 'This week I will mostly be eating . . .' man, the worlds were fully formed in the performers' heads. This is why the standard of the shows was so high.

Of course Paul and Charlie helped with costume and other ideas, and they also wrote some great characters for different people, but people still come up to me and ask me if I wrote my *Fast Show* characters, which is a bit frustrating. For the record I conceived and wrote Billy Bleach, Dave Angel, Competitive Dad, Monkfish, Tommy Cockles and Gideon Soames. I wrote stuff for Ron Manager, Carl Hooper and other things too. It sounds a bit 'Ner-ner', writing that down, but as I say people still attribute lots of stuff on that show to Paul and Charlie when in fact some of the credit lies with other cast members.

On the other side of the coin, P and C gave John the part of Louis Balfour in *Jazz Club* and I was given the part of Carl Hooper from *That's Amazing!* People would come up to John in the street and say, 'That *Jazz Club* is genius,' and John would say, 'Cheers.' It was an all-round win/win situation for everybody.

The other benefit of being a cast member was that we said our funny stuff and then went down the pub, while P and C had to edit, produce, write and perform. They may have got the most credit and the most money, but it was very hard work and if it wasn't funny or didn't get enough viewers the pressure was on them, not us. They also had to deal with the BBC and the press and all the other boring stuff while John and I were eating Thai food and being waved at by builders and fat girls.

Of course we all moaned about money and writing credits, and about our sets not being right and our costumes not fitting properly, and our cars smelling of fags and our dressing rooms being too small and dark, and our scripts not being bound properly and the food being tasteless, and our lines being cut and tea being cold . . . But apart from that we were a pleasure to work with.

Considering the actual amount of work we did on the show, the core cast had incredible success. Most people came up with a couple of good characters in each series, but we became very well-known throughout the country. Paul once said to me: 'I wish I could come in, do three hours, steal the show and then go home.' I'd never thought about it like that.

My Attention-Deficit Disorder meant I still found it difficult to focus on work. I found read-throughs fun but if I had to stay and work on something the old childish 'I want to go home' refrain would start playing in my mind. Once I got immersed in the work I'd love it and stay, but it seems my brain will always say, 'Go! Go on – go and do something less constructive.'

All through my life I've had to go, to get to the next place or thing, and when I've arrived there I've always done whatever I had to do in the shortest space of time then leave again. For instance, it takes me about thirty-five minutes to do the whole of the Tate Modern, all the floors, cup of coffee on the secret balcony overlooking the river, and the gift shop (for a book of superb black-and-white photos by an Eastern European, which must be hidden from wife as is too expensive). Do I appreciate art less than you? No, probably not. I only visit galleries early, ten on the dot: I can't have people photographing pictures on their phones while I'm trying to look at something. Some people now don't even look at things, they just hold up their camera and move on – what's that about? Actually I love an art gallery, the high ceilings, the light, the sense of time standing still and moving forward at the same time; paintings can transport me. It has to be quiet, though: I can't have seventeen schoolkids sitting on the floor trying to sketch a Turner or a Rothko. I'd rather leave the room and go buy a Grayson Perry tea towel.

I skim, scan and eat culture but I very rarely digest any of it during the meal. I've left football matches, films and theatre early (thank god); days out have become mornings out and holidays have become weekend breaks. If I have to be somewhere I always get there very early because I can't stand being in the house too long. I have to go – 'Bye!' – but am then forced to wait around and usually end up buying a CD I already own or a director's cut of a film with an incompetent director, or I might go to Pret and eat right through the card and feel a bit sick.

'It's not easy being you, is it?' a friend once said.

'No,' I replied, and left.

I'd have made a good nomadic tribesman: 'Come on, let's fuck off. It's only an oasis – plenty more where this came from . . .'

Chapter Sixteen

Rehearsals for the *The Fast Show* were held in the American church in Tottenham Court Road – which was, coincidentally, where we'd rehearsed *Saturday Zoo*. It's a good place for actors to rehearse because afterwards they can go and look at curtain fabric and silly lamps in Habitat (first series) or Heals (second series).

Paul and Charlie would have loads of printed scripts with different characters on, which they distributed among us, saying, 'This might be good for you, Mr Day,' or, 'I thought you could have a crack at this, Mark.' People soon began proffering their own stuff, which Charlie scrutinised as if it was a collection of ancient sea scrolls. I remember John and I reading 'Ted and Ralph' early on and asking if we could do it. 'No,' said Paul, 'we're doing that.' And very good they were too. I love seeing things done in the creative world that I couldn't do better myself. That's why I have no time for a lot of modern art: if you're so good, go and paint me a bowl of fruit or a horse eating a bit of sugar held by a charming kid; don't put a brick on top of an ice lolly or hang different-coloured skipping ropes over a washing line. Vic Reeves did that years ago and treated it appropriately – he laughed and everyone else laughed too.

Paul and Charlie gave me a character called the King for the first series. The joke was that I'd sit on a throne and various people would be brought before me – a jester, a serf, a landowner or whatever – and they'd talk to me for a bit then I'd say, 'Feed them to the pigs!' or 'Chop their head off! I love being King – *ha ha ha* – best job in the world!' in a sort of Sid James voice. I took everything in my stride in those days and although I hadn't written the character myself I was sure it would be hilarious on the day.

I was always a bit more wary of doing stuff written by other people, though. If I came up with a character their personality was rock-solid in my mind: you could sit me down and ask me thirty questions about him and I'd answer them straight off. Where did he go at Christmas? What kind of car did he drive? That kind of thing. The night before filming the King I thought about him before I went to sleep and had a slightly uneasy feeling, but I banished all negative thoughts from my mind, drained the last of my red wine from a chipped mug and tried to sleep.

When I arrived at Television Centre Paul and Charlie were very excited. 'Wait until you see the set for the King – it's brilliant!' I was led into one of the studios and was stunned when I saw a huge stone (fibreglass) staircase about forty feet high; it was like something out of *Raiders of the Lost Ark*. They also had burning torches, people in full medieval costume – everything bar chickens and wild boars roaming about.

I had a great costume and wig, too, and I walked up the staircase amazed by the trouble they'd gone to. Extras playing minstrels started playing medieval music and jigging about, then John appeared as a jester and did some funny stuff. By the time he got up the stairs the sketch was no longer 'fast'. I said my lines rather uncertainly and someone shouted 'Cut'. Paul nipped up the staircase and said, 'Not like that. Like Sid James: you've got to have more fun with it.'

The takes came and went and Charlie and Paul got more and more short with me. 'For fuck's sake, you're a *king* – be more evil!' They tried good cop/bad cop to get the right performance out of me but it wasn't how they'd imagined it nor indeed how I'd done it in rehearsal when the character was first mooted. Somehow I just wasn't doing it right; it wasn't funny.

I was at a loss as to how to achieve what they wanted. The longer it went on the more nervous I got and inside I reverted to childhood, as if I was being told I should understand a maths problem I didn't get.

There were quite a few characters like this, ones that seemed funny on the page but were not on the day. Fuck knows what they did with the staircase afterwards. I'd have liked to have kept it to practise award-show entrances but I thought it best not to ask.

At all times in *The Fast Show*, however inspired a character was, however much the crew was laughing, however funny the performer looked and however original the dialogue was, Charlie would be there saying, 'What's the joke? Yes, I see, but what's the joke?' The joke being an all-round reference to the meat of the character or sketch, the stuff the audience could chew on and then swallow.

Among the valuable advice Paul gave me was this: 'We're not doing this show to make Steve Coogan laugh. Harry Enfield gets nine million viewers; I want as many people as possible to understand this.'

I understood what he meant. I was often odd for odd's sake when I started out, trying to make Bob Mortimer laugh, or John Thomson. Also, when I was playing for *Big Night Out*, we thought what we were doing was more interesting than observational comedy, mainly because it was in no way political or angry – yet we all loved genuine funny-men like Freddie Starr and Frank Carson. Personally I thought that Jim and Bob were pursuing more lofty ideals, and this was borne out by those sections of the press who raved about Jim and Bob. I remember I'd suggested on one tour that we should kick footballs out from the stage into the audience; after we did so one review in a so-called quality paper described it as Dadaist! We were just copying Rod Stewart – not an overly surreal performer.

I was very lucky with P and C, because they always put my stuff in the finished show. They rated me, which brought out the best in me. Like little Joe Cole I'm an arm-round-the-shoulder player, though I'm taller than him and not as greedy. Arabella suffered the most on the cutting-room floor, she said, and would get very upset about her stuff not going in. She was convinced that there was a conspiracy against her and that it was a lad's show, a sort of geezer-fest if you will. To an extent this was true. It was definitely the lads' decade, with *Loaded*, Madchester, the rise of the Premiership and, er, Chris Evans, and expressions like 'You know you love it' and 'Let's have it' being bandied about. (Although of course eventually for the key players in that scene it all went 'Pete Tong' and now they're happy to be 'lightweights'.) But plenty of females loved *The Fast Show* and for that matter the Happy Mondays too. I'm not sure how many bought *Loaded* but you get my drift.

Historically the comedy teams of the twentieth century did seem to treat women as sex objects, though there's no definitive reason for this as far as I know. I think men and boys in general are more relaxed in their own company than they are with women. The public-school system has produced a lot of the important comedy teams, people who met at university and played silly buggers together, joshing and japing about, shaping their shared sense of humour. 'It is a world of men,' as Ricky Roma said in *Glengarry Glen Ross*, the excellent play/film written by the ultimate man's man, David Mamet (he hunts, he plays poker, he has balls of iron and a pen of steel; the people in his films don't half repeat themselves, though).

Generally the girls aren't in on the joke as much. Most men will try to make a girl laugh so they can bonk her eyes out, but they have a different set of agendas when they're entertaining other men. Men will invite women into their comedy teams but usually they must be good-looking *and* funny – think Pamela Stephenson, Carol Cleveland and Sally Phillips.

Often men like to have sex with good-looking women but they don't want to hang out with them for ever. Most guys would prefer to sit in a dark room watching *Goodfellas* with a few mates, getting pissed and rewinding the violent bits. Then hugging/fighting each other and getting more pissed watching televised sport, shouting, 'Don't text her back!' and 'Has she rung again? Fucking hell: this is England playing! Don't call her – *don't* call her!' before going home to wifey and shouting, 'If I told you what I've been doing you wouldn't understand.'

Gore Vidal said, 'If only they knew how much we hate them.' He was referring to the fairer sex, not Millwall, and it was a shocking statement – so dark. And he was gay. His rich, sensuous voice lends the words resonance and weight. I can see him in the garden of his beautiful home in Ravello, a sweaty piece of ham draped over a bowl of figs before him while a blond man lies in the shade reading a yellowing letter from F. Scott Fitzgerald. Until I heard this I'd always thought all gay men adored women, put them on pedestals. There are so many female gay icons, everyone from Bet Lynch (completely understandable) to Baby Spice (is there much to admire there?).

For straight men of my generation the main icon is James Bond. I think most men would like to live their lives exactly like his. I watched all the Bond films at a dangerous age, when my brain was very vulnerable to ideas and images. Every woman wanted to fuck him right there and then! Forget the gadgets and the harpooning of foreigners, to me he had ultimate power over women – like Dracula, another of my heroes. But while Dracula is in no way a homosexual I reckon James Bond's probably a closet: he tries too hard to be a real man. To me, then, are all real men homosexuals? The beefy weightlifter, the tattooed football star, the sixties gangster – all camp as Christmas. It seems the harder you try not to be gay the gayer you become.

I must admit, I'd love to have been mates with Gore Vidal – drinking Barolo and gossiping about Hollywood while Henry Kissinger made fresh pasta. I've been accused of homosexuality a number of times, mainly by girls I'd stopped having sex with. But then throughout my life I've hung around with different groups of men and often whoever wasn't in the room would be accused of being a poof. ('He opened the door to me in a towel the other day . . .') What were we scared of?

If not outright women-haters, comics have nonetheless always had issues with women. The 'nerd versus sexy woman' is a comic staple going back to Charlie Chaplin. But why does the clown think he deserves the girl? Why doesn't he lie down and think, *They're right: I'm a piece of shit*? We're all nerds, in a way, and greedy nerds too. Don't be mistaken: if we'd had the chicks already we'd have stayed at the back of the room.

In terms of *The Fast Show* the bottom line was that Caroline and Arabella provided a welcome batch of very funny characters. I particularly like the character Mizz Weir did when she was a no-nonsense career woman who started talking like Goldie Hawn whenever a man came into the room. At the time, though, we were all desperate to get on in our careers and there was a lot of bumping and boring on the way down to the start line.

You can't have such a diverse group of people all straining to make it without some cliques forming, and this wasn't simply a gender thing. John and I were already mates. Mark got a bit of stick from Paul and me for being an 'actor', with all the terrible implications of creaking boards, breathing exercises and pecks on cheeks. John escaped this because he'd written characters like Bernard Righton, even though it was always very important to him to be accepted as a proper actor by the rest of the world. I did my best to ingratiate myself with my twin bosses, being blokey with Paul and listening respectfully to Charlie.

I was always capable of bitching about people, questioning their comedic chops, but I soon realised I didn't need to in this set-up: my job was safe. It was one of the first times in my life that I felt like that, and it helped my performances.

The first series got an awful review from Matthew Norman in the *Evening Standard.* He really went to town. I think it was a bit beyond him, not what he was expecting. Their usual TV reviewer, Victor Lewis-Smith, had been on holiday at the time of airing; on his return he reversed the decision, saying the show was the best thing since Monty Python.

The other person who helped it get noticed was good old John Peel, who had a TV column in the *Radio Times,* which people still read in those days. He applauded it every week, and when Peely spoke people listened. His list of discoveries is astonishing.

After we'd finished the first series I was skint again. I didn't do voiceovers and Jan couldn't get me acting work or stand-up gigs, so I was broke. At some point I moved in with Mark Williams in Cannon Street in Wapping. He was and is a kind man and cooked me curries (good) and showed me tapes of him acting in *Casualty* (bad). I'm not a fan of East London. I like the Indian part but the 'good old Cockney' thing and the trendy vibe leave me cold.

It was a grim winter, walking round the Eastern block. I asked for gravy in the pie-mash shop and the bloke came out from the kitchen and said, 'We only do liquor here, mate.' I was still doing drugs a bit, a lot, a bit, a lot – though not with Mark: he was a grape man. I'd fallen back on some old pals from South East London and would hang out there, going back and forwards from the mirror on the table.

By now the raving and loved-up party scene had given way to the moaning and spiteful Charlie scene. We sat indoors and did Es that didn't work any more and piled coke on top and watched the Champions League; bottles of rum and grams of coke for *Midweek Sports Special.* We stopped going to nightclubs. It was like trying to push custard uphill: you'd get into the club, buy a drink, queue up for the toilets, have a line and a half and E, come out, all meet up on the dance floor and sort of sway about for a few minutes, then someone would say, 'Shall we go?' and everyone would say, 'Thank god you said that,' and we'd start getting the coats from the cloakroom. I remember the days when we'd spend half an hour talking bollocks to the girl in the cloakroom then half an hour out on the pavement looking at flyers and discussing DJs before finally piling into someone's car. Those times seemed like ages ago. Now we'd get straight back home, put the kettle on like the old people we were and see what was on the telly. We got so bored of the edgy acrid buzz but – like thousands before us – we carried on until it was all gone every time. Cocaine starts as an invigorating slalom through interesting people and places and ends up a repeated ski jump: up the ladder, teeth chattering, then boom – down to earth. You go back, Jack, and do it again, by the law of diminishing returns – much like our behaviour in the nightclubs.

We stopped making any pretence of it being a party. It was as dull as ditchwater mostly but it was what I knew how to do best: sitting about with other men, slagging people off and ordering pizzas we never ate. As Bez says: 'If you're celebrating, carry on; if you're hiding, stop.' And if you don't follow Bez's advice, you're *really* in trouble.

Suddenly Mark sold up and moved to Brighton. I'd finally split with Camilla by then so I went with him. As we plotted up in La-La Land spring was in the air and I was youngish, free and single (and on telly). There's nothing quite as gay as two actors living together in Brighton. History was in, on and around us: the haggling at the farmers' market, bringing interesting pebbles home, making each other's beds together . . .

Of course I'm not gay, though I sometimes wish I was – I would have gladly taken the pink pound as well as the King's shilling. Had I just said, 'Ooh ducky, they really were marvellous times,' as Tommy Cockles I'd have had a whole new fan-base. Instead I've proved beyond doubt I'm not gay time and time again with loads of girls – and just look at my characters: Dave Angel, Billy Bleach, Competitive Dad. All real men. And I love boxing and pies so leave it.

I've lived with many different men. It's easier than living with girls – you can have a row and just say, 'Fuck off now, please.' (Provided your flatmate isn't a good fighter, that is: I'd never live with a bloke who was capable of beating me senseless.) But telling a girl to go fuck herself is problematic at best; that sort of statement is beyond the pale, really. *The Sopranos* was a fantastic show but Tony using the word 'cunt' to describe his wife really shocked me. My wife fancied Tony quite a bit but still I doubt I could get away with calling her that. Both Tony Soprano and Homer Simpson, two big male icons of the nineties, were appalling role models and addicts too – Homer with food, beer and TV, and Tony with food and violence. Both of them also treated their respective partners as mother figures who they used and abused and both of those partners gave them free rein to behave as they did. To my mind you can say to a lady, 'I'm sick of you,' or, 'Just leave me alone,' but 'Fuck off' is too much and should be used only on very special occasions. After such a remark you'd definitely have to run after her and end up in that awful scenario, the row in the middle of the street. This could mean stopping her getting into a cab or on a train, in which case you'd have to grab her arm – and if she's attractive and it's a Friday or Saturday night this could mean the involvement of another man, who might want to strike you. At best you'd have to speak/shout in a high voice, which is very undignified. I used to think it was love that made me shout and scream at girls in the road but it wasn't. It was my personality and alcohol mainly.

Men love living with men. It's both liberating and childish. You don't have to behave like an adult, or do things out of a sense of duty at which you've arrived via a vaguely guilty feeling you never fully understand. And anyway you have so much more in common. 'Show me a man who understands women and I will show you a liar.' The crafty Cockney Eric Bristow said that – imagine what a laugh living with him would be! No tampons in the bathroom, no hairs in the sink (in my experience men are much more anal than women around the bathroom – a nice Freudian slip there), no dull girlfriend's girlfriends coming round who resent you slightly and in whom you have to pretend you're interested, and no good-looking girlfriend's girlfriends coming round either – the ones you fancy and who make you behave slightly bitterly towards your partner.

Eventually I left Jan Murphy and signed up with the dreaded Avalon in order to get live work – I needed to earn more money. I find acting work elusive at best – even when I was hot because of *The Fast Show* I was getting only three or four jobs a year. Avalon get a bad press sometimes but I've come to realise this is largely undeserved. My man there was Rob Aslett, tenacious in the tackle and he could score goals too. He'd not only fight for me on the phone and in person but was also prepared to listen to me moan on for hours about how I'd not been offered more film and TV parts. (And it wasn't all Avalon's problem: I once blew out Michael Winterbottom two days running because of drink and drugs – not clever at all.) Later Rob was a good friend to me when I had some rough times in my private life too. All in all being with Avalon was a good experience.

By the time we began work on the second series of *The Fast Show* I'd settled nicely in Brighton. I knew it well from old holidays anyway, and at the time it suited me perfectly. But as much as I loved the idea of Brighton I never really felt properly at home there. For all its party-party atmosphere there's an undercurrent of sadness, a kind of uneasy breeze floating about – especially in winter. A lot of people end up in Brighton at the end of a personal struggle, thinking they might find a pot of gold on the beach. And the cheap accommodation and plentiful casual work in summer attracts runaways, crusties, the mentally ill . . . One thing it is good for is slightly unhinged but attractive twenty-something girls in need of father figures: hooray!

A friend of mine once said, 'Brighton: the only place you'll see a didgeridoo in Waitrose.' There's certainly something for everyone there. It helps if you're a piss-head, though: there's a pub almost every ten feet and in the summer it feels like the best place in the world.

While I lived with Mark he made jam and biscuits, and he smoked chickens, cured his own salmon and even pickled some eggs. He mended things, washed his car, studied maps of the Downs for walks and planned meals. He was a bit like my dad, I think, which may have drawn me to him. Most of the men I've lived with have been the handy-with-a-screwdriver type: sensible with money and such but also very anal. (In fact most men I know are anal to a degree – the collecting, the filing, the obsessive tidying . . .)

Mark and I were the Odd Couple, him playing the Jack Lemmon role to perfection and me being Walter Matthau. It was funny sometimes and other times not so funny. We really were chalk and cheese.

A typical day would start with me lying in bed hungover and Mark downstairs, having risen early despite his own bad head. He'd start the morning doing his books: taping meal bills and cab receipts into a huge book to be handed to his accountant later. Then he'd make several phone calls to friends and associates, frequently whooping with laughter and cheering. I'd hide my head under my pillow in disgust at this point – how could you cheer with a hangover? After that he'd then consult his board of notes and reminders before tearing off to the butcher's or the market to buy fresh produce. When I heard the door slam I'd creep down like an adolescent and drink a glass of warm water from the tap, looking round and thinking, *Here I am in another home which is not quite my home.* Then I'd skulk back upstairs and hurl myself back on my bed, hoping for more sleep. On Mark's return I'd come back downstairs and avail myself of any coffee that was on the go. Mark would maybe cheer or say, 'How you doin'?' too loudly on my entrance, which would disgust me even further. Sometimes he'd be in a bad mood and there'd be a frosty silence. This might have been my fault – anything from sweet wrappers left down the back of the sofa or a cleaning error – or it could have been triggered by a feature in the paper about an actor who was doing well. We are strange in this way, us lot. We have actors we think are brilliant (good ones) and no one is more happy than us when we see them thriving, but there are other people (for me it's limited but hard-working character comedians) whose success can cause serious distress. Mark once went crazy when a female journalist wrote: 'Alan Davies had made the duffel coat sexy again.' He had to go down the pub over that. I have no problem with the curly Gooner, but of course I begrudge others their day in the sun.

That summer, though, the sun was shining and we were largely in good spirits. It was red hot and I used to go for a run listening to Oasis then jump straight in the sea: fan-dabby-dozy. I was still missing Camilla and felt guilty but she was better off without me.

Often at about eleven Mark would say, 'The sun's over the yardarm – pub!' and off he'd go. I stopped going with him at lunchtime because of the extraordinary number of people he'd befriend: anyone from old racists and lesbians with dogs to barmaids, students and van drivers. 'This is Simon,' he'd say to a man with a pipe or a seventeen-year-old boy who worked in a shop. I found it unbearable, being very particular about who I drink with even when I'm very pissed. I'd just slump off and return to my proper friend, the fruit machine. He wouldn't ask me questions about Jack Dee or discuss the relative merits of the Saddler's Arms and the Green Man. No one ever managed to bring me out of myself until my kids were born, though plenty tried.

Mark's capacity for friendship might have touched a nerve somewhere. Was I jealous? Well, not of the bloke with the pipe who talked about cricket, but yes when there were girls of course. Any two men who live together must compete over all girls they come into contact with; they're driven to it for all the wrong reasons.

All in all we had a crack in Brighton, though. We were on the way up in our careers and that is a special time. If we'd made a documentary about living together it would have been an instant classic. He helped me a lot on set as well, taught me lots of stuff about movement and suchlike. He's a good actor, too, and should have been Doctor Who years ago. Still, if he has a rummage down the back of his sofa he'll find some chocolate wrappers I left for him, and you can't say fairer than that.

For the second series of *The Fast Show* I'd come up with what I thought was my best character so far, Competitive Dad. Obviously I had no children of my own but I had once seen a dad desperately trying to defeat his small kids in a race at a swimming baths. The look on his face as he rested panting after reaching the side first was disturbing: a kind of maniacal glee mixed with genuine triumph. The kids were really young – the boy was only about six and the girl about four. I thought, *Right, I'll have you, son*, and I nailed him.

Lots of dads have come up to me over the years and said, 'My kids say I'm Competitive Dad because of you!' But it's not *because* of me, is it?

A guy of about eighteen approached me on a train once; he looked a bit like Bret Easton Ellis, pale and nervous. I could see he wasn't at a happy stage of his life. He said, 'You do Competitive Dad, don't you? My dad was like that – he was just like that.' He sort of perked up as he said it, then something seemed to come into his mind very suddenly and he faltered and looked at the floor before flicking his eyes around the carriage. He looked like he was going to cry and moved away from me, then stared out of the window, turning back occasionally looking embarrassed and sad. I felt for him between London Bridge and Charing Cross – that was the exact distance of my compassion – but then I left the train and moved through the station into London, which washed my mind clean.

I also wrote Monkfish for series two, which was in response to this terrible habit TV producers had of choosing a star, giving him a ludicrous job and putting him in an unlikely but picturesque environment to do it. Like a lot of things we try to look down on, the format proved to be very successful and now we've even had Amanda Holden in a fucking African game park – someone who'd struggle to survive in the Rainforest Café let alone the bush.

A day filming *The Fast Show* at Television Centre would usually begin with a car picking you up from home. The driver would offer you a paper and then talk about traffic or football. The best drivers were those who seemed to enjoy being connected with showbiz and if prompted would tell you stories about incredible acts of rudeness by established BBC stars or incredible acts of kindness by BBC stars. The latter were less interesting: they might involve Stephen Tompkinson giving the driver his paper or a young actress from *Holby* buying them a cup of tea along with her own latte.

People would arrive at work in dribs and drabs depending on the filming schedule. The first thing I'd do on arrival was buy a slightly disappointing bacon roll from one of the badly lit food places near my dressing room. If we had a late start the majority of the cast would usually have been shopping before work. I'd buy mainly CDs and perhaps an overpriced shirt that didn't quite fit me. Arabella would barge in and absentmindedly finish off my bacon roll while we had a gossip, then she'd drift off to talk to Charlie, eager to find out if her character was going to be filmed or dropped. John would come in clutching some imported Japanese jazz-funk CDs and maybe a robot that told your fortune or a gorilla that sang 'Feeling Hot Hot Hot' by Arrow. Mark would arrive with an overpriced Scandinavian canvas bag with compartments for everything from hunting knives to cheese. He'd also have purchased a tool for cutting corduroy and a decanter, while Charlie would have got a couple of games for his computer.

If I was worried about my shirt fitting I'd go to Wardrobe, where they'd say very positive things about it; the Make-Up people would always do this too.

Filming a character was for me always a joy. Providing you knew your lines you could dick about with the crew, making them laugh between takes, and Paul and Charlie would often come over and laugh genuinely at your work. This was in marked contrast to live work, where the whole room would go quiet if you got it wrong and you'd have to build up the audience's confidence again. Also my agents at Avalon were rumoured to attend stand-up gigs that featured their acts: they'd enter the auditorium, stand in the stalls and laugh, stand at the back and laugh, walk down to the front and laugh, then leave in a large black car.

The next day they'd ring and say, 'I came to your gig; it was very funny.'

Chapter Seventeen

Performing in *The Fast Show* opened many doors for me, but the main door I wanted open was the door to huge critical and popular acclaim as an actor. As I said earlier, when the child first dreams of fame and fortune he doesn't have a cut-off point. I'd forced my way on to television, on the very same channel as my heroes Monty Python. I'd been called out at in the street by both prole and toff. I was a bit-part player in a grand design – so why could I not go further? Who's to say I couldn't follow Sellers to Hollywood or at least play a caretaker with a facial tic in a Mike Leigh film?

I love Mike Leigh's films. I was obsessed with *Meantime* for ages and would show it to people whenever I got the chance, delighting in their amazement at how funny it was, how poignant and how much better Phil Daniels was than Gary Oldman. I rather fancied myself in a Mike Leigh film – or any film for that matter, but the roles I was offered didn't quite match up to my expectations. I was offered *Heartbeat*, which was ironic as it was exactly the type of programme I'd attempted to satirise with Monkfish in *The Fast Show*. It was good fun to do, though. I was put up in a fantastic hotel in a little village inland from Whitby and got to work with Selwyn Froggitt and Wicksy from *EastEnders*.

It was also the first time I experienced actors moaning in earnest. There were two old boys, both of pensionable age and living in splendour in the aforementioned hotel. I winkled out of them that they were being paid ten grand a week each and yet once the rioja came out the moaning began.

'I should be in the West End, Simon. What am I doing here?' (*Banking ten grand a week, for a kick-off.*)

'The menu doesn't change in the restaurant you know.' (*It's still free . . .*)

'My agent got me a meeting with Stephen Poliakoff but I'm trapped up here with the sheep and Wicksy . . . There's a chance of me doing a film in Italy with Nessie Redgrave – have you ever worked in Italy?' (*What do you think, you daft old twit?*)

I found it hard to believe. They both had suites looking out on to hillsides dotted with sheep and dry-stone walls wending their way up and around and not many lines to learn – and they were both seventy years old! No actor is happy, whatever he's doing: they all want to be doing something else. Showbusiness is a discontented ship and given a chance everyone will try to steer it. I used to complain to my agents about the paucity of my acting offers. Again going to Soho House or the Groucho didn't help, as gushing female agents would rock up to me as I fought back cocaine-based facial tics and say, 'Did you go for a casting for this? I know the director loves you . . .' and, 'Why are you not doing films? Who's your agent?' I'd hurl a double dark rum and Coke down my neck and hope it would make me feel like I did before I'd had the line of coke – which is a bit silly, no?

When they'd planted the seed of uncertainty in my bonce they'd leave and I'd look at their arses furtively then go and have another line.

In 1996 England hosted the European Football Championships. We had a decent team, with Shearer in his pomp and Gazza – world-class players. Terry Venables was at the helm, an excellent coach and tactician, underrated in my view: I think he was England's last great manager.

We'd trounced the Dutch and were now playing Spain in the quarter-finals. I was watching the game in a pub called Hardy's in East Greenwich with the usual suspects. There was a small cloud on the horizon that night, though: I was due to appear in Epsom in my one-man show as Tommy Cockles. It being an afternoon kick-off I'd worked out that if I left at the end of ninety minutes I'd make it via two trains. I was fairly pissed but hadn't taken any drugs, as was the unwritten rule. Most stand-ups who indulge in chemicals force themselves to hold off until after a gig. Festivals are a nightmare, obviously – people keep offering you joints and other bits and bobs. Stand-up comedy is the performance discipline that suffers the most from chemical intake. DJs and people in bands can breeze on through but we're fucked without a clear head; you don't need drugs when you're doing a gig. You're all alone on stage and if people aren't laughing your brain will automatically reproduce a veritable checklist of drug side-effects anyway:

Paranoia
Dryness of the mouth
Shrunken balls
The need to urinate
Mood swings (if you get a laugh)
Head swelling to twice its normal size (if you're turning the gig around)
Nosebleeds (that's torn it)

Back in the pub we proudly sang along to the second-best England song of all time: Keith Allen and New Order pip it for me with 'World in Motion'. Alternative comedy has covered itself in glory in regards to England anthems. I wish I could say the same for the players on the pitch.

Guess what? The match ended in stalemate, extra time. But my time was up – I had to get my little bag containing a pair of glasses, a blazer and an apple and hot-foot it to Epsom. People around me said, 'You're not going, are you? We could win this! This is a once-in-a-lifetime thing!' Fucking Epsom. More voices were raised in protest. 'Extra time is only half an hour. Get there a bit late! They can't start without you – you're the star of the show.'

'You're right,' I said. 'Pint of lager, please.'

The half hour was up and still no goals. In Epsom the townsfolk were ironing garments and confirming babysitters. I was smashed by now. The no-drug rule was crumpled on the floor along with empty Charlie wraps, fag ends and betting slips.

In Epsom a twelve-year-old *Fast Show* fan pushed away his fish fingers, too excited to eat.

Penalties. The game went to penalties. I thought I should take out some insurance on the inevitable defeat looming in the penalty shoot-out, and took a couple of Es.

Well, we won – we fucking won on penalties! England, an England team won a quarter-final on penalties! The pub erupted. We went bonkers, drinks flying everywhere, dancing in the street. Once everything had calmed down the people who'd begged me to stay all started saying things like, 'You better hurry up . . .' 'Are you going to the gig now?' 'You can't just blow out a gig . . .'

Smiles were playing across faces. I was gone, over the moon. I was ecstatic about the football. I am of that rare breed of people who don't support a club – I support England. The white cliffs, pie and mash, Charles Dickens, the Jam, light and bitter . . . The E was pushing my euphoria higher and higher. The good people of Epsom faded and dwindled in my mind, briefly appearing now and then, as if in a snow globe, then vanishing again. I'd taken the love drug and I wanted love but not the love of an audience: they had become an abstract idea. It was as if I'd taken the cow to market, met a bloke and swapped the cow for a handful of beans and then eaten them. The gig was at the top of the beanstalk but I had no beans left and I had to explain the lack of cow at some point too.

There was a girl I really liked who lived in Notting Hill. My serotonin levels and my loins combined to produce a phone call. Being a lady she was totally unaware of the football but nonetheless charmed by my cheeky psychedelic banter. She invited me round.

The irony was that I could have got to Epsom and back in the time it took me to get to Notting Hill. I kept stopping to talk to football fans in the street.

'Amazing, wasn't it!' (An attractive girl.)

'I can't believe it!' (A spotty youth.)

'We could win this . . .' (A cab driver.)

'Fucking Spanish cunts.' (A man with no shirt on.)

'I should be in Epsom.' (Me.)

Everyone appeared to enjoy my football chat but seemed bored and confused by the Epsom bit at the end – though probably not half as bored and confused as the audience in the theatre.

Bear in mind it was fucking hot too.

I really fancied this girl and was up for some hot E love action. Maybe we could just sit about in towels listening to something Balearic and stroking each other. I'm not greedy . . .

I ran the last 200 yards. She lived in a council flat and I buzzed the door.

'Hi, Si. Come up.'

Ooooooh I'm excited . . .

I burst in. 'Football's coming home, it's coming home; football's . . .'

The room was in pitch darkness and there were three people lying on the furniture. They all said, 'Ssshhh!' I clamped my mouth shut. It was very hot. They were watching *2001: A Space Odyssey* with the curtains drawn. My heart sank. There was still two hours of the film left.

I felt a bit silly.

One of the people was a ridiculously good-looking black guy I knew the girl fancied. I peered at the tiny black-and-white screen: Hal wasn't letting the spaceman back on the ship.

I wasn't going to get my leg over.

I felt a bit sad.

I was offered a cup of tea.

I hate tea.

The black guy was wearing a vest. He had a superb torso. *Maybe I should try to get off with him to muddy the waters a little . . . Create a diversion: that'll show her.* Truth be told I didn't fancy having a big black guy pounding away at me. Not in this weather.

In Epsom people were getting their money back.

The England squad had moved on to tequila.

I moved on to the couch and smoked a Benson, tapping the ash into my hand like the stinking cur I was. Either the film ended or they turned it off because I kept talking. The curtains were thrown open and I started banging on about the football again. No one was interested. I wondered whether I should slip down to the video shop and rent *Dr Strangelove* and pretend we weren't in the semi-finals of the European Championship.

I started thinking about Epsom, the grim reality seeping through my euphoria. I was in so much trouble. I hadn't even called the venue and made up an excuse: unforgivable. I'd sold 300 tickets. Just then I realised I was still off my chump. I dropped to the floor and put 'Long Train Runnin'' by the Doobie Brothers on the stereo. I felt that little frisson of excitement you get when you put a record on when you're on drugs. It's fine if everyone else is on drugs too but everyone else here was on tea. I jigged my legs around a bit and nodded. *A good choice*, I thought, *the Doobie Brothers*. 'Talk about love, talk about luu-a-uve . . .' The black guy stretched and laughed like the big sexy cat he was. 'Wow, this is a bit lively,' he said.

People were still drinking tea and talking about Stanley Kubrick. The music sounded all wrong now he was chuckling.

I'd really been enjoying it. I thought, *I'm on telly, you cunt. I've blown out a small town in Middle England to be here and you don't even like the girl who I'm in love with – plus I saw* 2001: A Space Odyssey *at the pictures when I was twelve. Yeah: at the cinema! Besides, I wouldn't sully this glorious English sporting occasion with any film unless I was in it.*

My mouth was dry. The girl kept trying to be nice to me but I had misjudged things somewhat. The record ended. I had a nasty metallic taste in my mouth and that hollow chemical feeling in my stomach. I needed about four pints then I'd be back on track, but of course she had no beer – why would you have beer in the middle of summer during the European Championships?

I left, went back home to South East London, home of Rodney Trotter and other idiots. I found the gang and took some more drugs.

On Monday I was in a lot of trouble. The people of Epsom were not pleased; Dave Gorman, the support act, was not pleased. I was really hungover, in a nasty, jittery, guilty malaise. The mighty Avalon had me in the boardroom at the end of a long shiny table. The walls were covered with pictures of comics less gifted than me who didn't take drugs. I wished they would give me the cane and send me home. I was very ashamed of myself. I told them I couldn't make it to the gig because of the football. Apparently my agent had watched the game at Wembley with Frank Skinner and David Baddiel, then gone to see another stand-up. Why couldn't I have done that? Baddiel and Skinner had been on the front page of the *Sun* that day, first-name terms with the players, I expect.

Frank Skinner didn't even drink any more; he'd stood up to his demons. 'Football's Coming Home', the song they'd helped to write, had sold vast numbers of copies and it was rumoured they were millionaires off the back of it. Any figure earned by any other figure in showbusiness is always a lot bigger in the mind of the person not earning it, and in my mind it was huge. They were my agent's top bananas, a hard-working and intelligent double-act who wouldn't go to a girl's house unless they were sure of a bunk-up.

I looked at a photo of Frank Skinner; he was smiling. My agent was not.

I was told to stay out of Epsom. I was told in no uncertain terms to never again blow out a gig or I'd be shining shoes at the Royal Variety Club. I was told to apologise to Dave Gorman.

I didn't: I still had some self-respect.

I never blew out another gig, though. I actually learnt something. Amazing.

After the second series of *The Fast Show* had been aired I got offered a part in the television series *Jonathan Creek*, written by David Renwick and starring Alan Davies. It was something of a gamble as a show for Saturday night, as it was at times quite off-the-wall and Davies was a complete unknown. Caroline Quentin played the female assistant somewhat against type: she is no bimbo. I came up at the same time as Alan Davies. We did stand-up together many times and it's always nice to see people move from stand-up comedy to acting – though a lot of 'proper' actors are hurt and disgusted by it.

While I was doing *Heartbeat* I'd got into a heated discussion with an actor who didn't like the way the wind was blowing in regard to stand-ups getting acting work. I suppose he saw me as one of them. He'd pointed out that all the great sitcoms featured 'comic' actors: Len Rossiter, Tony Hancock, Ronnie Barker . . . I took his point but I couldn't understand why he was so angry. A lot of actors think what they do is above other disciplines in showbusiness but in no way are they superior to stand-up comics. Stand-up comedy is a hard-man's game: you've got to run things. Certainly it's a more selfish platform but don't tell me Sean Penn doing *King Lear* in Norwich is a higher or more valid art form than Sean Lock doing stand-up in Nottingham.

But of course we clowns, we want to be actors – we want to do straight acting – which is where we fall down. It's a bit like a BNP member wanting a sun tan: you can't have it both ways.

The *Jonathan Creek* episode I appeared in was called 'House of Monkeys'. There was a family of four who lived in a spooky house and I played the son, Jordon. Apparently I was nuts about monkeys and had several different types wandering around the house, including a full-sized gorilla (not a real one of course). I was married and my wife lived there too. I didn't fancy the actress who played my missus, which was a shame. It's always interesting to see who Casting think you could be in a relationship with. Jordon's father had impaled himself on a pikestaff in his study and Curly had to work out what had happened. It all sounded like a good laugh and I was looking forward to the first day of shooting, which was on a Tuesday.

On the Sunday beforehand I had a big lunch in town, which became an early drink, which became a full-on night out. I wasn't worried: I still had Monday to recover and I planned a long lie-in eating Kettle Chips followed by some line learning. I got in at three in the morning, punched the button on my old-style answer machine and was horrified to hear a voice tell me that a car was coming for me in three and a half hours to take me to Buckinghamshire, where I'd be filming scenes 14a, 67, 83 and 98.

I'd been drinking for twelve hours and trying to force cocaine up nostrils already too blocked and knackered to take any more punishment for the last five. I was furious and terrified in equal measure. On the way home in the cab my body had begun to shut down in anticipation of sleep. I felt like someone had killed me, dug me up and killed me again. Three and a half hours! I didn't even know my lines. I poured myself a massive rum and Coke and lay on the sofa waiting for my car, sweating like a malaria victim.

It was midsummer. I slept fitfully as we sped through the empty streets towards the stockbroker belt. Cocaine attacks the central nervous system and mine had been under attack for hours. Fear and paranoia were my enemies and were winning the battle. In my head I was like a member of the Home Guard armed with a broom trying to repel the entire German army. After a heavy cocaine session just coming down in bed is fraught with potential disasters and calamities; going to work, acting a part you don't understand, saying things you haven't learnt and all surrounded by fucking live monkeys is not good, my friend, not good.

I arrived and luckily was not in the first scene. It was already getting hot and I was a bit clammy. Around me young crew members grinned stupidly in their shorts remembering a far-off *Fast Show* sketch I didn't want to discuss. I knocked back the offers of breakfast and coiled up in my tiny trailer trying to make sense of the script. I wasn't the first actor to have a late night then come into work but I felt stupid and guilty. Why did I keep getting twatted? Why could I not write down the correct date of filming? Every time I lay down I felt a sickly sleep washing over me and I'd lurch to my feet, drink some more water and bite off a mushy piece of banana from a black-and-yellow phallus. A lot of performers drink Red Bull in such situations, but trust me it doesn't work. There was a knock at the door and a cheerful lesbian appeared wearing a boiler suit.

'Hello. Are you Simon? Do you want to come and meet the monkeys?'

I was led towards the huge house that was our film set. It had been done up with suits of armour and nice rugs. Light shone through a stained-glass window. We went up to the second floor and it all got a bit shabby. Round a corner I was suddenly face-to-face with a group of smelly, hairy monkeys. They bared their teeth at me and flung themselves at the bars of their cages shrieking. The man from the Home Guard in my mind threw down his broom and let his incontinence take over.

'They're all ex-animal-experiment creatures but they're fine now,' volunteered the lady wearing the boiler suit. She clearly loved the little blighters and cooed and purred at them. I was less enamoured of my fellow thespians: they could smell fear on me like gun smoke and I smiled grimly as the handler gave me a list of instructions. These included: don't make any sudden movements; never, ever put your hands near a monkey's face; and don't walk around behind them. Was she having a fucking laugh? I'd only just perfected walking and talking last year on *The Fast Show* and now I had to act with monkeys who could leap ten feet into the air and had fangs – monkeys who'd been forced to smoke endless Benson & Hedges by men who smelt and acted just like me.

The other problem I had was not really having a handle on the character. Almost every time I'd performed on telly I had written at least some of the lines myself; when I did do acting I often changed the dialogue, sort of personalised it in order to perform it better. Unfortunately David Renwick – who is without doubt one of our most gifted television writers – didn't allow people to alter his dialogue. On this occasion it didn't need changing anyway: it was the actor who needed changing. I didn't have a lot of lines, which was handy, but I couldn't work out who my character was. I approached the director, Sandy Johnson, a lovely guy I've worked with on several occasions. He's a whimsical Scot of subtle intelligence and directs a lot of comedy; I know him to be both inspiring and a safe pair of hands. On this occasion, however, he didn't help me at all. When I asked him about my character he just smiled enigmatically and said, 'You'll be fine.' As I was about to go he called me back and informed me that in the story my dad had been fucking my wife. 'Just bear that in mind,' he said.

I was completely thrown. How the hell was I supposed to act that emotion? I didn't even have any scenes with my dad, just my wife. I went back to my trailer and practised looking hurt and angry. I tried to remember how I'd felt in my kitchen when I'd listened to the answer-machine message. I scowled a bit in the mirror. It wasn't quite Ben Kingsley.

My mother was being played by Annette Crosbie OBE, winner of two Baftas and Victor Meldrew's wife in *One foot in the Grave*. Obviously I felt a bit insecure about the prospect of working alongside an actor of her calibre. She was quite scary but luckily she'd seen *The Fast Show* so I was all right. Besides, it wasn't as if we were doing *The Iceman Cometh*.

In my first scene I was sitting in a chair and my wife was confronted by Annette with her infidelity. How was I going to act that emotion? The creeping worm of fear slid up my leg. I was wearing tight slacks and my nether regions were soaked in sweat. I thought that at the moment of my wife's confession I'd raise my bum slightly from the chair to indicate my displeasure. There was a monkey wandering about, his tail in the air, leaping from sideboard to chair with consummate ease; just as Sandy said 'Action' I noticed a small coil of pooh emerge from its bunghole.

'Ooh look – he's doing a pooh!' I said in a strange, high, girlish voice I didn't recognise.

'No, he's not,' replied the handler firmly, as if admonishing a schoolboy.

A bit more came out as the monkey peered round at me from behind a mock-Ming vase.

'He is – he is! Look, look! Eerrr – dirty!' I hadn't realised my voice could go that high.

In one expert movement the handler swooped down with a tissue and wiped the monkey's arse and the filming carried on. Funnily enough, at the crucial point when I had to deliver my line, my face twisted in rage at my wife, the monkey hopped on to my shoulders and started looking for things in my hair. I was so shocked I forgot to show my wife my full displeasure. It looks good, though.

While I was filming that scene I was worrying about the next one, in which I had to do another acting face – this time registering the shock of seeing my father impaled on a pikestaff through a leaded window. I was at a loss as to how to display this emotion.

And of course I'd also found out that Pa had been bonking my wife, so that emotion had to be displayed across my fizzog too. I thought I'd base my look through the window on Munch's *The Scream* with a bit of a Peter Glaze double-take thrown in. I showed Caroline Quentin my facial plans and she burst out laughing.

It was about eighty-five degrees by now and the beer was pouring out of me. I desperately thought of film scenes I knew in which people discovered dead bodies. I kept getting the *Psycho* shower scene in my brain and for some reason Marlon Brando's death scene in *The Godfather* (the best death scene ever). Could I put some orange peel in my mouth and crash through the window then keel over on my dead dad?

Annette Crosbie called me to the window: 'Jordon – Jordon! Come quickly!' In the script my line read: 'Mother wh-at?' When I acted it I said 'wh-at' phonetically, exactly as written – a two-syllable word. The director was laughing long before I'd raced round to the window. As I ran I felt as if I was about to do a pole vault without a pole: I had no idea what face to present. The camera was inside of the room. I looked through at it and for some reason let out a Kenneth Williams shriek – it was all I could do to stop myself saying, 'Oooohh matron!'

We did the scene quite a few times, with my face variously inspired by babysitters from *Halloween*, gargoyles, my mum finding me covered in oil paint and people being killed by Daleks. I never got it quite right.

The weather that summer plus my ongoing involvement with *The Fast Show* started to cheer me up. I'd never had any doubts that the show would be such a great success – it had too many things going for it to fail. Firstly there was Paul Whitehouse – an all-time great character comic – desperate to step out of Harry Enfield's shadow, backed and harnessed by Charlie Higson. I think with Ted and Ralph they showed what they were about: a subtle chemistry, lovingly crafted and beautifully shot by John Birkin. Then there was John Thomson, the man who won the Perrier but didn't, and me, a guy who'd clawed his way out of various prisons of his own making. Then there were the girls, Caroline and Arabella, who had their own things to prove.

I'm not saying the show was made in the spirit of some global revenge on mankind – far from it. The majority of the time for me and I think the others it was a time of great joy and release. But no one is driven purely by joy and love in this game, no one. We also want to win.

Chapter Eighteen

The Fast Show had really taken off when the second series was broadcast: we'd entered the public consciousness and the catchphrases were shouted across the land, all over town and country. When I'd had my first meeting with Paul and Charlie they'd described the idea as 'lots of short sketches: catchphrase and out'.

Funnily enough I was not a big catchphrase man within the show. I had 'marvellous times' left over from Tommy Cockles, but I didn't have one for Dave Angel, Competitive Dad or Billy Bleach. I suppose that was me being 'obtuse', as my dad would have put it. Let's face it: the show had enough.

When we were filming the *Dr Monkfish* segment in a hospital Charlie came to see me. It was a bit like a visit from the man from the Ministry of Comedy. He sat down patiently and said, 'Have you got a catchphrase for this character?' I think I said he didn't need one, my theory being that real people don't say something over and over again and last thing before they leave a room. I think I got a bit pedantic about my comedy and other areas. He looked at the floor and then said in that careful way, 'Everyone has a catchphrase, even James Bond.'

We went through the script and after a bit of haggling decided on a line I'd already written: 'Put your knickers on and make me a cup of tea'. This was derived from John Thaw's great line in *The Sweeney*, 'Put your trousers on', which would be delivered dripping with disgust and menace to a hapless villain. I used to watch that show with my dad and it was quite radical at the time – certainly a big step up from *Softly Softly*. The sad music at the end left me feeling morose, though; I think because it coincided with me having to go to bed. (*The Likely Lads* theme was sad too – it was enough to make you want to jump off a bridge.)

The Monkfish catchphrase did OK for that character. Charlie was right, I suppose. Before when people used to see me in the street they'd sometimes pause, not knowing what to say, before shouting, '*Fast Show*!' or Mark's line, 'You ain't seen me, right?' Apparently Mark was once walking down a street in Central London when a fire engine pulled up and four firemen got out and stood in a line before him shouting that.

This is the kind of thing that you never dream could actually happen but does. Policemen and soldiers all loved *The Fast Show* – any group of people who worked together and had time to sit about doing nothing for ages would either discuss it or watch it. It was very popular with ex-pats too, for obvious reasons. It's very English and a bit sad in places, which is the template for anyone living abroad unless they're loaded. (It's a hard life: the gin, the baked beans and the heat. Not for me.)

If you didn't like one character another would be along in a minute. It was a very good idea, and well executed. A lot of bands watched it on tour – everyone from Tom Jones to Bryan Ferry to Oasis (Meg Matthews asked me for my autograph for Noel once, which is odd to think of now). Paul Weller too. This really used to blow my mind, as I've always thought of music as more important than comedy. It was for me anyway; I'd been hooked ever since I bought 'Dance with the Devil' by Cozy Powell. When my family was gone and I had no fixed abode, Paul Weller and others were there for me on *Top of the Pops* every week without fail, pointing the way politically and personally and offering sensible fashion tips. Weller particularly has remained a constant reassuring presence throughout my life, with his different albums meaning different things at different stages of my journey. And now he was a fan of the show I was in! After thirty-five years in the business he even came and did *Jazz Club* for us, at the last gig we ever did.

For Billy Bleach, my pub know-all, the catchphrase became 'There's someone sitting there, mate'. That was exactly the sort of thing people like him – the guys in dead-end jobs who were just unhappy all the time – would say just for the sake of it. You might also get this sort of treatment from people if you walked into the wrong pub. One day I was talking to Mark Mylod, esteemed director of series three and lots of other stuff, and suggested how funny it would be if Billy uttered this remark to people in crazy locations, like by a waterfall or next to an ice floe or outside the Taj Majal or whatever, and the next thing I knew we were going to Iceland. Apparently there was some money left in the budget and the Icelandic tourist board had promised to foot part of the bill if we showed the frozen island in all its glory.

I was very lucky to be the only cast member who went – it was just me, Paul and Charlie and Mark Mylod, plus a couple of crew. The trip had stemmed from my idea, I suppose, but Paul was going to do some 'Brilliant's too and Charlie was going to look at the scenery and think about stuff while staring out to sea. It's a great place to do that: throughout the trip people would be found on their own in a car park or by a small glacier gazing wistfully at the horizon and thinking about the big picture.

If you haven't yet been to Iceland I suggest you go at once. It's probably the most profoundly beautiful and affecting landscape I've stood about in. The sheer diversity of physical geography available is overwhelming: it's like the end of the world and the beginning of the world all at once. Fields of crazy purple and green lichen give way to charcoal mountain ranges, and strange clapperboard churches sit defiant on hillsides covered in scrawny sheep and giant icy craters. It's like people were scared to build anything permanent for fear of the wind lifting it off the landscape; every building seems cowed by the prospect of god's wrath. Here geography rules. It's all about maps and torches and beards – and of course Björk, who put the place on the map in the first place and lends it a weirdly trendy vibe that sits uneasily with the howling winds and biblical crashing seas.

On the first day of filming I did my catchphrase next to a huge waterfall. We had no safety equipment and it was a long way down. I was shitting myself and nearly had a tantrum. But as Charlie said: 'It was your fucking idea to come here, you idiot! We've climbed halfway up a mountain because of you so get nearer the edge!'

I couldn't fault his logic so I put away my fear and we got the shots we needed.

That night we went to the best restaurant on the island, a revolving space-station affair. It didn't move very fast but it was a bit weird. As I tucked into my roast lamb (which tasted of iodine because of the sheep's seaweed diet) I thought to myself, *I'm being paid to do this – I'm the luckiest person in the world; I really have cracked it.* I pledged a toast to all concerned and then sent the wine back on the grounds that it was corked.

The following day we all piled into a giant Land Rover thing and took off across country. We were in high spirits and listened to *OK Computer* by Radiohead and *Aladdin Sane* by David Bowie, two good albums that sounded almost perfect when presented as the soundtrack to the science fiction outside. We barely spoke, just looked out of the window as bits of ice broke off and crashed into the sea. Paul was like a little kid losing himself in the music, singing, impersonating Bowie's phrasing. Charlie asked occasional questions about the Radiohead songs like a Japanese person, formal and polite as always. It was nice to see them so relaxed after all their hard work. They'd planned a big bank job and pulled it off: this was their reward.

After some herrings accompanied by some sort of berry compote taken at speed in a shed that served as a café we clambered up on to a sort of ice-sheet field thing that was dimpled and bobbled and in places translucent underfoot. There were six of us, including Mylod, the cameraman and the sound man. We were pretty high up and Paul had to march along shouting his lines before holding his arms aloft and exclaiming, 'Brilliant!' I got a funny feeling, a kind of nudge from somewhere in my head, like a double image. I felt spooked but blamed the iodine and Thom Yorke's voice, which at times is a little too stringent and can affect one's mood.

'I don't like it up here, Paul,' I said. 'It feels wrong. Besides, we should have harnesses and stuff.' The ice field was hemmed in by rock formations but at either end there was certain death of the 'smashed into tiny fragments amid a pink spray' kind. 'I'm going down,' I said and went and sat in the car.

I couldn't face Radiohead again so I dug out some reggae. After a while I got bored, as you do with reggae, and climbed back up. It was very still just then, calm and quiet. Suddenly a gust of wind blew across the ice shelf and all six of us were blown still upright about ten feet across the ice; we had no control over ourselves. It was terrifying, so quick and clean that not one of us even fell over. We were just moved like Subbuteo figures.

'Fuck off!' said Paul. 'Fuck *off*!' Another gust of wind and we were blown another ten feet or so like cheap sail boats across a pond, ever nearer the edge and our obituaries. We'd been humbled by the weather and the landscape like a lot of people before us. Fair play to Mark Mylod: he wanted to carry on filming, and it's that sort of determination that marks out the true artistes. But as we sat in the truck we all knew how close we'd been to an hour-long documentary on BBC2 and the crocodile tears of the corporation's big-wigs.

Chapter Nineteen

I decided to go to Australia just for the hell of it. I love going abroad: is there anything better? Years of poverty and milling around South East London had left me desperate to see what was beyond, plus I now had money so I could do it in style. I booked a flight on Thai Airways to Sydney with an overnight in Bangkok. Billy Connelly's late tour manager, Malcolm Kingsnorth, had recommended a hotel in Sydney called the Sebel Townhouse, which had once been a great rock 'n' roll haunt. I also planned to fly up to the Gold Coast and do some diving, drink some wine, read books and meet interesting people.

Business class: so exciting the first time you use it – turning left, as they say. I deliberately wore a suit jacket so the nice lady would put it on a hanger like in the adverts. I sat in my huge Jimmy Savile chair, adjusted my bollocks and did what everyone else does in business class: ate shammy-leather smoked salmon, beef en croute and pineapple cheesecake, drank white wine, red wine and brandy and finished up with chocolates and a scented towel. Then I ate a sleeping pill, lay down and farted in my sleep for eleven hours.

For the second leg of my journey I had an Australian man next to me. He was a proper Aussie: loud, positive, patronising, racist and sexist in equal measure. My kind of guy! Apparently he had a big raft thing in the sea up off the Gold Coast, for diving, swimming, cold beer and a motor boat or two. He gave me his card. I noticed his pudgy brown fingers and white teeth. He kept winking at me and lightly prodding the diminutive Thai stewardess in the small of the back as she went past.

The wine trolley arrived. 'Have you ever had Australian wine, Simon?' he said.

'Yes,' I replied. 'Loads.'

'Try that, Simon – it's called Shiraz and it's made in Oz.'

'Cheers – I've had it before, though.'

'What do you think? It's called Shiraz.'

'Nice. I've had it before.' A bit louder this time.

'Smooth, isn't it? It's called Shiraz. It's made here in Oz.' (Were we now in Australian air space?)

I slumped back in my seat and sipped the red liquid. He was pissed, I realised – had probably had a few beers at breakfast. *No worries, mate*, I thought, and we carried on drinking, me agreeing with him a lot. When the stewardess next approached our seats he suddenly grabbed her wrist and turned to me. 'Have you ever had one of these women, Simon? They're ever so easy to dominate.' I looked across at his fat hand holding her thin wrist. She smiled and squirmed. 'You're all right, aren't you, darling?' he said. She maintained her fixed rictus grin. He released her and patted her arse in one motion. She walked off and he proceeded to discuss the merits of the Thai girlfriend he kept at his Gold Coast resort. The main thrust of his argument was that the 'tops and tails all match' – which after more wine I realised meant that he and his princess were exactly the same height and could therefore enjoy a '69' with little or no difficulty. The other benefit was that she never argued with him and cooked him five-course meals on a regular basis. (Nothing wrong with that.)

'You wait till you see the harbour as we fly into Sydney, mate: best view in the world.' He was really drunk now, drunker than me. This was no surprise: when I'd realised he was comedy gold I'd retreated into the mode of watchful character comedian, making him do all the running in the conversation, prompting and probing. This is my job. And it wasn't hard – he was an Aussie after all. He kept repeating himself: the harbour, the Thai women, great wine, the view, the harbour, tops and tails . . . As we made our final approach he staggered to an upright position – all five feet five of him – and peered through someone else's porthole. 'Ah jeez, mate: it's cloudy – you can't see a thing!'

I smiled inwardly and said, 'Never mind. I'll buy a postcard. What was that wine called again?'

'Shiraz,' he said, slumping back into his seat. 'It's made in Australia.'

What I didn't know then was that this conversation on the plane would be my last for nine days.

For the next few days I went all about Sydney, eating, drinking, looking at people and generally behaving like a tourist. Apart from the odd greeting no one spoke to me and I kept quiet too. Like a lot of performers, I'm painfully shy and struggle to start conversations with strangers unless I'm drunk. Sydney is a city like any other and people were busy. Had I expected people to strike up conversations with me on the street?

My evening routine went something like this . . . Having chosen a restaurant from my guide book, I'd choose one of the seventeen short-sleeved shirts I'd brought with me. (There were some terrific shirts among these – shirts in which I'd enjoyed great success with the ladies and had held people spellbound with my invigorating conversation. The shirts made me feel good.) Around six-thirty I'd climb into a cab to my chosen restaurant, which would often be empty. I'd choose some wine, order a lot of food and eat it. No book or newspaper. The whole thing would be over by nine o'clock and I'd wander out into the night stuffed to the gills, feeling tired and emotional.

In London at that stage in my life I was, of course, taking cocaine a lot. Now, without any 'help' (as they call it in Deptford) the prospect of drinking more alcohol left me cold. I could have tried to score but I imagined Sydney would produce slim pickings on that front. Besides, one of the reasons I'd chosen Australia was a perceived lack of the white lady. Though I was very tempted, I hadn't dared go to Brazil for fear of dying of a massive heart attack brought on by having cocaine blown into my ears by a dwarf with a hair-dryer while a series of underfed and overpaid lady boys attempted to worry my penis into something approaching an erection. My funeral would have been held atop Sugar Loaf Mountain, a small and sober service with Ronnie Biggs singing 'Desperado' by the Eagles as a long line of sex workers filed past my open coffin stooping to kneel and cross themselves while searching my pockets for any coins not confiscated by the *polícia federal.*

The longer I went without human contact the more paranoid and strange I felt. I started feeling spooked. There was a meagre rooftop pool and gym at the hotel and I'd go up there and swim up and down; it took about four seconds to swim a length. There was never anyone else there, ever. Where was the lonely widow smashed out of her mind on Valium, desperate to rediscover her sexual identity? Where were the lithe blonde German students, their tanned thighs covered in goose-bumps, ducking in and out of the blue water, their hair plastered to their foreheads – laughing, sharing cigarettes, their eyes bold and questioning as they walked slowly towards me through the shallow waters of the pool, finally peeling off their swimsuits to reveal . . . ?

There I was in my new swimming trunks with an old towel, in splendid isolation, staring down on the great metropolis that was Sydney – a city that seemed to have been named after a caretaker or someone who worked at a bank.

One morning excitedly I ran up to the roof and did that thing with my camera where you photograph part of the skyline then move your camera along and take another shot from the edge of the last photo and so forth until you have the complete picture. I had planned the project the night before while eating an excellent

Thai meal and staring at a couple who didn't speak to each other all night. (Why do so many couples do this?) I should have struck up a conversation but just stared instead. At least I gave them something to discuss on the way home.

'Who was that weird guy staring at you with tom ka gai down his shirt?'

'I don't know, but did you notice he had nine starters?'

Sadly my contemporary-art project took only about ten minutes. I still had nine hours to kill.

I'd go down to the hotel bar early doors, drink beer and look at the floor. I was consumed with shyness and the more I thought about it the worse it seemed. When I ordered more beer I'd smile like the stewardess on the plane. I felt like the guy in *American Psycho*, though I had no desire to cut off anyone's lips.

I watched videos in bed on my own during the day, scoffing chocolate from the mini-bar like Liz Taylor.

It wasn't panning out like I'd imagined.

One evening I thought I saw George Melly in a restaurant and after drinking a lot I went and said hello. It wasn't him; it was just a man in a hat.

I had a Walkman and went jogging in the mornings past the yachts and the big houses by the harbour, listening to the Verve's big hit album. *But I'm a lucky man*, I thought. *With fire in my hands. I'm on telly, the master of my own fate.* After the initial endomorphic rush of the run had been washed off in the shower I'd be starving, and would catch the lift downstairs to eat some exotic fruit and then bacon and eggs. This would be my favourite part of each day. The coffee was good and I'd be sure that today would be the day I'd start to enjoy myself. A chance meeting with an attractive *Fast Show* fan in the Aboriginal museum? Perhaps a maid would come to my room and say, 'I've noticed you've been on your own for the last few days, Mr Day. Would you like to come to my parents' place in the Blue Mountains? We could go riding and swim by the waterfall. Mum runs the winery and Dad is a big fan of Dave Angel.' Maybe the Happy Mondays would be staying at the Sebel during an Australian tour.

I'd catch the lift back upstairs feeling full of partly digested food and hope. Unfortunately the combination of the run and the enormous breakfast would result in me going back to bed again and watching some girls in leotards doing aerobics by the Opera House on the telly.

I felt utterly alone. I'd lie in bed and listen hard to see if I could hear last night's room-service tray being removed before dropping off to sleep. Then I'd get up and go buy something I didn't need.

The Gold Coast is up the top of Oz, on the left. There are a number of islands offshore that serve as holiday resorts. I couldn't afford to go to the best one and felt a bit miffed but got a package deal to one of the others – flight, a week in a place on the beach. Wicked. Surely I'd do better there? Stoners, girls with flat tummies in bikinis playing Frisbee, maybe some dolphins?

On the boat from the mainland I wound up with a bunch of honeymooners. By this time I'd not had a proper conversation for a week and was very paranoid. I seemed to be taller than everyone else and my long white limbs clashed horribly with the tanned forearms of the laughing passengers. I looked around furtively and saw I was the only singleton. Great. Still, the sun was setting and the sea spray was in my nose: life was good, wasn't it?

As the boat grew close to shore I saw to my horror that tables had been set up with brightly coloured cocktails. Some tables had four on them, some had two. This was a disaster. Was there going to be a table for one with a lonely piña colada awaiting me? This was enough to finish me off. I wanted to dive in the water and swim home to Blighty.

Once ashore I realised there were place names on all the tables. I was doomed. When everyone else was seated the reps started to do that funny thing where one person speaks and the other stands behind them with their arms pushed under the first one's armpits and pretends these are the front person's arms. Everyone was laughing. I didn't laugh but stood at the back and moved my mouth upwards in an approximation of a grin. I approached the comedy guys and told them I couldn't find my name on any of the tables. The one in front stopped speaking and the one standing behind withdrew her arms. I'd ruined their act.

As they consulted a long list of names I felt eyes in my back. Somewhere there was the putter of an outboard motor, the whoop of a monkey.

'Jeez, mate – you're on the wrong island!'

I went bright red and some people laughed behind me. I was led into an office and given a seat but no cocktail while one of the reps made a telephone call. Twenty minutes later I was led down the beach and helped on to a small boat by a rep with a slightly patronising Australian manner. 'Whoa! There you go, big fella. Sit down. You're all right, mate. As I squatted/fell into the boat the tepid water in the bottom rose up to greet my genitals and a small amount of seawater swept unchallenged into my bumhole.

I reached the correct island under cover of darkness, which suited me. I had a simple lodge-style room and I fell asleep determined to make the most of the amenities on offer the next day.

The next morning I got my mini-disc player and sensible shoes and took myself off into the jungle interior for a stroll. I was keen to see whatever wildlife I could, as it seemed I wouldn't be experiencing any wild nightlife during my stay. Silence is the key to observing any creature in its natural habitat. As I've said, my Chinese sign is the tiger, a skilful and deadly hunter. Unfortunately a six-foot-two, sixteen-stone man crashing through the undergrowth listening to the Doors' first album at full volume will not be privy to much action from any local creatures.

After exhausting myself and having a disappointing swim in some shallow rock-strewn bay, I sat down in front of the TV in my room. I was thrilled to discover a Best of British satellite channel and spent the afternoon watching endless reruns of *The Bill* while half a mile to my right was the Great Barrier Reef, one of the Seven Wonders of the World.

I had a small bit of hash, which I smoked during the daytime as I pounded around the island. I saw a snake and a big lizard one day. The lizard flicked his tongue at me for about ten minutes then made off into the undergrowth. On the third night I decided to take my chances in the bar. I put on one of my best shirts, a Hartford original button-down in blue (half sleeve). As I approached I heard a huge roar of laughter. In the Clubhouse, as it was called, I was greeted by the sight of thirty people screaming with laughter. They were watching the centre of the room, where a girl was sitting on a chair with a balloon covering her thighs and another balloon covering her chest and with a man attempting to sit on her and not burst the balloons (or burst them; I wasn't sure). People were whooping, bent double in mirth. I watched for a moment, paralysed, then fled. I never went back. *The Sweeney* was on most nights anyway.

I never went diving, never saw the brightly coloured fish. You can see the Great Barrier Reef from outer space anyway, so I can do that one day in the future.

In 1998 we performed *The Fast Show* live at Hammersmith Apollo: thirty nights sold out! This was the cherry on the cake for me personally. I was an experienced live performer, and it was a relief to be doing sketches and characters with my friends in front of an audience hellbent on laughing at things that weren't even supposed to be funny. It was very different from doing my one-man show, where it was just me on stage for an hour and a half.

I think Charlie and Paul were a bit nervous. They'd done a tour with Harry Enfield years before but Paul especially was not a lover of live work. There was also no guarantee it would work.

How would we get people on and off stage quickly enough? Would the characters work in a live format? Was it physically possible for Paul to do all his characters? We all gave advice to Paul and Charlie, some of which they listened to and some of which they ignored. But they left nothing to chance and hired a theatre director called Ros to help with staging it all. It must have been a shock dealing with us lot.

The set was huge, with numerous balconies and windows where people could pop out and shout their catchphrases. The set designer did a fantastic job and it looked brilliant. The whole thing really moved at pace. The show was a double-header with *Shooting Stars* and for some reason Bob Mortimer decided they'd go on first; it looked a bit like we were being supported by *Shooting Stars*, which gave us an edge. There was a friendly rivalry. I think it was most important to Paul to be the best but we were all aware of the need to grind our heroes and mentors into the dust.

In fact *Shooting Stars* did suffer in the live format: no one knew why and it never really took off. However, as I write this it's once again the funniest show on TV, reaffirming the boys' position as the twin kings of comedy they always were. At the time, though, I was delighted to be part of the show that was getting the good reviews and I didn't spend any time worrying about how their quiz was faring with the paying punters. We sat around crowing about how much better than theirs our show was and how the audience had come to see us, not them.

One comedian who attended likened it to a Hitler Youth rally. Certainly as a performer you were carried along on a wave of love and bonhomie from the audience. You'd walk on stage and the whole place would erupt; by the time the cheering died down you were off stage again and someone else was in your place. From a performing point of view it really was like shooting fish in a barrel and I loved every minute of it. The only thing that didn't work as well as I'd have liked was Competitive Dad, which seemed to elicit less laughter than everything else.

After the show we'd sit about as the great and the good came backstage to a little Portakabin in the car park to drink free beer and tell us how amazing we were. People would whisper to me, 'You were the best thing in the show,' while across the room someone else would be whispering to Paul, 'You were the best thing in the show,' and outside John would be smoking a fag and yet another person would be telling him, 'You were the best thing in the show.' If you saw it and bought this book in hardback you'll probably agree when I whisper, 'I was the best thing in it.'

It's hard to remember it now, it passed by in such a blur. If ever my son or daughter are involved in something like that I'll take them aside and say, 'Make sure you enjoy every second of it. Be nice to everybody, write a diary of everything that happens and don't buy cocaine off the stagehands – it's always shit.'

There was some quality stuff in that live show. Paul doing Arthur Atkinson, the Ted and Ralph song at the end, Mark's Drunken Man . . . It was an incredible thing to be part of. One night we even got some groupies: they screamed and ran to the front of the stage, hopping up and down. A right rough load of tarts they were too – we refused them entry to the backstage area, a bit miffed they weren't underwear models.

No one drank before the show, perhaps just one beer. Paul was very strict about that sort of thing. Of course as the dates wore on it became more difficult to police us, though. John and I were borderline alcoholics at that stage and I was a proper coke head too. I always waited until after the show, but after we had taken our bows (trying to gauge who was getting the loudest cheers) I'd really put my foot down on the gas. Why not? I was single, I didn't drive and my septum seemed indestructible. I was the toast of the Portakabin and was often the last one there, downing beer after beer and snorting line after line. By the time I got back to South East London it would be three in the morning and I'd have a few more lines just to be sociable with myself. A few rum and Cokes then listen to classic rock on the headphones. I used to listen to a lot of hip-hop too, but one night I had the Wu-Tang Clan on and the sound of a gunshot gave me such a shock I jumped out of my skin and farted uncontrollably, my drink cartwheeling through the air and landing on the stereo. One morning when I emerged blinking like a mole from my rented one-bedroom hovel my next-door neighbour congratulated me on my performance in the sack the night before.

'You were at it for about six hours! Blimey, she was certainly enjoying herself – she screamed the house down!' I was too hungover to tell him that what he'd heard was a porn film playing over and over again.

Some days I'd get up just in time for my car to take me back to the theatre. It's tiring being a coke head and having another job too. The addiction's a job in itself and becomes your whole life. A lot of people take drugs a lot then stop but there are lots of others, like me, who just carry on regardless, bobbing and weaving, rolling with the punches, limping on and never getting so bad they have to stop. But how bad is bad? Driving from Lewisham to Wembley at five in the morning to buy something you know won't work? Seeing bloodstains on your tenners when you buy your morning paper? Having a long conversation with Tony Slattery and telling him you think he's brilliant? I mean *come on*: that is the lowest of the low.

In the Groucho I used to see people in their forties taking drugs when I was in my thirties and I'd think, *How awful. I'll have stopped by the time I'm that old.* But of course it's not that simple. Christmas comes and a big New Year's Eve mash-up. 'Never again,' you say and by February you're back at work, unwrapping little white packets, smoking fags and talking rubbish to people who don't care about you, blowing out dates with girls who do.

A great thing about our residency at the Hammersmith Apollo was that I had my name in lights – at the front of the building, up high, which was incredible really. As I've said before, I'm not wildly ambitious; I didn't think, *I'll come back and fill this place on my own – and then Hollywood.* The annoying thing was that you couldn't see your name properly without standing in the middle of the one-way system, where you might get run over. (Although that would have been a great way to die and a fantastic last image before the lorry smashed into your legs.) I used to like lying on the stage in the afternoons, looking up at the ceiling of the auditorium, with the tired red seats fading away into darkness and the sound desk glowing.

We owned the place for a month and everyone was nice to us because we were making them money, but the people who were most nice to us were the ones paying the money. In the evenings we ate pie and chips or sandwiches and worried about our weight. Someone would pipe up about how a particular character wasn't getting laughs and they'd receive reassurance from the other performers. We might convene in Jim's dressing room (he had a whopper) and listen to a bit of Robin Trower or Uriah Heep. Bob would be there plotting and planning, a fag on the go. Underneath the building there was a tunnel, which enabled large things to be carried from left to right, and we'd bustle past each other down there in various states of undress. It was an eerie airless tomb and often you'd see strange men you didn't recognise who'd stare at you unsmiling.

Obviously my cocaine intake meant it could prove difficult to stay sober for the show. One night I fetched up in London's fashionable Notting Hill and managed to stay up all night. The next day (surprise, surprise) I couldn't sleep and sat head in hands watching the clock tick round till show time. My only companion was Madonna's silver book, *Sex*, which people always used as a cocaine table. It kept me occupied for hours, like that bloke in the Carry On films. ('Phwar!' 'Wahey!' 'Ooh blimey: you don't get many of them to the pound!') I was convinced in my paranoia that I'd be denounced by Charlie or Paul, like a Jew in the Reichstag building, pushed and pulled apart by my comrades for being so stupid. I arrived at the venue twitching and jittery, my pupils enormous, and stole up the dark twisting stairs to the dressing room where I hid my face from my accusers. I expected Paul to grab me and stare into my eyes like Larry David in *Curb Your Enthusiasm*. I tried to eat a banana to give me energy, so drenched in paranoia it was hideous. Suddenly the door burst open and my saviour arrived: little John Thomson, pissed out of his mind. He'd spent the preceding thirty-six hours in much the same way as I had, minus the Charlie, and was like a clockwork pirate, all unintelligible growls and bawdy remarks.

'For fuck's sake!' said Paul. 'Look at the state of him.'

My paranoia vanished and I shook my head. 'Silly cunt,' I said, feeling my wits returning relatively intact. (As I write John Thomson is four years clean and sober, by the way, which is more than me.)

Looking back now I do regret not taking more advantage of my profile. In terms of my career I rested on my laurels and fiddled while Rome burnt at the same time. But I was earning well, and as long as I had a few grand in the bank I was happy.

The Fast Show was, of course, replaced with lightning speed by *Little Britain*. At the time we were all a bit miffed, though on reflection it's a great show – and we pinched as much from Harry Enfield as they did from us. When I first saw it I thought it was good but too gay to break through; clearly I underestimated the British public's love of camp. Plus there were some very strong characters there – 'the only gay in the village' and Vicky Pollard, of course, among others. Actually my favourite was the David Walliams character who always tried to get off with his mate's gran.

It was weird at first. My face used to fall when my friends raved about *Little Britain* and when asked what I thought I'd give a glum professional opinion, pointing out minor errors while people's faces glazed over.

Little Britain was transmitted around the same time as my vanity project, *Grass*, a ten-part comedy drama commissioned by Jane Root just before she hopped over the pond. Half the money for the show came from Stewart Murphy, the BBC3 wunderkind who, in a crazy blast of commissioning, spent his whole yearly budget in three months: 100 million quid! This included two *Fast Show* spin-offs, so you won't see me knocking him as I was in both. At the end of the day, though, spin-offs are rarely successful. People view them in much the same way as they do dodgy solo albums. I mean, you might be a fan of Queen but are you going to buy a Roger Taylor solo album? A lot of folk see a spin-off as sullying the original show and just switch off. Sadly for me and my orphanage in Botswana *Grass*, although well reviewed, was deemed not good enough for a second series. The new BBC controller Roly Keating said he really enjoyed it but he didn't know why. Which is a strange thing to say but channel controllers are a bit like Premiership referees: they have a lot of decisions to make and they cannot get them all right.

Another problem suffered by the BBC is a lack of aftercare or back-up service for writers and performers. If your show is cancelled you're shown the door. Anyone who saw *Grass* could see it had lots of things going for it, including some excellent characters. I think someone should have said, 'This was a near miss. Why don't you take this office and we'll go through your new ideas and see what you come up with.' I know people who put in proposals every three months and get knocked back continually. Not everyone has such thick skin, though. There should be some attempt at a nurturing process for writers. It's all a bit cold otherwise. Obviously I thought my show was good, but it was swamped by plaudits for *Nighty Night* and *Little Britain*. I think it was maybe a bit slow, with not enough shock and awe. And that other important thing: it might not have been funny enough.

Epilogue

There came a time when on any given night I'd half run, half skip the last few yards towards my front door and sanctuary, fumble the key into the lock and push the door into the small hallway. I'd drop the keys, pick them up, my heart beating like a tiny angry drum, and enter my flat: *yes*! There was my coffee table and my stereo, all I needed. I'd begin pulling things from my bag – a plastic water bottle, a biro, some Blu-Tack – and in five minutes would have built myself a crack pipe. I'd unwrap the little parmesan parcel of damage, stick a crumb on the foil, stick the biro on it and suck that filthy ghost spirit deep into my lungs. Then I'd fall back on the couch and feel utterly bereft.

After I'd finished my lump, and if I couldn't get any more, I'd get the bread knife and saw the bottle in half to scrape the thick, greasy yellow residue from its shoulder where it had gathered like pigeon shit on a statue. The first scraping would give me a small hit; the second scrape not much. By the third and fourth I'd be smoking plastic mixed with tar. That was my nightcap, before the searching began – the searching for spilt crumbs.

Smoking crack produces a peculiar psychosis wherein you actually want to believe you've found something on the carpet that is crack. Often it's dirt or sometimes a crisp or even cheese; you might prepare a whole new bottle just to smoke a bit of old cheddar. I was on my hands and knees in my bedroom looking for crumbs once and my friend came in and said, 'Simon, we haven't even been in this room.'

I'd been smoking crack for about a year. You may be shocked to hear this but the problem's far more widespread than you might imagine. People just keep quiet about it because they're ashamed. There's no glamour here. For me, as a long-term drug pursuer, it was the natural conclusion to my drug career: you smoke pot and it stops working, so you eat it and smoke it pure; you snort cocaine and it stops working, so you start smoking it . . .

I was in a bad way at this point. A lot of drug-taking friends had withdrawn from my table, not prepared to go down the crack route, but others had sprung up and filled their shoes. It's a fucking sinister, earth-shattering drug and it nearly finished me off. I survived somehow but it really was touch and go. I was earning a lot of money by then – hundreds of thousands of pounds a year – and I thought I could afford to watch a good portion of it go up in smoke. I'd think, *What does that mean?* My thought processes were fucked. I was in full addiction, no different to when I was jailed for stealing to play fruit machines, and I had no choice. I needed to be forcibly removed from society and put in rehab, but who knew? I had no family around me; I was just being rock 'n' roll.

The Fast Show was part of a huge upsurge in upfront British culture: Oasis, Blur, Damien Hirst, Kate Moss . . . I was on nodding terms with all of them. Everyone seemed to be having it large but whatever I had it wasn't enough. I was an XXXL kind of guy – life begins at forty, shaking in my good shoes, Nobu on Tuesday, New Cross on Wednesday, bed on Thursday, the Groucho on Friday. I remember a drunk bloke saying to me in Soho one night, 'I would love to be you – you're so fucking cool!' I'd have laughed but my mouth was twisted up and around as if I'd just got life at the Old Bailey.

Another night I went back to a media girl's flat somewhere. Our courtship had lasted about ten minutes and I was now pawing her on the sofa, trying to get somewhere away from myself, like a sixteen-year-old on New Year's Eve. Suddenly she leapt up.

'I can't believe you're behaving like this! I expected so much more from you.'

'Why?' I said.

'Because you're in *The Fast Show*,' she said mournfully, standing by her bookcase.

I laughed at that, I really laughed. Then I was off into the night like Ichabod Crane without a horse.

The binge culture covered my back. Everyone was on something, weren't they? My job and income gave me a veneer of respectability that stopped me from ever confronting my demons. I'd usually sober up for TV work and no one knew what I did in the privacy of my home. It wasn't as if I was smoking crack at the bar in the Groucho. I just had a cough and a cold, it seemed.

I cannot make light of this period. I had all kinds of lunatics around my house – giant lesbian prisoners on the run, working girls, one-legged Africans who made me soup, plastic gangsters . . . Anyone who could get me crack was admitted, day or night.

I had stuff nicked, windows broken. I once borrowed a load of bicarbonate of soda off the woman next door to wash up some coke, telling her I was making a cake. She came round and knocked on the door to ask for a slice and my gang and I froze, all spoons and Bunsen burners. All that mad shit was and is horrible and perhaps someone you know is doing it right now, right at the end of their tether, and in a few days they'll start all over again.

Some people think addiction is a joke, a lifestyle choice for people with more money than sense. They see famous bods being ushered into the Priory and say, 'Look at them, off for a rest. Probably had a breakdown 'cause they ran out of shampoo. Grow up.' I can only speak for myself, but I thought that too: *Grow up*. I'd say it to myself over and over again as the half-light filtered through the curtains, as I pushed on, having baths and making myself respectable for dealers, waiting for the sound of the engine outside. It was my only defence when I had black geezers on motorbikes buzzing my doorbell and dragging me down the cash point without a helmet. *Pull yourself together*, I'd think, then I'd have a lie down, my heart hammering like someone locked in a cellar, my brain churning, and I'd vow never, never, *never* again.

But addiction is real, I'm afraid; it's not a game played by anyone. I have a bug in my head who wants me on my own trying to destroy myself. 'You didn't have a gun to your head,' I hear you cry – but what if I did? What if I had a little man with a gun saying, 'Take that, drink this, sniff this, eat that'? I'm not talking about schizophrenia, but why didn't I stop? I had money, attractive female companions, talent, a good career – all I had to do was go to bed without picking up the wrong things. But I couldn't stop. Do you think I enjoyed my drug abuse? I wanted to stop in the early eighties. All the things I said about giving up coke I'd already said about cannabis years and years earlier. What I needed was love but I sidestepped that whenever it reared its ugly head. I couldn't deal with love: it was too emotional, too real. I'd have had to break myself into little pieces. I met a few girls who were good at jigsaws but I wouldn't even let them open the box.

I wouldn't wish an addictive nature on anyone. As I've already said, it's cunning, baffling and powerful. My inner addict played me like a monkey on a barrel organ for years and years and I should be dead. I'm not trying to be dramatic or sell books here: if I can get one person into rehab or to a meeting through this book I will be overjoyed, absolutely overjoyed.

Everyone else in *The Fast Show* had by this point bought a large house and pretty much paid off the mortgage. I was living in a drab brown rented flat. Then one night I wandered into a restaurant and met my wife.

As is often the case, it was a girl that saved my life. I met Ruth in 1998, when she was working in the fashionable and glorious folly that was Notting Hill's Pharmacy restaurant. She looked like a film star and still does. I was amazed to discover that she was prepared to go out with me and had never heard of *The Fast Show*. An African kitchen porter took her aside and said, 'Boss, that man is David Angel the Eco Warrior: you must go out with him.' His opinion didn't sway her judgement but I like to believe we were brought together by a Nigerian with lemon-check trousers who did not pay any tax. (I am a romantic, after all.) She'll never be what people call a groupie. Her favourite comedy TV show is *You've Been Framed*; and when I've been funny on radio or TV I often return home and eagerly burst through the door to watch myself only to be told, 'Oh, sorry. I forgot to tape it . . .' She loves me for who I am and at the beginning I found that hard to believe.

She's what my friend Tony would describe as a 'raving sort', which means beautiful. (And she turned out to be a beautiful person too – which was of course lucky for me, because she put up with my post-fame blues and Me-Me-Me-based shit for years.) When I first saw her I couldn't take my eyes off her: she was beyond sexy, beyond glamorous. The great thing was that because she worked in a restaurant I didn't have to ring her up and ask her out. I didn't hang about – I reasoned that someone who looked like that would not stay single for long, so I dived in there the following Sunday. I talked to her right through lunch-time service, went back to her flat for tea, then back to the restaurant for dinner, where I carried on talking while she ran the place with grace and a steel resolve. (Did I see these qualities and hope she might apply them to me?) At chucking-out time I asked her out on a date and she agreed before cashing up.

I invited her to see me perform at Prince Charles' fiftieth birthday, a variety bill at a West End theatre in honour of Britain's least-favourite royal. She had to sit through three hours of watered-down comedy and musical bilge that among other things included Ginger Spice performing 'Happy Birthday, Mr Prince' à la Marilyn Monroe. It was one piece of confused merchandising serenading another and to witness it first-hand was one of the most disturbing and sickening things I've ever experienced. He peered over the gilt shelf, guffawing in embarrassment, his ears twitching like leathery satellite dishes as Geri Halliwell tore the stockings off Hollywood's most enduring icon. There wasn't a dry eye in the house but plenty were rubbed in disbelief.

We then had dinner at the Guildhall, where we were sat on a table full of doctors and bankers who'd each paid 100 quid to sit with a 'celebrity'. Needless to say they did not recognise me. She was charming and elegant, and the best-looking person in the room. (I'm shallow, but so what?) I'd been given a big car to collect me, which I donated to her because of romantic torrential rain. Outside I, her caddy, jogged along beside her holding an umbrella over her perfect form before she slid inside and was driven back to her pied-à-terre in Notting Hill. I walked back to the Guildhall for my cheesecake and birthday brandy soaking wet but happy. Later I got a minicab back down the Old Kent Road towards home feeling like John Travolta in *Saturday Night Fever*.

My front door made its usual noise as I shut it and went into my living quarters, which were still in disarray from the previous night's Big Night In. On the shelf lay a smudged and sticky CD case, covered in cocaine residue, and U2 stood clad in black in the desert judging me. I put on *Let It Bleed* and sat down on the sofa with a drunken *whumph*. At least I wasn't as bad as Keith Richards: he took heroin. No, but he also had a lot of money in the bank – 'fuck you' money, they call it. I didn't even have any 'wank me' money. I saw my one glass and my one ashtray and my one mucky dressing gown tangled on the floor and it looked like a crime scene with me as the villain of the piece. I vowed not to let this extraordinary creature out of my clutches.

Ruth and I started going out and I flew back and forth between my place and her cosy little one-bedroom flat in Notting Hill. People slag off Notting Hill but I loved it. It seemed like a sort of imaginary Hollywood, where everyone appeared to be basking in the glory of being in the right place at the right time. And there were loads of people who wandered about in the day not really knowing what to do with themselves, so I fitted right in. When Ruth left for work I'd walk up and down the Portobello Road buying cheese or silly magazines, CDs from Rough Trade, occasionally turning down weed from deranged crusty Rastas. I was by accident the archetypal Notting Hill resident: slightly famous, slightly trendy and slightly (enormously) into cocaine.

I joined Ruth's gym, which was across the street and called Lambton Place. I was amazed by the sheer number of high-end celebs in there: it was only a small room but at any given time you could be sweating alongside Peter Mandelson, Dave Allen, Brian Eno, Elvis Costello, Paul Simonon, Mariella Frostrup . . . Some of these people just went in the steam room. I certainly don't recall seeing Eno bench-pressing any weights, but I did try to engage him in conversation about *Remain in Light* one morning as we left the place. After looking up at me nervously a few times he ran back inside claiming to have left a towel somewhere. To this day I don't know if this was a lie – whether he was watching me through the smoked glass like a murderer, peeling a clementine. It might be that he just could not bear one more conversation with another middle-aged man about such an '*important album*'.

Peter Mandelson used to occupy one of the stationary bike machines on the upper floor of the gym. He always sat on the same one – it gave him an excellent view of the whole room in case anyone was planning to hurl a grenade at him. He'd pedal furiously, his upper body remaining still, in a manner that was remarkably similar to his political behaviour. He'd read a copy of the *Economist* one-handed, his eyes flicking up and raking the room at short intervals. I would be below, pounding along on a treadmill like a punch-drunk bear with a charity marathon ahead of me. Whenever I caught his eye he'd look away coyly. I never knew if this was the first signal in complicated homoerotic courtship or whether he was just unsure of himself when wearing shorts. He was banished from the government briefly soon after this point, for buying a house in the wrong way. What a strange dance politics is.

I had a conversation with Elvis Costello once, by the lockers. Unfortunately he was naked. I tried to act casual but was appalled by his behaviour. I have no idea why men think it's OK to talk to you while drying their genitals and arse-crack. They say you should never meet your heroes; well, I would add the caveat that you shouldn't meet your heroes when they're stark-bollock naked.

Dave Allen was always in the steam room and we had many a chat about comedy and the BBC's reluctance to get our respective projects off the ground. He was a lovely man who inspired a great many comics of my generation. Goodnight and may your god go with you.

I was happy with Ruth just hanging about. She inveigled me into the crazy world of spa treatments and yoga and in return I instructed her in the finer points of Bob Dylan and Steely Dan. She encouraged me to stop picking my nose and eating it and trying to bite my toenails, and made me get my teeth whitened. (They need doing again, actually, but I think they'll fall out before I get round to it.) She slowly but surely encouraged me to repair my relationships with my close family, and also got me cooking meals for her on a regular basis.

I did very well in the nineties and we went on holiday a lot. We went all over the world and I think it drove my agent mad – after all, it wasn't as if I was tired out and on the verge of a nervous breakdown. Quite the opposite, in fact: I was glowing with health, my scalp massaged, my chi centred, my nails manicured to within an inch of their lives. Whenever nothing was happening we fucked off somewhere: a weekend in Bruges drinking beer from funny glasses; the South of France, sneering at the Russians and making sure we drank every last drop of expensive Bordeaux (which tasted revolting); two weeks in the Maldives looking at tropical fish up close . . . We pretended to be rich – we *were* rich

– but it could not last. I used to look around the Mexican restaurant in the Japanese hotel at the foot of the Cambodian mountain and think, *Most of these people are getting their companies or parents to pay for this.* For me it all came from bits and bobs of a career that was floating along with no destination in mind. We went to the Ritz in Paris on New Year's Eve once. I bought a box of matches that cost a tenner and we couldn't afford to have the set dinner. I had a fag outside and was ignored by the doorman.

What did it all mean? The hot-stone massages, the dry cleaning of things that were already clean, the iced hand-towel in the black Volvo that picked us up from the airport from where we were whisked off to the Amanpuri in Thailand. There no one said hello at breakfast. Americans from novels by Bret Easton Ellis ate very little while we ate a lot and the waiters seemed terrified of the people they were trying to put at ease. The jungle sat steaming, not expecting a tip. Only the monkeys laughed, nicking things from handbags and once raiding our mini-bar, baring their teeth as they expertly popped open the Pringles. I used to swim out to sea, look back at the hotel and tread water, trying to remember whether I'd had a Valium that morning. Was *I* a character in a Bret Easton Ellis book? Did they have fat bald people in his books? *Oh well, it'll be lunchtime soon . . .*

I was like a lottery winner who hadn't won the lottery. Once, in Malaysia, an English couple told us that David Dickinson was staying at our hotel. That night I rushed down to the bar hoping to meet the perma-tanned totter but found he'd checked out that morning. I drank my £5 beer and ate some cashew nuts the size of conkers. Was I really so bored that I ran down a corridor in order to meet David Dickinson? Had my life become that flat, to think that his leathery skin and crazy jewellery would somehow cheer me up? I was in one of the best hotels in the world – why did I need cheering up?

Perhaps I'd meet him somewhere else. In the middle of a tropical rainforest, perhaps; in another jungle – the one run by the chimp kings, Ant and Dec? But then we'd be in competition with each other and would be forced to eat bugs. Showbusiness: it's the hardest game in the world. 'More nuts, my friend, more nuts. The night is young . . .'

Woody Allen said that marriage was the death of hope and I believed him – until I saw him French-kissing a young girl in one of his films, the liver spots showing up like gravy stains on the back of his hands. Then I thought I'd take my chances with what I had, rather than waiting to see what I might get.

Ruth and I got married on 15 June 2002. I was nervous but it was a cracking do. She looked amazing and I sweated and cried in equal measure during my speech. Ruth was also very happy that I wasn't gurning during the wedding video. Crazy days and crazy nights . . .

When I met her I was a crack head, and I persevered with that lifestyle for a bit longer in South East London before realising I had to shape up or ship out.

I moved in with her and deleted all my numbers. I toughed it out. I say that but of course I still did coke: a lot of Ruth's crowd were users and I felt entirely comfortable among them. I am a chameleon and can fit in anywhere. Besides, as Malcolm Hardee used to say, 'My face is my passport.' To the people in Notting Hill I was a TV star, which was big currency there. There's no such culture of South East London – there you're 'nothing special' – but on the Portobello Road I was welcomed with open arms and numerous toasts and gradually all my old dodgy acquaintances fell away. The dealers dealt to someone else and the people who'd been round my table got round someone else's table.

I had once again pulled myself out of the fire. Or so I thought. I still had a coke problem.

One day I was invited to an NA meeting up the road from Ruth's flat. I knew I had no choice but to go. I went into a brightly lit room, sat down and listened to a vastly different array of people all tell stories similar to mine. This was a real light-bulb moment. I felt part of something – something real and with integrity.

I was horrified to discover that I wasn't allowed to drink alcohol, though, and (like many people before me) I left determined to not take any class-A drugs but to still drink, just moderately. Guess what? It didn't work. When I drank I took coke, end of story, and over the next ten years I was in and out of those meetings. I'm clean and sober now: I can say that after writing this catalogue of addiction. I had to do it, one day at a time.

Ruth made me feel safe and I found I could just do nothing with her and still be happy. Time moved on. I got less famous; she remained good-looking. She noticed a hole in our life when her friends started having kids, though. It was different for me: I was already in touch with my inner child. He'd surface and start playing up whenever I didn't get my own way. I didn't need any competition.

For three years, until 2007, I was the star of a very well-paid ad campaign for Powergen. I was proud of all the ads, in which I hugged wind turbines and talked about positive energy – they were funny (which is rare) and everyone involved knew what they were doing. It was great to see what it's like to be rich, too, albeit for just a short while. We bought a house in a good area and spent loads of money doing it up. I ate raw fish at lunchtime and bought some flat art, but time was still marching on and the person I'd decided to spend the rest of my life with was slowly going mad with grief about something she'd wanted since she was a little girl. I counselled her as best I could but you're either pregnant or you're not – no amount of spa breaks and fantastic shoes can fill that void. What could I do? Fortunately, thanks to the German energy company I was promoting, we had lots of money to throw at the problem and eventually science beat nature and we got our dumplings.

On 2 February 2007 Lloyd Theodore Day came into the world out of my wife and on to the floor, where he was scooped up by a man who didn't seem bothered by all the blood and gore. After a quick rest my missus gave birth to another baby, on 7 October 2008. We called her Evie. I was present at both births, as is the fashion, but found the ejaculations a bit distressing. My wife had a few problems after Evie's birth (like losing five pints of blood) and was whisked away for surgery. I was left literally holding the baby, being told wildly different things about my wife's state of health by people of various ethnic minorities before a posh white lady came before me and told me she would live.

Ironically the ad campaign ended exactly when Lloyd was born and over the following three years my earnings plummeted. Suddenly I was on thirty grand a year and staring at two young people who were hungry and tired and upset in no particular order. We sold up and moved to a not-so-flash area and shouted at each other a bit more often, but slowly – ever so slowly – I started to change.

When I was in my twenties and people I knew started having kids I was about as interested in their offspring as Simon Cowell is in Vic Chesnutt. On numerous occasions these new parents told me that I should never have kids: 'You're too selfish,' or, 'You wouldn't be able to handle them.' I used to shrug and play with their kids really well. For twenty minutes. I was never in a relationship long enough to discuss children, certainly not to father any. I thought that being left to my own devices was what I needed – especially when I became an artiste, when all my bad habits and wonky character traits become permissible. I was on telly: I could behave as I liked. I just didn't get it.

I get it now. I'm very lucky to have the life I have these days. I look forward to going home at night and I look forward to getting up in the morning. I'm amazed that no one conveyed to me the sheer joy that children can bring you. The main thing that hit me was how happy they were: provided you do exactly what they tell you to everything is fine. They laugh when they get up and frequently are laughing as you read them their bedtime stories. They are crazy and sensible, loving and kind. Also they are who they are already – their personalities are fully formed. Speaking as a self-obsessed person prone to mooching about and watching televised sport, I can report that my kids have solved many of my problems just by being alive. They will completely run riot if you don't watch it, though: sometimes I have to go and lie down. I am old, remember. (I got accused of being Evie's granddad in Center Parcs the other day. I didn't mind too much; I'm just happy I have her in my life.)

It's all about them – everything. They are faster, stronger, more cheeky and more cunning than me and as I get older they get even better at getting their own way. I have my hands and my brain full. Parenthood is an enormous human project that I will never finish. Every decision I make involving them is important and every move I make has consequences that are further-reaching than I can imagine. All that matters is that they're safe and loved-up.

It didn't take me long to work out that I really couldn't drink and take drugs at all while they were around. If something goes wrong I have to be alive, alert to that problem; anything else isn't fair on them or my spouse. At this precise moment I'm clean and sober but all that can change in an instant; I have to watch myself. Sugar, gambling, booze, sleeping pills . . . I'm just an all-or-nothing person. But ultimately if you don't stop your body will stop for you – and I don't want my kids writing a book about their wonderful complex father who died in his pants drinking Campari from a vase and eating Es in his wardrobe when they were still at nursery school. I want them to have proper jobs, like saving the world! Lloyd and Evie get up around six every morning and are ready for action. I need to be on my mettle or what's the point in being there at all?

Being on TV doesn't define my life any more; nor does being funny. My family are my life and that's it. Having kids so late and going through the hall of mirrors that is IVF has made Ruth and me stronger as a couple and more appreciative of our luck.

This year we went to Wales on holiday. It rained all week and I didn't even have time to read a newspaper but it was hugely enjoyable; it just felt right all the time. Even when they puked up in the night, even when they grabbed the barbed-wire fence, even when Lloyd threw a rock at a goat, even when Evie stuck a pen in my eye – it was still somehow fantastic. I know it won't always be like this. And (don't get me wrong) I'm not Super Dad; I still fight the desire to *not* interact with them.

I'm in Somerset writing this book and the peace and quiet is wonderful. I can really appreciate it now. Before the little people all I had was peace and quiet: I'd honed my life down to a series of quiet pleasures interspersed with earth-shattering and toxic benders that would leave me reeling for weeks afterwards.

Last night at seven the phone rang. It was Ruth: 'Hi. Someone wants to speak to you.'

'Hello, Daddy.' It was Lloyd.

'Hi, Lloyd. How are you?' Silence: just breathing. 'Are you OK?'

'I'm watching *Ben 10* with Evie and drinking my milk.'

'Did you have a nice day?'

'Yes, Daddy, but I'm a werewolf and I can kill you.' He says this in a gravelly whisper. (The kid's already good.) The phone goes dead. Later I learnt that after hanging up he hurled the phone into the bookshelves with such force that it broke into pieces. Then he climbed on to my wife's head and farted on her hair.

An hour later, the phone rang again. It was a mobile. Again there's a pause: a little heart beating and a little set of lungs hammering away.

'Hello, Daddy. I missed you.' The phone went dead and I felt that emotion I'm now getting used to: wanting to cry and burst out laughing at exactly the same time.

That will do for me.

Acknowledgements

First of all, Matthew Hamilton for instigating the book after hearing me talk in a room. Mike Jones at Simon & Schuster and Monica O'Connell for her wonderful editing and general positivity. Martha for her shed, ditto Polly. Mum and Dad for giving me books and the time and space to read them; without the books I have read I would be nothing. Everyone who ever gave me a roof over my head and treated me with kindness, all the music that kept me going, the funny people on TV, the sun and the moon, the sea and the sky, and of course, televised sport.

Index

(CD = Camilla Deaken; N = Natasha; SD = Simon Day)